THE SON OF A BLACKSMITH, William John Watson was born into a Gaelic-speaking family in Easter Ross in 1865. He was the rector of Inverness Royal Academy from 1894 to 1909, and of Edinburgh's Royal High School from 1909 to 1916, when he was appointed Professor of Celtic at Edinburgh. He edited two standard anthologies for An Comunn Gaidhealach, *Rosg Gàidhlig* and *Bàrdachd Ghàidhlig*. However he is best known for his major contributions to place-name studies, *Place-Names of Ross and Cromarty* and *History of the Celtic Place-Names of Scotland.* William J. Watson was married twice and was the father of six sons. He died in 1948.

SCOTTISH

PLACE-NAME PAPERS

William J. Watson

Steve Savage

LONDON AND EDINBURGH

Steve Savage Publishers Ltd
The Old Truman Brewery
91 Brick Lane
LONDON
E1 6QL

www.savagepublishers.com

Published in Great Britain by Steve Savage Publishers Ltd 2002

ISBN 1-904246-05-2

British Library Cataloguing in Publication Data
A catalogue entry for this book is available from the British Library

'*Place Names of Scotland*, A Review' was first published in 1904 in the
Inverness Courier; 'The Study of Highland Place-Names' was first published
in 1904 in *The Celtic Review*, vol 1; 'Paisley' was first published in 1904-5 in
The Celtic Review, vol 1; 'Tara' was first published in 1904-5 in *The Celtic
Review*, vol 1; 'Some Sutherland Names of Places' was first published in
1906 in *The Celtic Review*, vol 2; '*Innis* in Place-Names' was first published
in 1907 in *The Celtic Review*, vol 3; 'Note' was first published in 1907 in *The
Celtic Review*, vol 4; 'Topographical Varia' [I] was first published in 1908 in
The Celtic Review, vol 5; 'Topographical Varia' [II] was first published in
1909 in *The Celtic Review*, vol 5; 'Topographical Varia—III' was first published
in 1910 in *The Celtic Review*, vol 6; 'Topographical Varia—IV' was
first published in 1911 in *The Celtic Review*, vol 7, this revised version first
published 2002; 'Topographical Varia—V' was first published in 1912 in *The
Celtic Review*, vol 7; 'Topographical Varia—VI' was first published in 1913 in
The Celtic Review, vol 8; 'Some place-names in the Cairngorm region' was first
published in 1916 in the *Cairngorm Club Journal*; 'Place-Names of
Strathdearn' was first published in 1920 in the *Transactions of the Gaelic
Society of Inverness*, vol 30; 'Names of Places around Inverness' was first
published in 1909 in *Prints of the Past Around Inverness*, and this revised
version was first published in 1925; 'The Place-Names of Breadalbane' was
first published in 1928 in the *Transactions of the Gaelic Society of Inverness*,
vol 34; 'Place-Names of Perthshire—the Lyon Basin' was first published in
1930 in the *Transactions of the Gaelic Society of Inverness*, vol 35; 'Some
Place-Names of the North' was first published in 1930 for the Highland
Exhibition; 'Varia (Reply to a Review)' was first published in 1931 in *Scottish
Gaelic Studies*, vol 3; 'Annaid' was first published in 1933 in the *Transactions
of the Gaelic Society of Inverness*, vol 36.

Typeset by Steve Savage Publishers Ltd
Printed and bound by The Cromwell Press Ltd

The TransRoman Garamond font used to print this work is available from
Linguist's Software, Inc., PO Box 580, Edmonds, WA 98020-0580 USA
tel (425) 775-1130, www.linguistsoftware.com.

ABBREVIATIONS

Acall.: Acallamh na Senórach

CPNS: The History of the Celtic Place-Names of Scotland, by W.J.Watson

Ex. Rolls: Exchequer Rolls (Rotuli Scaccarii Regum Scotorum)

Geog. Coll.: Geographical Collections relating to Scotland made by Walter Macfarlane

Holder: Alt-celtischer Sprachschatz, by Alfred Holder

LL: Leabhar Laighean (The Book of Leinster)

Orig. Paroch.: Origines Parochiales Scotiae

OSM: Ordnance Survey Map

PNRC: The Place-Names of Ross and Cromarty, by W.J.Watson

Rel. Celt.: Reliquiae Celticae: Texts, Papers and Studies in Gaelic Literature by Rev Alexander Cameron

Ret.: Retours: Inquisitionum ad Capellam Domini Regis Retornatarum quae in Publicis Archivis Scotiae adhuc servantur Abbreviatio

RM: Registrum Episcopatus Moraviensis (Register of the Bishopric of Moray)

RMS: Registrum Magni Sigilli Regum Scotorum (Register of the Great Seal of Scotland)

TGSI: Transactions of the Gaelic Society of Inverness

PUBLISHER'S NOTE

In spite of the considerable duplication of material on the one hand and the variations in spelling on the other, I have not on the whole taken it upon myself to alter Professor Watson's words as originally published, except to correct the occasional literal misprint and to try to give the use of italics a rough consistency. (However the text of 'Topographical Varia—IV' has been altered to take into account the additions and correction originally listed at the end of 'Topographical Varia—V'.) Nor have I attempted to modernise Professor Watson's Gaelic spelling. Generally speaking, the intention is simply to provide the original papers in a convenient form. The order is basically chronological, which helps to give a picture of how Watson's thinking developed over the years.

I am particularly grateful to Professor W.F.H. Nicolaisen, and to the editor of Scottish Language, for allowing Professor Nicolaisen's thoughtful paper on the work of William J. Watson to be used as an Introduction to this book.

Gaelic-speakers may be interested to read Watson's paper *Ainmean na h-Alba*, which is to be found in *Rosg Gàidhlig*. Professor Watson was a member of the Gaelic Society of Inverness for the greater part of his life, and three significant papers in this volume were originally published in the *Transactions of the Gaelic Society of Inverness*. The Society is still going strong. Its website is at www.gsi.org.uk and it may be contacted at this address: Hon Secretary Mrs Anne Souter, 15 Green Drive, Inverness, IV2 4EX.

SCS

CONTENTS

In Praise of William J. Watson (1865-1948): Celtic Place-Name Scholar

by W. F. H. Nicolaisen

In his *Place-Names of Ross and Cromarty* [1904] Professor
Watson laid the foundation, in a compact and handy format, of
the scientific study of Toponymy in Scotland.

(MacDonald, D. J. 1932: vii)

The mature work [his *History of the Celtic Place-Names
of Scotland*] of 1926 deals with Scotland as a whole ... This
work has compelled the admiration of all serious scholars and
students of Scottish History and Topography in and furth of
Scotland.

(*Ibid.*: viii)

Where would one expect to find highly laudatory statements of
this kind? In an obituary after Watson's death in 1948? In a eulogy
praising his achievements on the occasion of the centenary of his
birth in 1965? As part of a retrospective assessment of his status
as a name scholar, in the 1990s? Not in any of these. These
quotations are actually part of a special introductory section,
complete with frontispiece, in Volume 33 of the *Transactions of
the Gaelic Society of Inverness*, in which the Council of the Society
celebrates, in the words of D.J.MacDonald (1932: v), 'our
authority par excellence in matters Celtic'. Published in 1932 but
covering the activities of the Society from 1925 to 1927, the
celebratory mood of this piece still reflects the pleasure and
admiration with which the publication of Watson's magnum opus
was received in Celtic Scotland in 1926 (Watson, W.J., 1926) and
we today, almost seventy years later, have no reason to distance
ourselves from that admiration and praise.

It is one of the great regrets of my life that I never had an
opportunity to meet the man on whose scholarship such praise

was lavished, since, at the time of his death, I was only just about to begin my studies as an undergraduate and had no inkling that these would one day lead me to Scotland and to a sustained interest in this country's place names. I know that in the last years of his life I would have found a kindly man, profoundly deaf, widowed since the late twenties and still suffering from the severe blow which the cruel wartime death of his son and successor in the Edinburgh chair of Celtic, James Carmichael Watson, had dealt him in 1942 (Macdonald, John, 1949: 216, for J. C. Watson see also Maclean 1942 and Calder 1940-2). Nevertheless, to have been in his presence would have been a great privilege, and I hope that this presentation will allow me to express now what I have not been able to say to him, especially in view of his close association with the university to which I am currently happily attached. (For other personal and biographical accounts see Watson, W. J. (ms); Obituary, *The Scotsman*, 10 March 1948, p9, 4e; Mackenzie 1914; Dundee, H.S. 1910-11, Vendryes 1950-51, and MacDonald, D.J. 1932.)

William John Watson was born on 17 February 1865 at Milton, in the parish of Kilmuir Easter in Easter Ross, as the son of Hugh Watson, a blacksmith. He was initially educated by his uncle James Watson, himself an accomplished Gaelic and Latin scholar, first in Strath Conon and later in Boath, Alness. In October 1880 he entered the Grammar School of Old Aberdeen, and two years later began his studies at Aberdeen University from which he graduated in 1886 with First Class Honours in Classics, having won both the Seafield Gold Medal and the Black Prize for Latin. After a session as an assistant to Sir William Mitchell Ramsay, Professor of Latin at the university, Watson entered Merton College, Oxford, as an exhibitioner. In 1889 he graduated with First Class Honours in Classical Moderations, and in 1891, also with First Class Honours, in Litteræ Humaniores. While at Oxford, he also gained a 'double blue' in athletics ('Hammer and Stone'). The most important encounter of that time was, however, with Sir John Rhys, the famous Celtic scholar, whose influence and inspiration Watson frequently and gratefully acknowledged in later years. After a short period as an assistant master at Kelvinside Academy in Glasgow, Watson was appointed rector of Inverness Royal Academy in 1894, at the early age of twenty-nine. Honours did come early to this remarkable man! It was during his fifteen years in the Highland capital that he became a staunch supporter and leading light of the Gaelic Society of Inverness, which elected him Honorary Secretary in 1903 and Honorary Chieftain in 1904. He seems to have joined it soon after his appointment as rector, for he is first listed as a member in Vol 20 (1894-96) of the Society's *Transactions*, published in 1897. His association with some of the leading Gaelic scholars of his time, particularly Alexander Macbain (1855-1907), resulted in a most fruitful period of publications, the most important of which for name scholars was his *Place-Names of Ross and Cromarty* (Watson, W.J. 1904*a*), which proved to be an eye-opener for those who had so far been familiar mainly with the 'old school' of Gaelic toponymists with its etymologies based often on no more than inspired guesses or wishful thinking. For all those with a keen interest in Highland place names Watson's study was a revelation; and Macbain himself, in a review in *The Celtic Review* (Macbain 1904-5: 89), termed it 'the first attempt by a Gaelic-speaking Celt, trained in modern philologic ways, to give in book form the results of a thorough investigation into the names of a large county, and, incidentally to give a practical epitome of Scottish place-names'. In Macbain's view, 'it lays a sound basis for the further study of Scottish place-names on modern philologic lines' (*ibid*: 92).

During his time in Inverness, Watson contributed widely to journals, newspapers and reviews; but mainly to *The Celtic Review*, the 'Acting Editor' of which was Elizabeth (or Ella) Carmichael, daughter of Alexander Carmichael (1832-1912), collector and editor of *Carmina Gadelica*. In 1906, Miss E. C. Carmichael became the second Mrs W. J. Watson. In the July 1908 issue of *The Celtic Review*, E. C. Watson for the first time contributed an article on 'Highland Mythology' (Watson, E. C. 1908-9); and at the 1909 annual assembly of the Gaelic Society of

Inverness, Mrs W. J. Watson was the first woman to give the Gaelic address (Watson, E.C. 1908-11). On 12 March 1910, their second son James Carmichael was born; but by this time the Watsons had moved to Edinburgh (Lamont 1940; G[illies] 1986), on the appointment of William Watson as rector of Edinburgh Royal High School, a position he held from 1909 till 1914. In the same year as the birth of his son, Watson was given the Honorary Degree of LLD by his alma mater, the University of Aberdeen—as I said, honours did come early to this remarkable man, who was only forty-five at the time.

On the death in 1914 of Professor Donald Mackinnon, who had been the first holder of the Chair of Celtic Languages, Literature, History, and Antiquities in the University of Edinburgh since 1882, Watson succeeded him in that prestigious position. It was, after all, and remained for more than half a century, the only professorial position in Celtic Studies in a Scottish university. Watson's appointment was warmly applauded by those who had known and admired him in Inverness and who had with great reluctance seen him move to Edinburgh five years earlier (Anon. 1915; MacDonald, MA 1969-70). In retrospect, one cannot even imagine anybody else being chosen as the second holder of the chair; although we may find it unusual for the rector of a High School to have been the outstanding candidate for a professorship and to have been acknowledged as such. Watson remained in this position till 1938 when he was succeeded by his son James Carmichael Watson, who was at that time only twenty-eight and had, by all accounts, a brilliant future before him.

One of the first honours to come Professor W. J. Watson's way was the invitation by the Society of Antiquaries of Scotland to deliver its annual six Rhind Lectures in 1916. Since these formed the nucleus of the book-length *History of the Celtic Place-Names of Scotland* published ten years later (Watson, W. J. 1926), it would have been useful to have been able to discover some details about their substance in order to establish the precise relationship with the later work. Unfortunately, the files of the Antiquaries do not contain anything but the barest information, and we have to rely solely on the rather brief reports in *The Scotsman*. Surprisingly, this source is somewhat coy about the actual lectures, introducing the series, in its edition of 14 November 1916, as follows:

> The opening Rhind Lecture of the season, in connection with the Society of Antiquaries of Scotland, was delivered in the Albyn Rooms, 77 Queen Street, Edinburgh, yesterday. The subject of the course is 'The Celtic Place Names of Scotland', and the lecturer Professor W. J. Watson, Edinburgh.

We do, however, learn that the lectures dealt with the following subjects:

Nov. 13: 'The Early Names: Their Celticity'
Nov. 15: 'The Names Recorded by Classical Writers, esp.
   Ptolemy'
Nov. 17: 'The Coming of Gaelic to Scotland'
Nov. 20: 'The British Element in Scottish Names'
Nov. 22: 'The British Element in Scottish Names'
Nov. 24: 'Alba's Earliest Celtic Speech' (river-names)

These five topics, in six lectures, appear to correspond roughly to the Introduction and chapters I and II, III, XI and XII, and XIII and XIV of the book, respectively, while chapters IV 'Territorial Divisions', V-VIII 'General Regional Surveys', IX 'Early Church Terms', X 'Saints' Names', and XV 'Some General Terms' had not yet been given their later individual shape and space. I will come back to the question of the gradual emergence of Watson's magnum opus and of its astonishing modernity at the time of its publication. In the meantime, let me just add that in the same year in which the book appeared (1926) the National University of Ireland awarded Watson the honorary degree of DLitt in Celtic Studies.

At this point, a more general charting of the development of Watson as a place-name scholar in Celtic Scotland appears to be in order, for his productivity as a publishing scholar in this field neither begins with *The Place-Names of Ross and Cromarty* nor ends with *The History of the Celtic Place-Names of Scotland*, as must be obvious to those who own the later edition of the book with its nine pages of 'Additional Notes', augmenting, improving, or correcting the original text The magnum opus was always in the making and never truly finished, it seems.

The claim that Watson was active as a name scholar before the publication of *The Place-Names of Ross and Cromarty* is not easily substantiated[1] except on the one hand, for the commonsense realisation that such a work does not come into being overnight (he himself admits to having taken four years to verify the mainland names of his native county [Watson, W. J. 1904-5*a*: 24]), and, on the other, for a statement in the 'Introduction' to Volume 24 (1899-1901) of the *Transactions of the Gaelic Society of Inverness* (published in 1904), that part of the book 'as will be seen in the present volume, was delivered in papers before the Gaelic Society'. Unfortunately, the introductory prediction lacks fulfilment and there is nothing in that volume or in the later cumulative Index to confirm that any of these papers were actually read before the Society. Nevertheless, I am inclined to

1 Since making this statement, I have become aware of Professor Watson's paper on 'The Celtic Church in Ross' which he read to The Inverness Scientific Society and Field Club on November 21, 1899 (Watson 1899). As is to be expected, place names figure prominently as evidence in this account, and one can see without much difficulty germs of the relevant chapters on his *magnum opus* (Watson 1926). Watson, who also chaired the meeting at which he read this paper, is referred to in the introduction as the 'retiring President' of the Club; and perusal of Vol 5 of the *Transactions* of the Field Club reveals that he became a member of its Museum Committee at the Annual Meeting on 19 November 1895, was appointed Vice President at the meeting on November 23, 1897, and was elected President at the meeting on 22 November 1898. I am grateful to Mr Hugh Barron, Honorary Secretary of the Gaelic Society of Inverness, for this information and for other biographical details. While still preparing his *Place Names of Ross and Cromarty* for publication, Watson read a paper entitled 'Study of Scottish Place Names' to the Inverness Scientific Society and Field Club (12 January 1904); according to a synopsis which appeared in the *Transactions* of the Club, the paper 'consisted of a summary of the sections which now form the Introduction to that valuable work' (Watson, W. J. 1904*c*: 279).

take the statement to be correct. In the absence of any tangible proof or documentation for earlier activities and without a close scrutiny of local Inverness papers like the *Inverness Courier*, the *Northern Chronicle*, and the *Highland News*, it is both prudent and beneficial to concentrate on 1904 as the year in which Watson's involvement in the study of Scottish place names was beginning to bear rich fruit. I have already highlighted the publication of *The Place-Names of Ross and Cromarty*, which would still bear critical examination today in terms of modern onomastic scholarship, methods and requirements: its one serious defect is its failure to provide any sources for the early spellings quoted, and indeed early references to the names discussed are employed very sparingly. It is significant that ninety years later this is still the major reference work on the place names of that part of Scotland.

In the same year, 1904, in the very first issue of *The Celtic Review*, we find Watson's seminal article on 'The Study of Highland Place-Names' [see p44] in which he not only charts a path for future studies, especially 'in districts where Gaelic is still vernacular' (Watson, W. J. 1904-5*a*: 23) but also touches on many of the themes which continued to preoccupy his writing on the subject for most of his life. Among these are his useful and still justified complaints about what he calls 'the fewness of investigators possessing the necessary qualifications of scholarship and opportunity' (*loc cit*) and about the fact 'that much of the work actually attempted is sadly lacking in trustworthiness from no other reason than defective method' (*loc cit*). The methodological principles which he himself advocates are as sound in 1994 as they were in 1904: a 'duty ... to ascertain with accuracy the native Gaelic pronunciation' (*loc cit*), verification of names on the spot, checking of variants, inspection of the places themselves, and the recording of names not found on the map. Obscuring Anglicisations and map forms may thus be penetrated, as he demonstrates in a brief discussion of the Sutherland name *Altnaharra* (Watson, W. J. 1904-5*a*: 24) which, in his time, had been explained variously as Harold's Burn, Burn of the Heights (*na Hearradh*), Stream with the pillar or rock (*earragh*), and Stream of slaughter (*marbhadh*). Local pronunciation, and spellings in 1834 as *Aultnaharrow* and *Aultnaherve*, led him to Gaelic *Allt na h-Eirbhe* 'Burn of the wall of turf or stones' (*loc cit*); and he supports his etymology further by the fact that the wall in question is still *in situ*. His particular concern is directed toward Anglicisations which may represent different Gaelic forms and may therefore be quite misleading (Watson, W. J. 1904-5a: 25); for instance, the River Garry at Kinlochewe is in Gaelic *a' Ghairbhe* while the Inverness Garry is Garadh; also the Anglicisation *Kil-* may stand for Gaelic *cill* 'church', *cùil* 'nook', *caol* 'narrow', or *coille* 'wood'. Kilmuir, Kilcoy, Kildary, and Killiehuntly would be respective examples. Watson also addresses the fate of Pictish, Scandinavian, and early Gaelic names in Modem Gaelic and, as far as Pictish is concerned, squarely calls it 'a Celtic language of the Cymric type, i.e. of the P-group', stressing that 'the Pictish element in our Highland place-names is much stronger and more widespread than is generally supposed', but also admitting that 'it is really only beginning to be investigated' (Watson, W. J. 1904-5*a*: 28). The seeds of the later *magnum opus* have been clearly sown here, and the early written sources which he recommends for a search for old spellings later form the nucleus of the reference works cited in *The History of the Celtic Place-Names of Scotland*. Among the Scandinavian names which have passed into English he singles out what he calls unconscious tautologies like Ardtornish or Glendibidale, and part-translations like *Blaven* (Gaelic *Blabheinn*) for Norse *Bla-fjall* or *Gaodabheinn* for Norse *Geita-fjall*, which is still represented by the Anglicised Goatfell (Watson, W.J. 1904-5*a*: 31). Altogether, this is an article which even at the end of the century at the beginning of which it was written could well serve as prescribed reading for students of place names. The only shortcoming to which I have drawn attention in the past is the absence of any consideration of a pre-Celtic Indo-European stratum; but it has to be borne in mind that such a possibility was not seriously suggested and investigated until after Watson's death, initially by his illustrious successor in the Edinburgh Chair of Celtic, Kenneth Jackson (Jackson 1953: 195 note 1, 1955: 132; see also Nicolaisen 1976: 179-91). In the absence of such a consideration, Watson tends to overestimate the Irish mythological influence, especially in his interpretation of certain river names such as Earn, Auldearn, Findhorn and Deveron; but it would be churlish to blame him for that.

When evaluating Watson's article on 'The Study of Highland Place-Names' and his achievements in the years which followed, one has to remember that what may sound to us self-evident was no less than revolutionary at the beginning of this century. This was the time of the second edition of the Rev James Johnston's dictionary of the *Place-Names of Scotland* (Johnston 1903), of D. Matheson's *The Place Names of Elginshire* (Matheson 1905), Dr H. Cameron Gillies' *The Place-Names of Argyll* (Gillies 1906), and the like, against which the new breed of Celticists and name scholars waged war in their reviews without being able to dislodge them from the shelves of the public libraries where they are still enjoying a shelf-life which they should not have been given in the first place. Watson himself reviewed Johnston's dictionary in the *Inverness Courier* [see p33] in that productive year 1904, more than generously acknowledging certain improvements which had been made since its first edition (Johnston 1892). Nevertheless, one can hear his disappointment and anguish in his judgement (Watson 1904*b*: 3):

> While giving the author due credit for the enthusiasm which has prompted him to attack so difficult a subject and the diligence which he has displayed in the collection of materials, we are bound to state much still remains that is capable of improvement. The author has not yet attained the necessary proficiency in the Gaelic language and Gaelic philology which alone can make him a trustworthy guide; nor does he seem to put in practice all the principles, most of them sound enough, with which he prefaces his Introduction.

It is quite clear at this point that Johnston had not learned very much from Alexander Macbain's biting criticism (Macbain 1892, reprinted 1922) of his first edition (Johnston 1892) in which Macbain concluded (Macbain 1922: 327-8):

... from the state of philologic knowledge in Scotland at present, we should have expected much better results. He [Johnston] confesses to only an amateur's knowledge of Gaelic, but he might have saved himself the confession. His work too plainly reveals the fact.

Macbain was also Matheson's severest critic: let me quote just three sentences from his review of *The Place Names of Elginshire* (Matheson 1905) in the *Highland News* (reprinted Macbain 1922: 313-23):

Mr Matheson stands by himself, and is a law to himself on language and history (p313).

Mr Matheson belongs to the old school of etymologists (p314).

We thought Mr Matheson knew Gaelic; we are now doubtful (p315).

Of the same book, the Rev C.M. Robertson had this to say (Robertson 1905-6: 289):

In the case of Gaelic words Mr Matheson does not follow authority, but attempts to supply the cognates on his own account. His independence is scarcely justified by the results.

Johnston and Matheson had a tailor-made bed-fellow in Dr H. Cameron Gillies. Professor Donald Mackinnon, a Colonsay man and first Professor of Celtic in the University of Edinburgh, who had himself published a well-informed series of articles on the Place and Personal names of Argyll in *The Scotsman* in the late 1880s, responds with obvious pain to Gillies' claim regarding his own *The Place-Names of Argyll*—'I believe it as nearly correct as any one could make it' (Gillies 1906: xi)—by saying: 'If this be so, one must despair of even an approach to accuracy in this branch of study' (Mackinnon 1906-7: 83). One can understand this despair in view of Mackinnon's own demand: 'Adequate knowledge of the roots, sounds, and forms and structure of the languages concerned must be brought to bear upon the names, and the results must be presented with clearness and, above all, with accuracy, without bias or prejudice of any sort' (*Ibid*: 84).

It is, however, again Macbain who is the most acerbic critic when, after several pages of corrections of obviously nonsensical derivations, he declares (Macbain 1906; reprinted 1922: 357):

> These are some of the errors which we find in Dr Gillies' *Place-Names of Argyll*. They are not all that we, or better still, one more acquainted with the county, could point out, but, as Mercutio says, ''Tis enough'.

I have referred to these three books and some of their reviews in so much detail because they demonstrate the contrast between their amateurish approaches and the new professionalism which was on the point of entering Scottish name studies, especially in the Highlands, at the turn of the century. It was into this changing world of scholarship, already inhabited by Donald Mackinnon, Alexander Macbain and, as Watson would have it (Watson, W. J. 1904-5*a*: 31), Dr Alexander Cameron of Brodick, of the *Scottish Celtic Review*, that William J. Watson stepped about a hundred years ago when he decided to study the names of his native county, after many years dedicated to the classics. Through his position as rector of Inverness Royal Academy and his close association with the Gaelic Society of Inverness and the editors of *The Celtic Review*—one of them Professor Donald Mackinnon, whom he later succeeded in Edinburgh; the other Ella Carmichael, his future wife, who provided a link with her father Alexander Carmichael—he had the status, the expertise, and the connections to translate his wide philological knowledge and educational ideas into sound onomastic scholarship and solid publications in this complex field of study. He was, at the time, the personification and synthesis of it all.

One is naturally inclined to concentrate all one's laudatory remarks on the *magnum opus, The History of the Celtic Place-Names of Scotland*, but it would be falsifying the picture if we were to perceive everything written by Watson on Scottish toponymy before 1926 as a prelude to the main work and everything published afterwards as a kind of postlude. Of course much of the earlier material made its way into the book, but this does not call into question its validity, its innovational impact or its influence as a methodological model at the time of its original publication; and anyhow, there is much that, for some reason, was never included in the book. As soon as *The Place-Names of Ross and Cromarty* had been published, Watson turned his attention to the neighbouring county of Sutherland: whether with the ultimate aim of producing a companion volume to his first book is difficult to say (Watson, W. J. 1905-6) [see p56]. If the publications which followed are anything to go by, he perhaps found the county as a geographical and administrative unit of study inappropriate or inadequate, preferring to roam more freely and more widely. His series of 'Topographical Varia' in *The Celtic Review* [see p80], probably starting with his short article on *'Innis* in Place-Names' [see p76] in the third volume (Watson, W. J. 1906-7), touches on a wide variety of questions and structural elements, such as the preposition *fo* 'under', the old adjective *loch* 'black', the element *ialo-s*, names containing references to the hazel, ecclesiastical place names, and so on (Watson, W. J. 1908-9; 1909-10; 1911-12; 1919-13).

After his move to Edinburgh, papers in the *Transactions of the Gaelic Society of Inverness* became fairly common: although hardly ever read by Watson himself because of, as the editors have it, 'the unavoidable absence of the author'. One is perhaps entitled to speculate that, in addition to his professorial obligations in Edinburgh, the main reason may have been the onset of his deafness. Among these papers are an account of the 'Place-Names of Strathdearn' [see p137] read on 9 March 1920 (Watson, W. J. 1919-22), followed by a study of 'Personal Names. The Influence of the Saints', read on 13 March 1925 (Watson, W. J. 1924-5), a survey of 'The Place-Names of Breadalbane' [see p163], read on 27 April 1928 (Watson, W. J. 1927-8), and 'Place-Names of Perthshire: The Lyon Basin' [see p193], the third part of which had been read to the Society on 17 April 1931 (Watson, W. J. 1999-30). Even if not designated specifically as dealing with toponymic topics, papers on other subjects—and we must remember that Watson was an all-rounder as a Celticist who represented the various aspects of the chair, Celtic literature, language, education, and archaeology, with equal competence—tend to include references to names, especially place names, when these can throw light on the subject matter in hand. Watson's fascination with name studies would not be denied, whatever the topic. A considerable portion of his article on hunting the deer is thus taken up by a detailed discussion of the place name *Elrick* and the like (Watson, W. J. 1913-14*a*: 162-5); and in a paper on 'The Celtic Church and Paganism', place names connected with *nemeta* 'sacred groves or meeting-places' are used as illustrations, and there are references to the deities of Glen Cuaich in Inverness-shire, of Loch Etive, and of the river Lochy (Watson 1914-16*a*: 276 and 266). His discussions of the *Cliar Sheanchain* 'Shenchan's Company' (Watson, W. J. 1907-8: 86), of 'Ciuthach' (Watson, W. J. 1913-14*b*), and of 'The Death of Diarmid' (Watson, W. J. 1914-16*b*: 357) are enhanced by the traditional localisation of events with the help of place names. It is probably not surprising that his Inaugural Address in Edinburgh on 13 October 1914 on 'The Position of Gaelic in Scotland' (Watson, W. J. 1914-16*c*), should make ample, or at least occasional, use of place-name evidence, as do his papers on 'The Picts: Their Original Position in Scotland', read on 14 April 1921 (Watson, W. J. 1919-22*b*; also a separate reprint Watson, W. J. 1921), 'The Celts (British and Gael) in Dumfriesshire and Galloway', read on 21 March 1924 (Watson, W. J. 1925), and 'The History of Gaelic in Scotland', read on 13 April 1939 (Watson, W. J. 1934-6, publ. 1946); but it is perhaps less to be expected that place names should figure prominently in support of arguments put forward in archaeological presentations on the 'Circular Forts of Perthshire', read on 9 December 1912

(Watson, W. J. 1912-13*b*), 13 December 1912 (Watson, W. J. 1912-14), and 14 December 1914 (Watson, W. J. 1914-15), which Watson wishes to ascribe to the Verturiones. The investigation of place names *per se* or as supporting evidence in all kinds of contexts—literary, linguistic, historical, archaeological, didactic—was in Watson's blood, and he never passes up an opportunity to make good use of them nor, as I have shown elsewhere (Nicolaisen 1982), to give credit to the Irish scholar P. W. Joyce, whose place-name books (Joyce 1869, 1875, 1913) served, at least in the initial stages of his researches, as providers of comparative materials and as stimuli for his own detailed examination of the Scottish Gaelic place-nomenclature. Both Joyce and the Rev Isaac Taylor (Taylor 1873) are mentioned as examples to be followed in the very first paragraph of his very first place-name article in *The Celtic Review* (Watson, W. J. 1904-5*a*: 22-3).

As I have already stressed, Watson's greatest achievement in the field of toponymic studies, his *History of the Celtic Place-Names of Scotland*, is the result of over thirty years of diligent and committed work by the author in acquiring and patterning the pieces of the mosaic which it represents. At some future date, it might be fascinating to trace in detail the gradual process underlying the emergence of this remarkable book and to catch glimpses into the workshop and mind of a great scholar. On this occasion we must content ourselves with following the shaping of two or three discrete items.

One of these has already been mentioned: Celtic *nemeton* 'a sacred place'. This is initially alluded to in *The Place-Names of Ross and Cromarty* under the name *Navity* in the parish of Cromarty: the Gaelic form is *Neamhaididh*, which Watson derives from *neimhidh* 'churchland', as 'the lands of Navity formed the endowment of a chapel in the Cathedral of Fortrose' (Watson, W. J. 1904*a*: 125). He compares it to *Nevity* in Fife, and also includes an extensive discussion of it and its cognates in the general Introduction to the book, under the rubric 'Ecclesiastical Terms' (*ibid*: xii-xiii). In his seminal article 'The Study of Highland Place-Names', this element is used as an example of how sometimes 'very old spellings, often unintelligible by themselves, at once light up when brought in contact with the modern Gaelic' (Watson 1904-5*a*: 26), citing *Nevoth* 1274 and Gaelic *Neimhidh* (apparently in reference to *Newmore* in the Ross-shire parish of Rosskeen, although this is not made clear). In his article on 'The Celtic Church and Paganism' (1914-16: 276), as we have already seen, *neimhidh* is used to illustrate the concept of sacred meeting-places, before finding its way into the fifth Rhind Lecture and from there into the *History* in a full and expert discussion taking up several pages in the section on 'Early Church Terms' (Watson, W. J. 1926: 244-50). Even after the publication of the *History* we find another brief discussion of it in 'Some Place-Names of the North' [see p211], a paper published by the Highland Exhibition, Inverness in 1930 (Watson, W. J. 1930: 9-10); and it apparently also became part of his classroom teaching.[1]

Secondly, the ancient Gaelic term *fortair* 'fortress' makes an appearance in Watson's series of 'Topographical Varia' in *The Celtic Review* (Watson, W. J. 1909-10: 236-7) where it is equated with a place of the Brigantes, called *Verterae*, listed in the *Antonine Itinerary*. Two years later, in Watson's account of 'Circular Forts in Perthshire', presented to both the Society of Antiquaries of Scotland (Watson, W. J. 1912-13*b*: 59-60) and the Gaelic Society of Inverness (Watson, W. J. 1912-14: 153); see also 1914-15: 17 *et passim*), it serves both to explain the tribal name of the Verturiones and place names like *Fortingall* and *Forfar*. A passage based on both these earlier examinations is then included in the *History* (Watson 1926: 68-9).

---

1 I am grateful to Mrs C.M. McClements, one of the last surviving students of W. J. Watson's and the first woman to receive a First Class Honours Degree in Celtic from the University of Edinburgh, for allowing me to examine her meticulously kept note-books containing her lecture notes of Professor Watson's classes. These not only reflect his teaching methods in general but also his extensive use of toponymic material whenever appropriate. Mrs McClements speaks of him in the warmest terms, both as a person and as a teacher.

Thirdly, the name *Paisley*, Gaelic *Paislig*, ultimately from Latin *basilica*, is the subject of Watson's very first reply to a reader's query [see p54] in *The Celtic Review* (Watson, W. J. 1904-5*b*), although he had already offered it a year earlier in his article on 'The Study of Highland Place-Names' as an illustration of how the modern Gaelic pronunciation of a name can throw light on the early written record (Watson, W.J. 1904-5*a*: 29). In the survey of the Celtic names of 'Ayrshire and Strathclyde' in the *History* (Watson, W. J. 1926: 194) this argument is somewhat extended but ultimately identical.

These are, of course, only very small bricks in the resulting edifice; but they afford us at least a glimpse of the patient ways in which that much and rightly praised *History of the Celtic Place-Names of Scotland* gradually found its final printed structure. I, for one, am happy that it did; because any work I have done on the Celtic place names of Scotland has had Watson's *History* as its starting-point and, more often than not, as its foundation.

Thus we take this opportunity to praise with reverence William John Watson, the greatest name scholar to have come out of the Gaelic culture of the Scottish Highlands, himself an accomplished student of the panegyric (Watson, W. J. 1914-18 and 1917-18); but our *laudatio* would be incomplete without also paying tribute to William John Watson, the educator and man of letters: after all, his *Rosg Gàidhlig* (Watson, W. J. 1915) and his *Bàrdachd Ghàidhlig* (Watson, W. J. 1918) are still university text-books today, the Scottish Gaelic Texts Society which he founded in 1934 is still flourishing, and his edition of *Scottish Verse from the Book of the Dean of Lismore* (Watson, W. J. 1937) was among the first to open our eyes to the riches of that most valuable Scottish Gaelic manuscript. And that is by no means the end of the achievements of this great man, just as the long list of publications at the end of this article is far from complete.

As someone who is very much in his scholarly debt, I hope that it is not too late for us to honour William John Watson, MA (Aberdeen), BA (Oxford), LLD (Aberdeen), and D Litt Celt (National University of Ireland), late rector of Inverness Academy and of Edinburgh Royal High School, also late Professor of Celtic Languages, Literature, History, and Antiquities in the University of Edinburgh, the continuing influence of whose achievements in the field of Celtic studies in general and in place-name research in particular is impossible to measure. We are privileged and content to live in his shadow.

BIBLIOGRAPHY

Anon, 1915 (1908-11). 'Complimentary Dinner to Mr W. J. Watson', *Transactions of the Gaelic Society of Inverness* 27, 170-84.

Calder, W. M., 1940-2. 'James Carmichael Watson, OS', *University of Edinburgh Journal* 11, 243.

Dundee Highland Society, 1910-11. *The Dundee Highland Society Year Book*, 12-13.

Gillies, H. Cameron, 1906. *The Place-Names of Argyll*. London (David Nutt).

Gillies, W, 1986. 'Elizabeth (Ella) Carmichael Watson (c1871 - 1928)'. In John H. Burnett *et al.* (eds), *The University Portraits*. Second Series, Edinburgh (Eyre Spottiswoode), 204-6.

Jackson, K. H., 1953. *Language and History in Early Britain*. Edinburgh (University Press).

— 1955. 'The Pictish Language'. In F. T. Wainwright (ed), *The Problem of the Picts*. Edinburgh (Nelson), 129-66.

Johnston, J. B., 1892. *Place-Names of Scotland*. First Edition, Edinburgh (Neill and Co.).

— 1903. *Place-Names of Scotland*. Second Edition, Edinburgh (David Douglas).

Joyce, P. W., 1869. *The Origin and History of Irish Names of Places*. Dublin (McGlashan & Gill).

— 1875. *The Origin and History of Irish Names of Places*. Second Series. Dublin (McGlashan & Gill).

— 1913. *The Origin and History of Irish Names of Places*, Vol. III. Dublin (The Educational Co. of Ireland).

Lamont, Donald, 1940. 'Elizabeth Catherine Carmichael'. In Alexander Carmichael, *Carmina Gadelica*, Vol. III. Edinburgh (Oliver & Boyd), xxi-xxiv.

Macbain, Alexander, 1892. 'A Review of *Place-Names of Scotland*'. *Inverness Courier*, 1 March; reprinted in Macbain 1922, 327-36.

— 1904-5. Review of *Place-Names of Ross and Cromarty*. *The Celtic Review* 1, 89-92.

— 1922. *Place Names of the Highlands & Islands of Scotland*, ed William J. Watson. Stirling (Eneas Mackay).

MacDonald, D.J., 1925-27. 'Professor W. J. Watson'. *Transactions of the Gaelic Society of Inverness* 33, v-x.

Macdonald, John, 1949. 'The Late Professor W. J. Watson'. *Scottish Gaelic Studies* 6, 215-6.

MacDonald, Mairi A., 1969-70; publ. 1971. 'History of the Gaelic Society of Inverness from 1871-1971'. *Transactions of the Gaelic Society of Inverness* 46, 1-20.

Mackenzie, Donald A., 1914. 'W. J. Watson'. *The Gambolier*, 3 December, 17-9.

Mackinnon, Donald, 1906-7. Review of *The Place-Names of Argyll*. *The Celtic Review* 3, 83-94.

Maclean, John, 1942. 'The Late Prof James Carmichael Watson', *Scottish Gaelic Studies* 5, 185-7.

Matheson, D., 1905. *The Place Names of Elginshire*. Stirling (Eneas Mackay).

Nicolaisen, W. F. H., 1976. *Scottish Place-Names: Their Study and Significance*. London (B. T. Batsford).

— 1982. 'P. W. Joyce and Scotland'. In *Topothesia*. Galway, Ireland RTCOG), 72-89.

Taylor, Isaac, 1873. *Words and Places*. Third Edition, London (Macmillan and Co.).

Vendryes, J., 1950-51. 'W. J. Watson'. *Études Celtiques* 5, 407-8.

Watson, E. C., 1908-9. 'Highland Mythology'. *The Celtic Review* 5, 48-70.

— 1908-11. 'Gaelic Address'. *Transactions of the Gaelic Society of Inverness* 27, 166-7.

Watson, W. J., 1899-1906. 'The Celtic Church in Ross', *Transactions of the Inverness Scientific Society and Field Club*, 6, 1-14.

— 1904a. *Place-Names of Ross and Cromarty* Inverness (The Northern Counties Printing and Publishing Co.).

— 1904b. '*Place Names of Scotland*: A Review', *Inverness Courier*.

— 1904c. 'Study of Scottish Place Names'. *Transactions of the Inverness Scientific Society and Field Club* 6 [1899-1906], 279-80.

— 1904-5a. 'The Study of Highland Place-Names'. *The Celtic Review* 1, 22-31.

— 1904-5b. 'Paisley'. *The Celtic Review* 1, 288.

— 1905-6. 'Some Sutherland Names of Places', *The Celtic Review* 2, 232-42 and 260-8.

— 1906-7. '*Innis* in Place-Names'. *The Celtic Review* 3, 239-42.

— 1907-8. 'Cliar Sheanchain'. *The Celtic Review* 4, 80-8.

— 1908-9. 'Topographical Varia'. *The Celtic Review* 5, 148-54 and 337-42.

— 1909-10. 'Topographical Varia—III'. *The Celtic Review* 6, 236-41.

— 1911-12a. 'Topographical Varia—IV'. *The Celtic Review* 7, 68-81.

— 1911-12b. 'Topographical Varia—V'. *The Celtic Review* 7, 361-71.

— 1912-13a. 'Topographical Varia—VI'. *The Celtic Review* 8, 235-45.

— 1912-13b. 'The Circular Forts of North Perthshire'. *Proceedings of the Society of Antiquaries of Scotland* 47, 30-60.

— 1912-14. 'Circular Forts in Perthshire'. *Transactions of the Gaelic Society of Inverness* 28, 151-5.

— 1913-14a. 'Aoibhinn an Obair an t-Sealg'. *The Celtic Review* 9, 158-68

— 1913-14b. 'Ciuthach'. *The Celtic Review* 9, 193-209.

— 1914-15. 'Circular Forts in Lorn and North Perthshire'. *Proceedings of the Society of Antiquaries of Scotland* 49, 17-32.

— 1914-16a. 'The Celtic Church in its Relations with Paganism'. *The Celtic Review* 10, 263-79.

— 1914-16b. 'The Death of Diarmid'. *The Celtic Review* 10, 350-7.

— 1914-16c. 'The Position of Gaelic in Scotland'. *The Celtic Review* 10, 69-84.

— 1914-19. 'Classic Gaelic Poetry of Panegyric in Scotland'. *Transactions of the Gaelic Society of Inverness* 29, 194-235.

— 1915. *Rosg Gàidhlig*. Inverness (An Comunn Gaidhealach).

— 1916. 'Some place-names in the Cairngorm region'. *Cairngorm Club Journal* 8, 133-6.

— 1917-18. 'Classic Gaelic poetry of Panegyric'. *Proceedings of the Royal Philosophical Society of Glasgow* 49, 134-56.

— 1918. *Bàrdachd Ghàidhlig*. Inverness (Northern Counties Publishing Co.).

— 1919-22a. 'Place-Names of Strathdearn'. *Transactions of the Gaelic Society of Inverness* 30, 101-21.

— 1921. 'The Picts: Their Original Position in Scotland'. *Transactions of the Gaelic Society of Inverness* 30, 240-61.

— 1921. *The Picts: Their Original Position in Scotland* (reprinted from *The Inverness Courier*, Inverness).

— 1924-25. 'Personal Names: The Influence of the Saints'. *Transactions of the Gaelic Society of Inverness* 32, 220-47.

— 1925. 'The Celts (British and Gael) in Dumfriesshire and Galloway'. *Transactions of the Dumfriesshire and Galloway Natural History and Antiquarian Society*, Third Series, 11, 119-48.

— 1926. *The History of the Celtic Place-Names of Scotland*. Edinburgh (Blackwood).

— 1927-28. 'The Place-Names of Breadalbane'. *Transactions of the Gaelic Society of Inverness* 34, 248-79.

— 1929-30. 'Place-Names of Perthshire: The Lyon Basin'. *Transactions of the Gaelic Society of Inverness* 35, 277-96.

— 1930. *Some Place-Names of the North*. Inverness (Highland Exhibition).

— 1934-36 (publ. 1946). 'The History of Gaelic in Scotland'. *Transactions of the Gaelic Society of Inverness* 37, 115-35.

— 1937. *Scottish Verse from the Book of the Dean of Lismore*. Scottish Gaelic Texts Society I. Edinburgh (Oliver & Boyd).

— (ms) Item 25B in Carmichael Watson Collection of Edinburgh University Library.

SCOTTISH

PLACE-NAME PAPERS

Place Names of Scotland, A Review

The new and enlarged edition of Rev J B Johnston's *Place Names of Scotland* (Edinburgh: David Douglas) consists of an introduction of about 100 pages, followed by a list of names extending to about 300 pages. The author has had the advantage of criticisms and notes, contributed by Dr A Macbain and others; he himself also has not been idle in the meantime, and the result is an advance in accuracy and fullness. Among the articles which have undergone a change for the better are such as Clachnacuddin, Conchra, Don, Glentruim, Glenshiora, Gravir, Hirsel, Killiecrankie, Knockando. From the Introduction some questionable matter has been excised, and the author's researches among records, especially the Coldingham Charters, have enriched the book with many additional old written forms of names, which enhance its value as a handy book of reference. While giving the author due credit for the enthusiasm which has prompted him to attack so difficult a subject and the diligence which he has displayed in the collection of materials, we are bound to state that much still remains that is capable of improvement. The author has not yet attained to the necessary proficiency in the Gaelic language and Gaelic philology which alone can make him a trustworthy guide, nor does he seem to put in practice all the principles, most of them sound enough, with which he prefaces his Introduction.

At the root of enquiry into the origin and meaning of Scottish names lies the great Pictish question—not necessarily who were the Picts, but what language did they speak. Mr Johnston tells us that on this point Dr Skene's verdict is generally held to be the true one; to wit, that the Northern Picts spoke a language closely akin to Gaelic, and that the change from Pictish to Irish Gaelic was a little thing. With regard to this, it is enough to say that Dr Skene's theory is not shared by Dr Whitley Stokes, Dr Macbain, Windisch, Principal Rhys, or indeed by any modern Celtic scholar of standing. Linguistic tests prove that the language of North Pictland was of the Cymric branch. Even Principal Rhys, who still clings to the theory that the Picts were non-Ayran as to race, has to admit that before Columba's time the dominant Celtic influence among the Picts must have been Brythonic. The outstanding test is the treatment of the primitive sound *qu*, which the Brythonic Celts made into *p*, while the Gadelic branch made it *c* hard. Mr Johnston applies this principle in a dangerously loose fashion. He seems to think that any Gaelic *c* may be equated with a Pictish *p*, e.g. Pathstruie he makes Cathstruthan, battle on the little stream. Such a nomenclature is in itself unlikely, but the serious thing is that Gaelic *cath* is Welsh *cad*, Gaulish *catu*, showing that the Brythonic and the Gadelic languages are in this case identical, and *p* could never have stood here. So with Spelvie, which he takes to be a Pictish form of Gaelic *sgealb*, a splinter; the Welsh is *ysgolp*, Breton *skolp*. Plean, he thinks, may be a Pictish form of Gaelic *gleann*; worse still, under Logie-Pert, he says 'Pert is probably G. feart, a small round fort, with Pictish *p*'. The Pictish *p* can be equated only with Gadelic *c* when the latter is derived from a primitive *qu* or velar *q*: to equate it with *c* not so derived is impossible, still less can it be interchanged with wholly different sounds such as *g* and *f*. Incidentally, it may be noted that the first mention of the Picts is by the orator Eumenius, c300 AD, not Ammianus Marcellinus, who, of course, does mention them, but who lived some 70 years later.

'Inver does not exist in Wales, and it is rare in Ireland; these facts point to it being a Pictish word.' Dr Joyce, who ought to know, says that Inver is common in Ireland, and it is a genuine Gaelic word, used in Gaelic with the article as a common noun. Pictish *obair* is never so used.

Dealing with names in general, Mr Johnston lays down the sound rules that it is important to ascertain the old written forms of names, while it is almost equally desirable that we should know their local, native pronunciation. To the former of these rules he adheres with zeal that often leads him into strange conclusions. The latter he enunciates only to depart from it in the very cases where a knowledge of the real spoken forms would have been of the utmost consequence to him, namely, in the verification of the current pronunciation of names of Celtic origin in districts where Gaelic is still spoken. Here he is seized with a profound distrust of the Celt. Yet if anyone knows the real name, as opposed to the attempts at writing it made by scribes ignorant of Gaelic, and of Gaelic phonetics and spelling, the native Celt, to whom the name descended from his fathers before him, ought to know it. '*Nota bene*, it will not always do to trust local pronunciations and interpretations, even when given by a true Gael. Loch-Maree, so universally and wrongly thought to be Mary's Loch, is a case in point.' Here, of course, the author confuses two very different things, pronunciation and interpretation. No place name expert who heard the native pronunciation of Loch Maree would imagine for a moment that it meant Mary's Loch. If the native tells him that it means Mary's Loch, that only proves that the native is not an expert at interpreting place names. 'It will be found that the "oldest inhabitant" (Gaelic) is apt to be extremely ignorant and misleading in his idea of Celtic etymology.' These characteristics are not confined to the 'oldest inhabitant', but what does Mr Johnston expect? Does he expect to find him armed with a copy of Dr Macbain's *Dictionary*, and capable of criticising the same? It will be time enough to fall foul of the honest man when we find him, in the excess of his etymological ardour—for he does etymologise—misrepresenting the tradition of the elders in the matter of pronunciation. But when the author has got hold of the real Gaelic pronunciation, as he has in a few cases only, his devotion to old written forms makes him underestimate its value. In dealing with Kilmuir (Ross), he quotes 1394 Culmor; 1482 Culmore; and derives thus: 'cùl mór, big back (of the hill); only to-day it is Gael. Cill Mhoire'. Here Mr Johnston is sinning against light. *Cill Mhoire*, Mary's Church, was of course the name all along; the early spellings are not for a moment to be taken into consideration here. Cromdale, Geanies, are further examples. The vagaries of early spelling lead the author to the curious conclusion that Gaelic names are in a state of flux. They change, he finds, from century to century. Of this Heraclitean doctrine the best example is that ill-omened name Glencoe: '1343, Glenchomyr; 1494, Glencole; 1500, Glencoyne; 1623, Glencoan. The form shows the word has been constantly altering.' If the author is sure that these are bona fide spellings of Glencoe, and that he has not mixed it up with another place, he may rest assured that the variations are careless scribal attempts at a Gaelic name difficult to spell. Further examples of the same doctrine will be found at Fortingall, Balquhidder, and elsewhere.

The value of written forms is greatest when these can be controlled by the genuine modern Gaelic pronunciation. The oldest spelling of Dundee (the author quotes it at Dundaff) is Obsessio Duin Deauae 696; the modern Gaelic is *Dùn Dèadh* (pron. as in *gèadh*, goose). This proves *Dun Dé*, Hill of God, to be out of the question. Kilravock, 1282 Kilrethuoc; c1286 Kilrevock; G. Cillrathag proves *coil riabhach*, brindled wood, wrong. Kincardine, 1227 Kyncardyn; G. Cinn-chardain, shows that the name has nothing to do with *gàirdean*, arm. Latheron, 1274 Lagheryn; 1275 Laterne; 1515 Latheron; G. Lathairn proves it, old forms notwithstanding, to be, as Dr Maclauchlan saw, the same as Lorne. Latheron-wheel, old spelling Latheron-fuil, G. *Lathairn a' phùill*, Latheron of the pool; not 'the forks or divisions of the spot of ground', as Mr Johnston would have us believe. Examples of this sort might be multiplied. It cannot be too clearly understood that the first duty of one who professes to deal with Celtic names is to ascertain the true native pronunciation. With this he is on sure ground; old spellings are merely ancillary. Mr Johnston's method, as may be seen from the examples quoted above, is to proceed placidly to interpret names on the strength of old spellings only, most of them illiterate, while, as a rule, he entirely ignores the Gaelic form which, after all, is the real name. This is little better than guessing.

'English speakers often put *the* before a name, as the Methil, the Lochies; in Gaelic the article is almost never prefixed to a place name.' Where *the* is prefixed in English, it is often a translation of the Gaelic article, for in Gaelic names the article is usually prefixed wherever the construction admits. In fact, the presence of the article is one of the surest tests of a genuine Gaelic name. In the records it is frequently translated by *lie*.

'The Gael almost always aspirates his *s*, and loves to speak of the "Shawms of David".' What is referred to here is not genuine aspiration, which results in *sh* being pronounced as *h*, but palatalised *s* before a slender vowel, as in *seas*, pronounced *shes*. Before a broad vowel *s* is never so palatalised, and the Celt who talks of 'Shawms' must have been affected as to his articulation by something stronger than himself.

With regard to Gaelic spelling, Mr Johnston complains that 'there is probably no language in the world in which the eye can give less help to the tongue. To an untrained eye the spelling is usually altogether misleading.' If in the above we substitute 'more help' for 'less help', the author will be right. Gaelic is not written phonetically, but its spelling has this advantage, that a word correctly spelled is pronounced with exact correctness by any person who can read Gaelic. And the rules of Gaelic spelling, arbitrary to some extent as they are, can be mastered easily. The present writer has before him a list of Gaelic names of places, spelled by a gentleman who knows the rules of Gaelic spelling, and though there are some which he has never heard pronounced, he has not the slightest difficulty with regard to the proper sound of any one of them. Of how many European languages could this be said? 'The untrained eye' is capable of many things; but in matters regarding phonetics we are dealing, or are supposed to be dealing, with the trained eye. It will be long ere we can evolve for Gaelic a system of spelling so well adapted, on the whole, as the present for representing the spoken word.

In dealing with influence of accent, the writer points out that in Gaelic the accent tends to fall on the first syllable. He should have added 'in uncompounded words and in compounds where the first part is an adjective, a noun used adjectivally, or a preposition'. In compounds formed on the ordinary model the adjectival part comes after the generic part, and therefore the principal stress accent is on the second part of the compound, e.g. *Ach-nan-gart*, Field of the corn enclosures, accented on *gart*.

In view of this, it is difficult to understand what the author means when, dealing with the slurring of unaccented syllables, he says 'seldom has the final syllable survived in a name; though we have, e.g. Achanancarn, Achanamoine, and Auchamore'. The whole section on accent seems to show some confusion of thought. He falls into a mistake of far-reaching consequences when he asserts that *achadh*, a field, has in hundreds of names become -*ach* at the end of words.[1] Terminal -*ach* has nothing to do with *achadh*, a field; it represents the Gaulish -*ācum*, place of; *ācus*, abounding in. Carnoch means not Field of Cairns or Stones, but Place of Cairns; Stony-place; so with Crannich, a locative form of Crannach, Tree-place; Dornoch, Pebble-place, and other instances innumerable. He also overrates the extent to which final unaccented syllables are liable to corruption. Thus, Logie, Eathie, etc, have not arisen and could not arise from Lagan, Athan; final -*an* does not become -*ie*. Logie, Tully, Dornie, and a host of other names are survivals from the period when the locative of Gaelic words ending in -*ach* was in -*aigh*, as it is still in Irish. Thus, Logie is the old locative of Lagach, Place in the hollow, and so on; cf Cairnie, Dornie, Blairie, as against Carnoch, Dornoch, Blarich.

Mr Johnston allows himself a dangerous laxity in the matter of hybrids, i.e. compound names in which the different parts of the compound belong to different languages. The genuine hybrid is a very simple and intelligible affair. In the west and north, for instance, the Norsemen left their Gaelic-speaking successors a number of Norse names, such as Shieldaig, Alladale, Dibidale, Tanera, meaning respectively Herring-bay, Ali's-dale, Deep-dale, Haven-isle. This legacy the Gaels accepted, and soon forgetting the meaning of the names, they prefixed their own Gaelic terms as they had occasion. Thus we get Ardshieldaig, Promontory of Shieldaig; Glenalladale, Glen of Alladale; Glendibidale; Eilean Thannara, Isle Tanera; in many cases, as will be noted, the Gaelic

---

1 Here the author has pointed out that his meaning has been misapprehended. But, as the misapprehension was a natural one, and as the author does not seem to know the true theory of -ach final, the passage has been allowed to stand.

element is merely a duplication of Norse dale or vik, or ness, as the case may be. In all it will be observed that the Gaelic speakers were ignorant of the meaning of the Norse name. And this is of the essence of hybrid formations. No names are found of a type involving the conscious use of two languages at once. Names containing words borrowed from Norse into Gaelic are not real hybrids; for these loans have become part and parcel of the Gaelic language, the visible sign of annexation being the prefixing of the definite article. We have observed about a couple of dozen of thoroughly bad hybrids in the book. For instance— Ardtornish—'G. àird-t(h)orr, cape of the hill, + Norse ness'. The word should be divided into G. Aird, cape, and Tornish, yielding the legitimate hybrid Cape of Tornish, i.e. of Thori's ness; a duplication of meaning. Arisaig—'Prob. Norse, Aross-vik, river-mouth bay'. This is correct; but it is immediately spoiled by the bad addition, 'or, Gael. aros, house + vik'; an unthinkable combination. Cadboll—'Place of the Cat or Cataibh with Norse bolstaðr. Possibly from G. Cath, old Gael, cat, a battle'. Both suggestions are untenable. Cadboll is pure Norse 'Cat-stead'. Wild cats once abounded in the rocks here; cf Teachatt, Cat-house. Easdale—'G. eas, a waterfall + N. dal, a valley'. Embo—'G. àthan, a little ford + N. bol'. This despite the fact that the author knows the Gaelic to be 'Eirpol' (properly Éiribol), an impossible vowel mutation. Embo is of course an English corruption, and a bad one at that. Eskadale—'G. uisge, water + N. dal'. The name is pure Norse Eski-dalr, Ash-dale. Kilham—'looks like Gael. coille, a wood, or cill, a church + OE ham. But Isaac Taylor is probably right in deriving from OE locative chillon, at the springs.' This is one of several cases where the author fails to recognise the right explanation when it is placed before him. Letham—'G. leth, a half, a share + OE ham, house'. On this principle why not also half-tigh, half-allt? Geanies—'G. gaothanach, windy + N. ness.' The s of Geanies is the English plural; the place was Gany, and it was divided into the easter, wester, and mid Ganys. But in any case the combination of a Gaelic adjective with Norse ness is a monstrosity. Other examples, neither better nor worse, are

Attadale, Criffel, Crichtoun, Idrigill, Kerrysdale (a modern name by the way), Kirkliston, Langavill (N. lang + G. bhaile!), Ledaig, Miavaig, Rutherglen, Restalrig (G. lios-talamh, garden soil + rig!), Saddell, and so on. Among Norse names wrongly explained may be noted Loch-Ranza, which is really Norse *reynis-á*, rowan tree river (Macbain), not Ransay, island of the house. The numerous names involving the common Norse name Thori need not, as the author is inclined to do, be referred to the great god Thor. One of the easiest Norse names on the map of Scotland is Carradale N. *kjarr-á-dalr*, Copse-river dale. This name, says Mr Johnston, may mean copse wood valley. So far not amiss; but he has failed to recognise the N. *á* river, with this result: 'Only there is a river Carra, and river names are rarely Norse; so perhaps cognate with Gael. *carraig* or *carr*, a rock or cliff.' This is sad work; the River Carra is just N. *kjarr-á*, copse river.

Trotternish, 'said to mean enchanted cape; cf Icel. trùdra, a juggler'. The Gaelic is *Trò(n)dairnis* (with strongly nasal *o*), which at once shows the name to be the well-known *Thróndar-nes*, Boar-ness. The derivation of Skibo, Gaelic *Sgiobul*, from N. *skeid*, a warship, is entirely doubtful, for Norse *ei* regularly becomes *ao* in Gaelic. Skibo is old Scithebol, 'Skithi's stead', as in Skeabost. Shieldaig, Gaelic *Sìldeag*, Norse *síldvík*, herring bay, the author takes to be N. *skjöldr vik*, shield bay. He ought to have known that Norse *k* never becomes *h*; it is always stable. He repeats this error in Glenshiel and Shiel, Adamnan's Sale, Gaelic *Seile*, which he coolly takes to be Norse *skáli*, a hut. The name is Pictish doubtless, and means something like 'fluid'; cf *seile*, saliva; *sil*, to drop. Flowerdale, in Gairloch which he takes to be Norse *flúr-dalr*, might be so; only it is a name of yesterday, like Kerrysdale, near it. In a fine piece of confused writing on Forres, the author suggests the name to be influenced by Norse *fors*, a waterfall. The Gaelic is *Farais*, showing the distinctive Pictish ending *-ais* (open *a*) seen in *Allt-ais*, Altas; *Cinn-it'ais*, Kinnettes, and numerous other names on the east coast. Garrynahine in Lewis shows borrowed Norse *gerði*. G. *gearraidh* a strip of enclosed land, very common in Lewis; but Mr Johnston makes it *garidh na h-aibhne*, copse, or rough land by the river side. Gartie comes from Gaelic *gart*, a corn enclosure; not from Norse *garðr*, which could not possibly show a *t* in Gaelic. From all this it will be seen that the Norse element in Mr Johnston's book requires a good deal of rubbing up.

We turn to the Celtic names, many of which are comparatively simple, many on the other hand difficult enough to put the best equipped Celtic scholar and philologist on his mettle. Here we require above all things accurate data, and, as has been already stated, Mr Johnston takes little or no account of the supremely important data afforded by modern Gaelic. Moreover he is often at sea in his phonetics. *Na h-Earradh*, the Gaelic name of Harris, he thinks to be Gaelic *àirdead*, which, even granting the existence in Gaelic of such a word, is clean impossible. Mintlaw, 'Probably Gael. moine t' lacha, moss of the wild ducks'. But whence the t? Excrescent *t* developed after *s* we know, but no developed *t* is possible here. 'Abriachan G. aber breacach, confluence abounding in trout'. The *c* of *breac*, trout is absolutely stable, and could never become *ch*. So in Achnashellach, where the author contemplates the possibility of *Ach-na-seilg*, Hunting-field; *g* of *seilg* is stable, and could not be anything other than itself. Again, the author does not possess the *feel* of the Gaelic language, which would prevent him from suggesting impossible combinations. Maggiknockater, a sufficiently curious word as it stands, he says looks like 'G. Màgach cnoc-a-tìre, hill with many arable fields on the land'. What this looks like, we should rather not say; we are content to suggest as a possible alternative *màg an fhucadair*, the fuller's field; the *fucadair* was a well-known institution when home-made cloth was in vogue. Kinkell G. Cinn-cheal, Head-church, is, so far as the present writer is aware, a derivation without any authority, and an un-Gaelic formation. In the matter of prefixed adjectives much greater caution should have been exercised; e.g. *cailleanach tir* as a possible explanation of Callander is quite out of the question. The Gaelic adjectives actually found prefixed in names of places are quite few in number, and in the main very common and familiar words of one syllable, referring chiefly to colour and size. A few names may be noted in conclusion.

Kirkintilloch has nothing to do with Kirk. It appears in the ancient gloss on Nennius as Cair Pentaloch, near the western end of the Roman wall, and is one of the names that prove Brythonic *pen*, head, to have been translated by the Gaels who succeeded the Brythons into their own *cinn*, locative of *ceann*, head. Kirkintilloch should therefore be divided Kir-kin-tilloch, where *kir* equals *caer*, fort. Carron, as the present writer has pointed out years ago, is primitive Carsona, rough river, and is not to be connected with *car*, turn. Contin, G. *Cunndainn*, in all probability means 'confluence'; Gaulish *Condate*; certainly not *cointin*, a dispute. Boleskine is in Gaelic *Both-fhleasgain*, withy-booth; the inspiration that derived it from *Poll-eas-cumhain*, pool of the narrow water-fall, with reference to the Falls of Foyers, was emphatically not a happy one. The fall itself is *Eas na Smùid*, spray-fall. Foyers, an English plural, is the name of the estate near it; Gaelic *Foithir*, a terraced slope; one of the commonest names in the west, if I identify it correctly with the West Coast *faithir*. Loch Hourn is Loch of the Kiln, or furnace-shaped gulley; G. *sorn*, borrowed early from Latin *furnus*; Gaelic *Loch Shuirn*; in Dean of Lismore phonetically *sowrnni*. Mr Johnston derives 'Loch of Hell'; a grisly suggestion, which he repeats with no probability, under Loch Katrine. 'Tomnahurich—Prof Mackinnon says, G. tom na h-iubhraich, hillock of the juniper bushes'. Here Prof Mackinnon, wrote 'juniper', inadvertently no doubt, for 'yew'; the name means Hillock of the Yew-wood; its old form is seen in Eboracum, now York. 'Iubrach (*sic*) also means "boat", as in Portnachuraich, Iona'. *Iubhrach* does mean boat, but only, we think, in fairy or heroic tales. Portnachuraich is *Port a' churaich*, Port of the *curach* or hide boat; no connection of *iubhrach*. As to Paisley, the Gaelic is *Paislig*, therefore the present writer suggests O. Irish *Baisleac*, a Church.

'Alness, at the mouth of the River Rusdale, called in 1608 Affron; G. ath 'n-innis, ford of the island (the Black Isle); influenced by Ness'. The Gaelic of Alness is *Alanais*, a Pictish name; there is no River Rusdale, nor ford to the Black Isle. 'Ford of the island' would be *àth na h-innse*; but the author habitually makes Gaelic genders suit the exigencies of the moment.

Some of the derivations suggested above ought to have been known to the author, for they have appeared in print under the names of reliable Celtic scholars. Many valuable articles on the subject of place names have within the last dozen years appeared in the columns of the northern press, e.g. the *Inverness Courier*, *Northern Chronicle*, and *Highland News* and the *Oban Times*, which should have proved a perfect mine of information to Mr Johnston, and not the least misfortune in connection with his book is that he has not availed himself of the work already accomplished by others to the extent that he might have done. In the above remarks only the fringe of a great subject has been touched, for there are few articles in the book which would not stand revision. But the labour involved in an authoritative work on Scottish Place Names is beyond the capacity of any single scholar.

The Study of Highland Place-Names

Although much has been written about our Scottish names of places, we are as yet very far from possessing anything like a complete or satisfactory account of them. Nothing on the subject so far approaches, for example, the work of Dr Joyce on the names of Ireland, or that of Canon Isaac Taylor on English Village Names. This may be ascribed partly to the great difficulty of the subject, aggravated as it is by the comparative scantiness of ancient and reliable written forms of names, partly to the fewness of investigators possessing the necessary qualifications of scholarship and opportunity. It must be admitted, however, that much of the work actually attempted is sadly lacking in trustworthiness from no other reason than defective method; and the remarks that follow are intended mainly to set forth some principles that the writer, and others of greater experience than he can claim, have found trustworthy and helpful in the study of names which occur in districts where Gaelic is still vernacular. There, with care and right methods, it is possible to attain a high degree of certainty in interpretation; in districts where Gaelic has long died out, and where, accordingly, our sole data are old spellings and modern English pronunciations, the case is different.

In dealing with the names of a Gaelic-speaking district the first duty of the investigator is to ascertain with accuracy the native Gaelic pronunciation. For small areas this is a comparatively easy matter; when one has to deal with the names of a whole Highland county it becomes formidable. Very little can be done by correspondence, unless one is fortunate enough to have as correspondent an expert in Gaelic spelling; and though Gaelic spelling is not really difficult, such experts are not to be met in every district. By far the most satisfactory way is to verify the names personally on the spot; thus variations may be checked; the places themselves can be inspected—always an advantage; in addition, one picks up names of interest not found on the maps, as well as local lore in the shape of topographical rhymes and other items of *Dinnsenchas*. Incidentally one becomes acquainted with local peculiarities of dialect, which is not seldom a matter of some importance. It is obvious that to deal with the whole of the Highlands in this manner is beyond the capacity of one man, unless he be endowed with exceptional enthusiasm and leisure. Even with the advantage of generous assistance it took the present writer quite four years to verify the mainland names of his native county of Ross, and another survey of the ground would doubtless bring much new material to light. There is therefore in our Highland counties ample room for many investigators, who may render inestimable service to the study of topography by simply writing down in orthodox Gaelic spelling the names as they are heard on the lips of natives. It is only after such a process of verification that we are in direct touch with the name itself as distinguished from Anglified corruptions or mere map forms. A good example of an Anglified form is the well-known Altnaharra in Sutherland. As to this name, *quot homines, tot sententiae.* It has been explained as Harold's Burn; Burn of the Heights (cf Harris, in Gaelic *na Hearradh*); Stream with the pillar or rock (*carragh*); Stream of slaughter (*marbhadh*); and so on. But one and all carefully avoid the genuine Gaelic form, which is *Allt na h-Eirbhe* (given by the Andersons in 1834 as Aultnaharrou or Aultnaherve[1]), involving the old Gaelic word *eirbhe*, a wall of turf and stones; O. Ir. *airbe*, a fence (primarily 'ribs'). In point of fact the old wall is there; a long wall across moor and hill, worth the attention of antiquaries. I give without comment some more examples of Anglified names with their forms in modern Gaelic:–

Toward Point (Rothesay)	*Tollard*: Hole Cape
Loch Eye (E. Ross)	*Loch na h-Uidhe*: Isthmus Loch
Inchberry (Inverness)	*Innis a' Bhàraidh*: Hurling Mead
Pitnellies (Tain)	*Bail' an Ianlaith*: Bird Stead
Killiehuntly (Badenoch)	*Coille Chunndainn*: Wood of the Confluence
Rhives (Ross)	*na Ruigheannan*: the Slopes
Rhives (Sutherland)	*an Ruigheach*: the place of Slopes

1 Anderson's *Guide to the Highlands*, 1834.

Pookandraw (Black Isle)	*Bog an t-Srath*: Bog of the Strath
Torris Trean (Dingwall)	*Torr a' Phris Draigheann*: Knoll of the Thorn Clump
Tornapress (Lochcarron)	*Treabhar nam Preas*: Bush Stead

This list—a fairly typical one—might be extended indefinitely. It includes one name in part Pictish (Killiehuntly), and one name involving an obsolete word (Inchberry). All that is required for the understanding of the rest is a fair knowledge of Gaelic. The question arises: What sort of explanation could be given of such Anglified forms if we did not happen to possess the genuine Gaelic ones? And arising therefrom the further question: Seeing that all Celtic names outside the Highland counties have been subjected to similar treatment in English mouths, how far is a reliable explanation possible where the Gaelic form has been lost? And there are further complications. The River Garry (Kinlochewe) is in Gaelic *a' Ghairbhe*; the Inverness Garry is *Garadh*; the Ross-shire River Bran is *Bran*, the Perthshire is *Breamhainn*; English *kil-* may stand for Gaelic *cill*, church, as in Kil-muir; *cùil*, as in Kil-coy, G. Cuil-challaidh; *caol*, as Kildary, G. Caol-daraidh, as also for *coille*, wood. Again, the Anglicised forms fail to show the quantity of vowels even in accented syllables; e.g. in Balfron, we cannot tell whether *o* was originally long or short. A knowledge of the Gaelic forms sweeps away all such difficulties and ambiguities.

The forms of names given in Gaelic spelling on the present Ordnance Survey Maps require verification in every case. I give a few typical examples from the map of Ross.

OSM	Local Pronunciation
Beinne na Diollaide (Alness)	*Bendeallt*
Cnoc Liath Fad (Alness)	*Cnoc Leithbhaid* (i.e. *Léith Bhaid*)
Cnoc a' Ghille Bhrònaich (Alness)	*Cnoc Gille Mo-Bhrianaig*
Cnoc Vabin (Kiltearn)	*Cnoc Mhàbairn*
Feachdach (Kiltearn)	*an Fhiaclaich*

Sgurr Marc-Suidhe (Contin)	*Sgùrr Marcasaidh*
Loch na Caoidhe (Contin)	*Loch na Cuithe*
Beinn Aonaclair (Lochbroom)	*Beinn Eunacleit*
Loch na Doire Seirbhe	*Loch Doire na h-Eirbhe*
(Lochbroom).	

It is satisfactory to know that this outrageous mangling of our Gaelic names will be largely rectified in the forthcoming issue of the Ordnance Survey. As far as Gaelic forms of names go, the present maps are most deceptive.

It will be legitimately asked: to what extent have the Gaelic forms themselves suffered corruption? All language changes, and Gaelic is not exempt. A distinction, however, must be drawn between the orderly phonetic changes that take place within the language itself in the course of its development, and those corruptions which are the result of transferring Gaelic names to a language so very different in its genius as English. Now through Gaelic we have had handed down to us three different classes of names, Pictish, Scandinavian and Gaelic. It is, I believe, safe to say that the changes undergone by names of purely Gaelic origin have been mainly, if not almost wholly, those incidental to the language itself. The modern Gaelic forms of such bear the mark of authenticity on their faces. Even old Gaelic words now obsolete are regularly found in perfect preservation; e.g. *eirbhe, fasadh, eileag, faithir, seòlaid*. The chief difficulty—and it is not serious—is in connection with unaccented syllables following on prefixed adjectives, nouns, and prepositions, where the strong accent on the prefixed part causes slurring of the rest. As an example of the prefixed adjective may be taken Loch na Shanish, dear to the skaters and curlers of Inverness. This is *Loch na Seanninnse*, Loch of the Old Haugh or Meadow. A prefixed noun is seen in *Plucaird* near Poolewe, from *Ploc-àird*, Lump-cape; here *à* is shortened. A good example of the prefixed preposition at work is Ettridge in Badenoch, G. *Eadrais* for *Eadar dhà Eas*, Between two Falls. Another is Ardroil in Lewis for *Eadar dhà Fhaoghail*, Between two Fords. The total number of such formations is relatively small. The general stability of Gaelic names may of course be tested by comparison with charter forms, to which they supply the best key. Very old spellings, often unintelligible by themselves, at once light up when brought in contact with the modern Gaelic: e.g. Kennachrowe, 1362, G. *Ceanna-ruigh*, Head of the Hill Slope; Nevoth, 1274, G. *Neimhidh*, Churchland (Gaul. Nemeton); Culderare, 1611, G. *Cuilt-eararaidh*, Nook of Parching, etc.

Norse names transmitted through Gaelic show great regularity of treatment as a whole, combined with local peculiarities. Gaelic regularly preserves the quantity of accented syllables; in itself a very great advantage, for the accented syllable is the business part of the name. In unaccented syllables the quantity is lost, e.g. *á-mót*, river-meet, confluence, becomes in Gaelic always *Àmaid*, Amat. Unaccented syllables are liable also to slurring and curtailment, e.g. *ár-skiki*, riverstrip, becomes *Àrscaig*, Arscaig; Inverasdale (a hybrid) is in Gaelic *Inbhir-àsdal*, but as old forms give Inver-aspedell, we know that we are dealing with Norse *aspidalr*, Aspendale. In this latter case without the old forms we should have been helpless, but fortunately it is an exceptional one. Detailed consideration of Gaelic treatment of the Norse vowels and consonants would occupy too much space, and I have attempted it elsewhere.[1] The account there given will doubtless be improved and extended in the light of further research. Among local peculiarities may be noted the treatment of *bólstaðr*, which becomes *Bosta*, and terminally *-bol*, *-bost*, *-bus*. *Lín-setr*, flax-shieling, becomes in Sutherland *Lianasaid*, Linside, in Lewis *Lìseadar*, Linshader. Examples of regular treatment are: Isle Tanera, G. *Tannara*, N. *Hafnar-ey*, Haven-Isle; Trotternish, G. *Tròndarnais*, N. *Thròndar-nes*, Thrond's Cape; Ard-heslaig, N. *hesla-vik*, Hazel Bay; Loch Ranza, G. *Raonasa*, N. *reynis-á*, Rowan Water; Miavaig, N. *mjó-vík*, Narrow Bay; Stornoway, G. *Steòrnabhadh*,

1 PNRC, p *lvii, seqq.*

N. *Stjórna-vagr*, Steerage Bay; Tòll, N. *hól*, hill; Slattadale, G. *Sléiteadal*, N. *Sléttrdalr*, Evendale; G. *Tòrasdal*, N. *Thóris-dalr*, Thorir's Dale.

The treatment of Pictish names in Gaelic is naturally a delicate question. One has to make up his mind as best he may as to what Pictish was: in the view of the present writer it was a Celtic language of the Cymric type, i.e. of the P-group. One of the most indubitably Pictish names in Scotland is Porin in Strathconon, G. *Pórainn*, cf Welsh *pawr*, pasture; *poriant*, pasturage. This is the root that appears so often in the aspirated form of -*four*, e.g. Pit-four, Bal-four, Doch-four, Inch-fuir. Another is Strath-peffer, G. *Srath-pheofhair*, cf Welsh *pefr*, sparkling. There are several Peffer streams in Scotland. With Welsh *cardden*, a brake, may be compared the numerous Urquharts, a name which Adamnan gives as Airchartdan; (*air* = on, by); Woodside; the Gaelic is *Urcha(r)dain*. The same element appears in Kin-cardine, G. *Cinn-chàrdain*, a fairly common name; also in Carden, Cardenden, and probably Pluscarden. With *Allt Aradaidh* in Contin and Inver-arity, cf Welsh *araf*, slow; Gaul. *Arar*. In these safe examples, which might be extended, we have the advantage of being able to compare with well-known Welsh words: they go to show that Gaelic preserves Pictish much as it has preserved Norse. Here also may be observed the natural tendency to drop unaccented syllables, e.g. Drum-derfit, of old Drumdafurde, Drumdervate, Drumdarwecht, is in modern Gaelic *Druima-diar*, with which may be compared the name of the monastery of Deer. Similarly Cromarty, Crumbauchtyn, 1264, is in G. *Cromba'*, based on G. *crom*, Welsh *crwm*, bent.

The Pictish element in our Highland place-names is much stronger and more widespread than is generally supposed. It is really only beginning to be investigated, and it is to be hoped that ere long we shall be able to speak more definitely about its representation in Gaelic. There are abundant remains of it awaiting discussion.

Reference has already been made to the use of old written forms. It is, of course, advisable to procure these when they are accessible, e.g. from the *Registers of the Seal*, the *Exchequer Rolls* and the *Retours*, now published in convenient form. Still older and far more valuable forms are to be met in the *Chronicles of the Picts and Scots*, in the *Irish Annals* (occasionally), in Adamnan's *Life of Columba*, in Nennius and others. Oldest of all are the few names preserved by the geographer Ptolemy and the classical writers. The value of charter forms, etc, found in the Record Publications and elsewhere, is best tested by confronting them with the modern Gaelic. Occasionally, especially in the case of Norse names, they are really important; as a rule, wherever the genuine Gaelic can be found, they are merely ancillary. A case in point is Paisley. The Records are quoted thus: 1157, Passeleth; 1158, Paisleth; but the modern Gaelic is *Paislig*, known widely in Argyll. Here there can be no doubt that the Gaelic is the real name, representing Old Irish *baislec*, Latin *basilica*, a church. In the Records either *th* was originally written for *ch*, or *c* was misread as *t*, as very often happens.

Of the numerous minor points which experience has shown to be important, a few may be noted.

In Gaelic names the qualifying part regularly follows the generic part—the adjective follows the noun. Quite often, however, there is met an old usage of prefixing the adjective, e.g. *Dùgaraidh* for *Dubh-garaidh*. This occurs only in the case of monosyllabic adjectives referring chiefly to colour, shape, size. In Norse names the qualifying part comes first, a rule to which there is no exception.

In both Gaelic and Norse compound names the accent falls on the qualifying word—noun or adjective—whether prefixed or not. Thus Norse names are always accented on the first syllable; the accentuation of Gaelic compounds varies with the position of the qualifying part. Gaelic uncompounded names are always accented on the first syllable; the same is true as a rule of compounds where the first part is a preposition, e.g. Conchra, Contullich, where *con* has the same force as Latin *cum*, together.

Names of pure Gaelic origin are regularly used with the definite article. Exceptions to this are rare and well defined. The presence of the article is usually a sure sign that the name with which it goes is either pure Gaelic or borrowed into Gaelic and naturalised. Norse names are very rarely found with Gaelic article, except in Lewis, where it is not so uncommon. No Pictish name has been found with the article.

In Celtic nomenclature the river regularly gives its name to the loch whence it issues, the strath, glen, or corry through which it flows, and the place where it falls into the sea or another stream. The loch is regarded as the reservoir of the river; thus Adamnan speaks of Loch Awe as *Stagnum fluminis Abœ*, and of Loch Ness as *Stagnum fluminis Nesœ*. A typical example is the River Naver, Ptolemy's Nabaros, which gives Loch Naver, Strathnaver, Invernaver. This is of great importance in dealing with names of lochs, straths, and glens, which are often Pictish and very difficult.

The names of parishes are usually taken either from the name of the ancient parish church or from its site. Examples of the former are the numerous parish names in Kil-, such as Kilmuir, Kilmorack, Kilmonivaig; the second part here is the name of the saint commemorated in the dedication. From the name of the spot where the church was situated come such parish names as Logie, Contin, Resolis, Nigg, Daviot.

In all districts where two or more languages have been spoken in succession, hybrid names are apt to appear, i.e. compound names, the constituent parts of which belong to different languages. These hybrids all arise in much the same way, and show the same characteristics. In the north and west of Scotland, for instance, the Norsemen left a number of names which remained as a legacy to their Gaelic-speaking successors. The latter, soon forgetting the meaning of these foreign names, or in some cases probably never having known it, added on descriptive Gaelic terms as they found occasion, the result being often unconscious tautology. Hence names such as Loch Seaforth meaning Loch Sea-firth; Ardtornish, Cape Tornish, i.e. Cape

Thori's Cape; Camastrolvaig, Bay of Trolvaig, i.e. Bay of Troll-Bay; Strathhalladale, i.e. Strath Holy-Strath; Glendibidale, i.e. Glen Deepdale. Here we have tautology. Slightly different are such names as Ardshieldaig, Cape of Shieldaig, or Cape of Herring Bay; Coir' Atadail, Corry of Attadale, and such like. In no case do we find a real organic union between the parts. It would be impossible to find Norse *vík*, bay; *ey*, island; *nes*, cape; *dalr*, dale; *fjörðr*, firth; *á*, river, qualified by a Gaelic adjective. Less unthinkable would be an old Celtic name qualified by a Norse adjective, but in point of fact this does not seem to occur. Here again there are some highly interesting exceptions, all curiously involving the same element. Goatfell is in Gaelic *Gaodabheinn*, N. Geita-fjall, Goathill; Blaven in Skye is *Blàbheinn* for Blá-fjall, Bluehill; Sulven in Assynt is *Sùilebheinn* for Sùla-fjall, Pillar Fell; cf also Busven, G. *Badhaisbheinn* in Gairloch. In these cases it appears that Norse *fjall* was translated into Gaelic *beinn*, hill. This proceeding seems unique.

In dealing with a large collection of names from a wide area where different conditions have prevailed in different localities, certain broad peculiarities or distinctions come into prominence, Among such is the geographical distribution of certain generic terms. In Ross, for instance, *baile*, a stead, Scottish 'toun', is extremely common on the east coast; on the west there is practically only one instance, Balmacarra. On the other hand, with *achadh*, field, exactly the reverse is the case: *achadh*, *acha*, *achd*, *ach*, swarm on the west coast of Ross; they are rare on the east coast. *Both*, a booth, hut, appears only once with certainty in Ross: Boath, G. *na Bothachan*, the places of Booths, paralleled in the Black Isle by *na Peiteachan*, the places of Pits. In Sutherland no instance of *both* occurs to me. But along the south side of the Great Glen *both*s swarm from Bunachton near Inverness G. *Both Neachdain*, Nectan's Booth, to Bohuntin in Glenroy, G. *Both (C)hunndainn*, Booth of the Confluence. Epidemics of *both*s will be found elsewhere also; but not north of the Great Glen.

It is but fitting to recall that to the departed editor of the former *Scottish Celtic Review* we owe, among other services, the first scientific treatment of Scottish names of places. May our new *Celtic Review*, now happily inaugurated, long continue to advance the work in which Dr Cameron led the way.

Paisley

No Roman remains have been found at Paisley, and there is nothing to indicate the existence of a temple or court there in Roman times. This, of course, in no way affects the derivation from *basilica*, as this term was borrowed at an early date into Irish as *baslec*, and into Welsh as *baseleg*. In Ireland it appears as a place-name—Baislec, Baslec Mór, Baslican, with genitive *Baislicci*, dative *Baslicc*. The Gaelic form of Paisley is *Paislig*, where the terminal consonant obviously must come from an older *c*. The name may have been originally given either by the Scots or by the Britons of Strathclyde; in view of the perfect correspondence of *Paislig* with Irish phonetics, more probably by the Scots. For *Paislig* becoming *Paisley* in English, cf the numerous names like *Beverley*, old forms of which are *Beoferlic*, *Beverlac*.—(Canon Isaac Taylor, *Names and their Histories*, p 374)

Tara

Tara, Ir. *teamhair*, means 'a place of prospect', commanding a wide view. This, according to Dr Joyce (vol 1, p271), applies to all the places of that name in Ireland. In Scotland the name seems to be rare, but I have come across one instance which seems fairly certain. Far up Glencasley in Sutherland (Gaelic *Gleann Charsla'*) there is *Dail Teamhair*, a level plain by the river side, of which the characteristic feature is a number of truncated conical mounds or hillocks, about thirty feet high, probably of glacial origin. These correspond to Dr Joyce's definition, and the meaning 'Dale of Taras' seems appropriate. Cf *templum*, τέμνω, τέμενος, 'a cut-off place'.

Some Sutherland Names of Places

Part 1

The county of Sutherland, in its present extent, includes three old divisions—Sutherland proper, the Reay country, and Assynt. Sutherland, South-land, was the name applied by the Norsemen to that southern part of their province of Caithness lying between the Ord of Caithness and the river Oykell, with its estuary, the Kyle of Sutherland. 'Mons Mound', says an old geographer (1165 AD), 'dividit Cathanesiam per medium'. Accordingly he writes of this whole north-eastern part of Scotland as 'Cathanesia citra et ultra Montem'. The Mons is of course the Ord, and is not to be confused with the modern Mound between Golspie and Rogart, which dates from the early part of the last century. The Reay country in the north from Durness to the Caithness border was, and is, the home of the Mackays; in Gaelic, *Duthaich Mhic Aoidh*. Assynt is the district on the western seaboard. In 1601, through the influence of the Earl of Sutherland, the south-eastern and northern districts were raised to the dignity of a separate sheriffdom, to which, in 1631, Assynt was added. Previously they formed part of the sheriffdom of Inverness.

Sutherland names fall into three classes—Pictish, Gaelic, and Norse. The two latter are found in varying relative proportions all over the country. The Pictish element is most pronounced in the south-eastern part, though by no means confined to it. This paper attempts to give specimens of the Celtic names, i.e. Pictish and Gaelic. The Norse names will be taken separately[1].

That the Picts, however much they may have been mixed with an older and non-Aryan stock in point of race, spoke a Celtic language of some sort, is generally agreed. It is also the view of most leading authorities that their language had strong Kymric affinities; that, in other words, it is today more nearly represented by Welsh and Cornish than by Scottish or Irish Gaelic. The place-names of Pictland, so far as they have been investigated, bear this out; and Sutherland, though early

1 See Part 2 of *Some Sutherland Names of Places*, p 66

56

subjected to strong Norse influence, contributes its own share to the proof. Our earliest authority for this district, Ptolemy of Alexandria, who wrote about 120 AD, mentions two Sutherland rivers, Nabaros and Ila, one place ὑψήλη ὄχθη, High Bank (of a river), and the tribal names Cornavii, Caerēni, Lugi, and Smertae. Nabaros is the modern river Naver, G. *Nabhair* (*bh* = *w*). Its ending -*aros* may be compared with *Tam-aros*, 'the Tamar'; *Sam-ara*, 'the Sambre', and others. The root *nab-, nav-*, appears in several river-names of Celtic origin (cf Holder), and is most probably the same as in *nūbes, nebula*, νέφος; Sanskrit *nabhas*, 'vapour'. For the idea may be compared the Ross-shire river Meig, G. *Mīg*, if that is rightly equated with ὁμίχλη 'mist', and its congeners in Greek and Latin. Many of our oldest river-names mean simply water or fluid. As a parallel may be compared the Welsh Nevern. Ila is now in Gaelic *Ilidh* (short initial vowel), the Helmsdale river, connected by Dr W. Stokes with German *eilen*, older *īlen*, 'hurry'. In point of meaning this is not exactly satisfactory. The river is about 21 miles long, with a fall of 362 feet. The Banffshire Isla falls 1,000 feet in 18½ miles; the Perthshire Isla, G. *Ile* (initial long vowel) falls 3,000 feet in 47 miles. The island of Islay is G. *Ile*, with long initial vowel. The latest theory as to the origin of these names, which seem all to hang together, refers them to the root *pi* seen in πίνω, ἔ-πι-ον, *bi-bo*, giving a primitive **pila*, initial *p* being dropped in Celtic. This has the advantage of explaining the island name, as well as *all* the river-names. High Bank, as was pointed out in the first number of the *Celtic Review*[1], is echoed by Norse *Ekkialsbakki*, 'Oykell Bank', where Ekkial, G. *Oiceil*, is taken to represent old *uxellos*, 'high', whence Welsh *uchel*, Gael. *uasal*. The idea is repeated in the name of the township on the bold left bank of the Oykell estuary—Altas, G. *Alltais*, 'bluff-stead'. Of the tribal names no trace can be found except in the case of the Smertae. These I discovered last summer as commemorated by the Ross-shire hill-name *Càrn Smeirt*, 'the Smertae's Cairn', in

1 In a note by Charles M. Robertson

Strathcarron (Kincardine), behind Braelangwell Lodge, and east of *Meall Dheirgidh*, 'lump of redness', forming part of the ridge between Strathcarron and the Oykell estuary. It does not appear on the OS maps. This indicates the location of the Smertae as at least partly in Ross. They probably occupied the valleys of the Carron, Oykell, and Shin. With Smertae is to be compared the Gaulish goddess Ro-smerta, πολύφρων, 'deep-thinking', from the root *smer*, 'think'. The Smertae were *smart*. This brings us to the end of Ptolemy's names, if we except his names of capes, which, however, seem properly to belong to Caithness rather than to Sutherland. Of the seven Ptolemaic names noted above, it will be seen that four survive to this day, a striking proof of continuity of transmission.

Seven hundred years after Ptolemy's time, the invading Norsemen found in easter Sutherland and Caithness a tribe who called themselves the Cats—*Catti*, 'wildcats'—whence the Picto-Norse hybrid, *Katanes*, 'Cat-promontory', now Caithness. That these folk were regarded by the Norsemen as Picts is sufficiently proved by the name Pentland Firth applied to the sea that washes their northern coast, which certainly means Pictland Firth. According to medieval Gaelic legend, Cat was one of the seven sons of Cruithne, the Pict, who divided Scotland into seven provinces, of which the most northerly is referred to as *Crich Chat*, 'bounds of the Cats'; *i Cataib*, 'among the Cats' (as Caesar says *in Sequanis*). This latter expression explains the term *Cataobh* (Cataibh), which is modern Gaelic for Sutherland. With these fierce, wildcat folk may perhaps be compared Herodotus' *Kynetes* or *Kynesii*, 'Hound-folk', most westerly of European peoples, and next neighbours to the Celts. This old tribal name has impressed itself strongly on the place-names. The southern uplands of Lairg are still in Gaelic *Braigh-Chat*, 'Uplands of the Catti'; northward is *Dithreabh Chat*, 'wilderness of Cats'; the Kyle of Sutherland is *An Caol Catach*, 'Cat-kyle'; the Earl of Sutherland was *Moirear Chat*, 'Mormaer', or 'Lord of Cats'; the Duke is *An Diùc Catach*; Sutherland men are *Cataich*.

In Gaelic the primitive Indo-Germanic *qu* sound becomes *c*; in Kymric it becomes *p*; and as primitive *p* is non-existent in Celtic, no place-name involving *p* can be of *Gaelic* origin, unless the *p* has arisen independently, or in borrowed words. If it is Celtic, it must belong to the Kymric branch. Applying the test thus roughly and generally indicated, we find in Sutherland six or seven *pits*; O.G. *pett*, Welsh *peth*, 'a thing', 'a part'. In Gaelic *pit* is usually translated, generally by *baile*, 'a stead', which is the meaning of *pett* in the Book of Deer. The Sutherland *pits* are confined to the parishes of Rogart, Lairg, and Dornoch in the south-eastern part of the county. There we have Pitfour (twice), G. *Baile-phùr*; cf Welsh *pawr*, 'pasturage', 'grazing'. Pitfour or Balfour is common all over Pictland, and *-fur* appears also in Delfour, Dochfour, Tillifour and Tillifourie, and Trinafour. Once heard in Gaelic, it cannot be confounded with G. *fuar*, 'cold'. The unaspirated form is seen clearly in Porin, G. *Pórainn* (Strathconon), cf Welsh *poriant*, 'pasture', and in *Purin*, older *Pourane* (Fife). The aspirated form is as old as the Book of Deer, *nice fúrené*, now Pitfour in Deer. Pitgrudie, G. *Baile-ghrùididh*, seems to mean 'grit-stead' or 'roughstead'. As a river-name Grudie occurs twice in Sutherland and twice in Ross, not elsewhere. Gruids (Lairg) is an English plural of G. *na Grùidean*. Pittentrail, G. *Baile an Tràill*, may mean 'thrall-stead', in which case it is a post-Norse formation, G. *tràill* being borrowed from Norse *Thræll*. The remaining *pits* appear only on record: Pitmean, Pitarkessie, Pitcarie, Petterquhasty. Another p-name is Proncy, near Dornoch; Promci 1222; G. *Pronnsaidh*, of which I have no derivation to offer. With it may be compared a' Phronntanaich, not far away, which seems to be from the same root with developed *t*, and well-known Gaelic suffixes.

Sutherland shows a fair number of streams with the *-ie* suffix, which is so common in Pictland, while it is scarcely known in the stream-names of Dalriada, still less in Skye or Lewis. This suffix probably often represents an old *-ios* or *-ia*, but there are other possibilities, e.g. we have seen that Ptolemy's Ila is now Ile. The two Grudies (Durness and Lairg) have been already noted. In

Golspie there are Lundaidh and Màilidh. Lundaidh or Lundie is an extremely common water-name, and has been referred to a nasalised form of G. *lod*, 'puddle'. Màilidh is also common: Invermaillie and Maillie river in Inverness; Polmaly in Glenurquhart; Dalmally and Allt-màilidh in Glenorchy, while Coire Mhàileagan (a double diminutive) occurs twice in Ross. These may possibly come from the root seen in Latin *madeo, madidus*, wet; *mad-l-ios, cf Holder's *Mad-onia*. O.G. *màl*, 'noble', from *maglos*, is also possible. The notion of nobility appears in Allt Eilgnidh (Brora), from O.G. *elg*, 'noble', whence Glen-elg, G. *Gleann-eilg* (where *eilg* is to be regarded as a stream-name), and Elgin, G. *Eilginn*. In Kildonan there is Tealnaidh, cf the Gaulish fountain god Tel-o(n), and (?) the river Tella (Holder). The Lothbeg river is Labhaidh, which points to an early **Labios, Chatter-y*. The river of Strath Terry is in G. *Tiridh*. Glengolly, G. *Gleanna-gollaidh*, implies a river Gollaidh, which it is just possible may be a dialectic variation of the common *Geollaidh* or *Geallaidh*, Geldy, etymologised by Dr A. Macbain from the root *geld*, 'water'; Norse *kelda*, 'a well'; German *quelle*. Sgeimhidh (Altnaharra) is a rapid stream with a delta, which suggests a comparison with G. *sgeith*, 'vomit'. On the north-west coast we have Malldaidh, based on G. *mall*, 'slow'. Further search would doubtless reveal several more stream-names of this class. The above will serve as specimens. Besides these there are two important river-names, Shin and Casley. Shin is G. *Abhainn Sin* (pronounced exactly like *sin*, 'that'). Ptolemy's name for the Shannon is *Senos*; in *Trip. Life* Sinonn and Sinna; in Irish *Sinainn*; and Dr W. Stokes derives from Sanskrit *sindhu*, 'a river'. Shin and Shannon are no doubt ultimately the same; the root, however, seems to be rather *sĭ, sei*, 'bend', as seen in σῖμος, 'snubnosed'; *sĭmius, sĭnus*. This applies physically to both rivers. Casley is in G. *Abhainn Charsla'*; its glen is Gleann Charsla', and its mouth is Inbhir Charsla'; an obscure name; *r* is probably a matter of development in Gaelic. Loch Alsh, G. *Loch Ai(l)s*, in Assynt, is no doubt the same as the Ross-shire Lochalsh, Ptolemy's Volsas; and Loch Awe is a repetition of Loch Awe in Argyll; Adamnan's

Stagnum fluminis Abæ, where Aba simply means 'river', now the river Awe.

Distinctively Pictish terminations, i.e. terminations unknown in Dalriada or in Ireland, are rare in Sutherland. Thoroughly Pictish, however, is the suffix -*ais*, seen in Alltais (Altas) already referred to, and described as to situation. It is also found in Allt Charrais, Rosehall, from root *kars*, 'harsh', 'rough', seen in Carron, *Carsona*. This burn flows by the site of an old broch, the stones of which were quarried from its bed. There is another Allt Charrais near Strathpeffer. The ending may be referred ultimately to the root of G. *fois*, 'rest', ἄστυ, *vostis*, 'a stead'. It is found in such names as Forres, G. *Farais*; Farness, G. *Fearnais*; also in Dallas, Duffus, Geddes, Pityowlish, Durris, Dores, and so on. Another appears in Tressady (Rogart and Lairg), G. *Treasaididh*; cf Navity, G. *Neamh-aididh* (Cromarty); Musaididh in Stratherrick, from root of G. *mus-ach*, 'nasty'; Welsh *mws*, 'rank'. For the root of Tressady may be compared O. Ir. *tress*, 'battle'; Welsh *treisio*, 'oppress'; *treisiant*, 'oppression'. There is a Tressat in Perthshire. A name which should perhaps have come under stream-names is Banavie, seen in Loch Bhanbhaidh, near Loch Shin. There is Banavie, near Fort William, several of them indeed; also Glen Banavie in Perthshire, and Benvie in Forfar. All these are to be referred to O.G. and Irish *banb, banbh*, 'pig'; Welsh *banw*, 'swine'. *Banba* was an old poetic name for Ireland, and the three pagan queens of Ireland were Eriu, Fodla, and Banba. *Banw* is the name of a Welsh river into which falls *Twrch*, 'hog'. 'Many rivers forming deep channels or holes into which they sink in the earth and are lost for a distance are so called.'[1] Whether this applies to any of the Scottish Banavies I have failed to learn, but the name is more probably a locative form of which our Banff (G. *Bainbh*) and Bamff are the accusatives. Dola, G. *Dóla*, is near Lairg; also Loch Dola (OSM *Loch Dúghaill*!), a name puzzling in both root and suffix. The ending -*la* has been seen in Carsla' (Casley); it appears also in Croyla (Badenoch), and in *Sruighla*,

---

1 *Archiv für Celt. Lexicographie*, vol 3, p45.

the Gaelic for Stirling, and is perhaps a reduced form of *-lach* or *-lann*.

In the south and north parts there are some names not necessarily Pictish, but at any rate of very old Celtic formation. G. *Magh*, 'a plain', appears commonly enough as *muigh* (genitive or locative), e.g. Drum-muie. It appears also in Morvich, G. *a' Mhor'oich*, 'sea-plain'; Ir. *muir-magh*. Such formations are comparatively modern. A much older formation, on the model of the Gaulish compounds, is seen e.g. in the Irish *Fearnmhagh*, 'alder-plain', repeated near Inverness in the obsolete Fearnaway, with which cf Darnaway (? *Durno-magos*). It is seen also in such names as Multovy (Ross), Muckovie (Inverness), for *Molto-magos, *Mucco-magos, 'wedder-plain' and 'swine-plain'. In Sutherland Rovie (Rogart) stands for *Ro-magos, 'excellent plain'. Rinavie (Bettyhill), Gaelic *Roinnimhigh*, stands near a sharp bend of the river Naver, forming a cape, and I take it to be for *Rindo-magos, 'point-plain'. Reay is in G. *Meaghrath*, in the Book of Clanranald Lord Reay is *morbhair meghrath*. The name has been equated with Irish *Moyra*, *Maghrath*, 'plain-fort', but in view of the Sutherland treatment of *magh* as *muigh*, coupled with the difficulty of the palatalised *m* in *Meaghrath*, the parallel is doubtful. In Ross we have *Coire nam Meagh* and *Meaghlaich*, both from *meagh*, which is our dialectic form—as it is also in Sutherland—for *mang*, 'a fawn', and Fawn-fort is an intelligible enough combination. In the Caithness part of Reay there is Downreay, G. *Dù(n)rath*, evidently a Pictish *Dūno-rāton, 'strong fort'. Reay itself is also heard as simply *Ràth*.

The prefix *far*, which is not necessarily Pictish, though common in Pictland, is seen in Farlary, G. *Farrlaraigh* (Rogart), 'projecting site' (*làrach*), which exactly suits the place. Elsewhere such places are called *Socach*, 'snout-place'. *Rudha na Farai(r)d*, Englished 'Farout Head', in Durness, has been wrongly equated with Ptolemy's Virvedrum. It means simply 'projecting cape', and there is another *Rudha na Farai(r)d* at the entrance to Badcall Bay, much projecting. An old spelling of Farout Head is *Farard* (*Orig. Paroch.* ii. 2. 701). With these may be compared *An Araird*, in Ross, and *Urrard*, in Perthshire, at the junction of Tummel and Garry. The parish name *Farr*, which recurs in Inverness-shire, is also to be compared. Some interesting names in *con-* occur. Ben More (Assynt), or at least its highest peak, is *Conmheall*. This has been rendered as from Norse 'Queen-fell', but as the name Convall occurs as a hill-name elsewhere where there is no possibility of a Norse origin, the true meaning seems to be rather *con-mheall*, 'combination of lumps'—which describes Ben More well, as it has four peaks. *Kuno-mellos*, 'high lump', is also possible. Between Altas and Lairg, a bold and striking rock of oblong form rises out of the moor, with distinct traces of an old hill-fort. This is *Conchreag*, probably meaning 'high rock'; cf the hill Conachar, near Lubcroy (Ross), which may be *Kuno-carson*, 'high rock'. The other Sutherland *Conchreag* I have not seen. There is also *Coneas* on the Glengolly river, 'combined fall'? In all these cases *con*, 'dog', is possible, but there are so many of them all over Pictland which are physically either 'combinations' or high places, that one doubts the applicability, especially as *cù* is quite rare in other combinations. All these names may be regarded as on the debatable ground between Pictish and Gaelic. It may be noted here that *Clais nan Cruithneach*, 'the Picts' hollow', is near Stoer in Assynt.

There are some interesting purely Gaelic names. *Longphort*, 'encampment', 'shieling', which becomes elsewhere Luncart, Lungard, Luncarty, Luichart, is in Sutherland *laghart*. *Seann laghard an t-sluaigh*, 'the old shieling of the folk', occurs in a poem contributed by Rev A. Gunn to the Gaelic Society of Inverness (TGSI vol 24, p8). Rob Donn has *Allt an Fhaslaghairt*, 'burn of the stead-shieling'. Evelix (Dornoch), Aveleche 1222, is an English plural form of G. *Eibhleag*, 'a live coal', and applies primarily to the sparkling Evelix Burn. Dornoch represents an old *Durnàcon*, 'place of hand-stones, or rounded pebbles', an accusative form, of which the locative appears in the common name Dornie, wrongly ascribed to G. *dòirlinn*, 'an isthmus'. Bonar, 1275 le Bunnach, is in Gaelic *am Bannath*. The site of the present Bonar was known up to the building of Telford's Bridge in 1812 as *Baile na Croit*, 'hump-stead'. The real *Bunnach* (doubtless a misreading for Bunnath) was half a mile lower down, where a long ford, which can still be pointed out, ran from near the beginning of the present wood on the Sutherland side to a spot near Kincardine Church on the Ross-shire side. Bonar must mean *Bonn-àth*, 'bottom ford', the lowest ford on the Kyle. Bona, at the north end of Loch Ness, is *am bàn àth*, 'white ford', from its white pebbles. There has been no ford there since the deepening of the outlet for the canal. A quaintly Anglicised form is seen in Pattergonie (Oykell), a corruption of G. *Bad a' dhonnaidh*, 'clump of the mischance'. Shinness on Loch Shin is commonly supposed to mean *Shin-ness*, 'Shin-point', a hybrid which may indeed be parallelled by Katanes, Caithness. The modern Gaelic, however, is (*Aird na*) *Sinneis*, and the oldest spellings are *Schenanes* 1548, *Schennynes* 1563, pointing unmistakably to *seann innis*, 'old haugh'. There is another Shinness in Strath Dionard, Durness. Dail Teamhair in Glencasley has been noted already (*Celtic Review*, vol 1, p286) [see p55]. No satisfactory derivation has been offered of the parish name Creich, 1223 Crech, G. *Craoich*. But for the old spelling, it might be explained as *Crao(bh)aich*, 'place of trees', but this can hardly hold. Of the common explanation *crìch*, 'boundary', is out of the question. Of the other Gaelic parish names Lairg, 1230 Larg, is from *learg*, 'a sloping hillside'; Clyne, 1230 Clun, G. *Clìn* is the locative (dialectic), of G. *claon*, 'a slope'. It has been wrongly ascribed to *cluain*, 'a meadow'. Farr, Dornoch, and Reay have been mentioned. Eddrachilles, G. *Eadra-chaolais* for *Eadar-dha-chaolais*, 'between two kyles'. Loth is O.G. *loth*, 'mud'. Kildonan appears to mean St Donan's Church, but 1223 Kelduninach points to *Cill-Domhnaich*, Lord's Kirk. There is no space to deal with the church-names, but it may be noted that there are seven *Cills* in Strath Brora: *Cill-Brathair*, 'the Brother's Kirk'; *Cill-Pheadair Mhór* and *Cill-Pheadair Bheag*, 'little and big Kilpeter'; *Cill Caluim Cille*, 'St Columba's Kirk'; *Cill Eadhain*, 'St John's Kirk'; *Cill Mearain*, 'St Mirren's Kirk'; and *Cill Ach-Breanaidh*. *Circ*, borrowed from Norse *kirkja*, occurs once or twice, e.g. *Innis na*

Circe, Kirk Haugh in Glencasley, not far from *Badintagart*, 'priest's clump'. The island on the north coast which appears on OS maps as *Eilean nan Naomh* is given in G. as *Eilean na Neimhe*. It has an old dedication to St Columba, and I suspect that it is really from O.G. *neimhidh*, Gaul. *nemeton*, 'a sacred place'. Another name which may be referred to this is Navidale, 1563 Nevindell, G. *Nea'adail*. There was a sanctuary here in olden times (Sir R. Gordon, *Earldom of Sutherland*), and though the formation is Norse, it is none the less possible that the Norsemen named the dale after the 'Nevie' which they found there. In addition to the Nevies noted in *Place-Names of Ross and Cromarty*, there is yet another at the head of Glenlivet. All these were doubtless pagan shrines of the Picts, later taken over by the Celtic Church.

In conclusion, some rare or obsolete Gaelic words may be noted as occurring. *Eirbhe* or *airbhe*, 'a wall of stone or turf', is found repeatedly, as it also is in Ross, e.g. *Eilean nan airbhe*, 'isle of walls'; *Allt na h-Airbhe*, 'burn of the wall' (at least thrice), Englished Altnaharra. Some of these walls are said to extend for many miles, disappearing in soft ground to reappear further on. *Uar* is the regular Sutherland word for a scree, a landslip, also, a waterspout and is extremely frequent in the names, e.g. *Coire Uairidh*, 'scree corry'; *Beinn Uairidh*, 'scree hill'; *Allt Uairidh*, applied to burns whose banks slide, leaving scaurs. It occurs only once in Ross: *Srath-uairidh*, in English Strath-rory, and the only other instance outside Sutherland known to me is *Allt Uairidh*, behind Abriachan, Inverness. It is probably a Pictish survival. Another term extremely common is *rabhann*, pronounced in some parts *rafan*, a species of grass growing in lochs of which sheep and cattle are fond. From it we have *Bada-rabhainn*, 'clump of *ravan*', and such. It is probably to be connected with Welsh *rafu*, 'to spread'; *rafon*, 'berries growing in clusters'. *Lòn* in Sutherland means 'a slow burn', as in Skye. *Saidh*, 'bitch', occurs several times, as in *Coire na Saidhe Duibhe*, 'corry of the black bitch'. *Preas* regularly means 'copse', not 'bush'. Diminutives in -*ie* are very common, e.g. *alltaidh*, 'a burnlet'; also *dailidh*, 'a little dale'.

Part 2

The Norse occupation of Sutherland and Caithness lasted from about 880 to 1200 AD, when William the Lyon finally established the authority of the Scottish crown in these northern parts. The names from this source, therefore, may be over 1,000 years, and cannot be less than 700 years old. While it is true that Norse names may be found almost anywhere in Sutherland, even in its very centre, there are several indications that the occupation was not nearly so complete as it was, e.g. in Lewis. There the old Celtic names have suffered a clean sweep; almost all the Gaelic names are 'phrase-names' of the type of *Allt na Muilne*. In Sutherland, on the other hand, there survives quite an appreciable number of Pictish names, dating long before the advent of the Norsemen. We also find a free use of suffixes in forming Gaelic names—such as -*ach* with its old locative -*aigh*; -*lach*, -*an+ach*, and other combinations of an antique cast, which could hardly have been formed after 1200, and probably date much earlier. The Norse element is very strong on the north coast, much weaker in the interior and in Sutherland proper. It is noteworthy, however, that many of the principal hills and dales are Norse. Freshwater lochs are mostly all Celtic, as also rivers. Village names are divided, with a preponderance in favour of Norse which does credit to their choice of site. The evidence of the place-names, then, goes to show that the Norsemen held the whole of Sutherland as its overlords, but did not occupy it to the extent of displacing the native population or their language. At the same time, it is highly probable that there was a good deal of bilingualism during this long period of 300 years; this also is, to some extent, reflected in the names.

We shall take first the principal terms found in combination:–

á, river, genitive *ár*, appears terminally in Brora, G. Brùra, N. Brúar-á, Bridge water, a name found in Iceland; also in

Borgie, Fort-water. The genitive case is seen in Arscaig, ár-skiki, 'river's strip', with which we may compare Ascaig, 'river strip'. Amat (Oykell and Brora), G. Àmaid, is á-mót, 'river-meet', 'confluence', found also in Ross. Calda Beag and Calda Mor are two parallel streams that flow into Loch Assynt: kald-á, Coldstream. The district between them is Edrachalda for Eadar-dha-Chalda, 'between two Coldstreams'. Abigil, G. Àbigil, may be á-bæ-gil, 'river-stead-gully'. Aberscross is in G. Àbarscaig and Àbairsgin; in 1512 Abbirskor, 1525 Estir and Westir Abbirschoir; 1563 Westir Abberscors, showing the modern English form to be a plural. The G. Àbarscaig would represent á-búr-skiki, 'river-bower-strip'; in Iceland there is Búrá, 'bower-stream'; but in view of the variant forms the last syllable must be held uncertain. In any case the initial long vowel shows that we are not dealing with a Pictish *aber*, as has been commonly supposed.

Bakki, a bank, is seen in Ekkiallsbakki, Oykell-bank. Hysbackie is hús bakki, 'house-bank', and Coulbackie, G. Callbacaidh, is kald-bakki, 'cold-bank'. The first part of Crasbackie is not clear. Backies, near Golspie, is an English plural, Banks.

Bólstaðr, *ból*, a homestead, is not uncommon. Arnabol is either 'Arni's stead', or, less probably, 'eagle or erne stead'. Gylable is gilj-á-ból, 'gully-river-stead'. Erribol, G. Éiribol, is eyrr-ból, 'gravel beach stead'. The Gaelic of Embo is also Éiribol, but it appears as Ethenboll, circa 1230; Eyndboll 1610; and may mean 'Eyvind's stead'.

Unapool in Assynt is Una's or Uni's stead. Kirkibol and Crosspool, Churchstead or Kirkton, and Roodstead, are two of the few Norse church-names in Sutherland. Leirable, 1563 Lyriboll, occurs in Kildonan, apparently mud-stead, N. *leir*, whence in Lewis Lurebost. With it may be compared Duible, 1527 Doypull, perhaps from *dý*, 'a bog', 'bog-town'. Colaboll is either 'Kol's stead', or 'charcoal stead'. Scrabster appears in the *Orkneyinga Saga* as Skára-bólstaðr, 'seamew-stead'. Torboll in Dornoch and Torrobol in Lairg both represent Thori's stead.

Eldrable, G. Eildirebol, 1563 Altreboll, 1610 Eltribol, has been explained as Altar-stead, but more probably contains a proper name such as Elldjárn. The N. *altari*, 'altar', is late and Christian. Skelbo means 'shell-stead', the Gaelic Sligo and Sligachan. Skibo, G. Sgìobul, appears about 1230 as Scitheboll, which may be either 'Skithi's stead', or, from *skíð*, 'firewood-stead'. The local authorities take it from G. *sgiobal*, 'a barn', but the ancient spelling has to be taken into account. Ribigil is in 1530 and 1610 Regeboill, which might be reyka-ból, 'reek-stead', but though *reykr*, 'reek', is common in Icelandic names it seems always to be applied to places near hot springs. A suggested derivation is rygjar-ból, 'housewife's stead'; the difficulty here is that Norse *g* between vowels would certainly have been aspirated. Ulbster in Kildonan is probably Ulfr's stead, but may be Ulli's stead, Ulli being a pet form of Erlend.

Borg, a fort, appears in Borve Castle, Farr, G. Borgh; here G. *gh* must have been sounded *v*, a pronunciation which we know from other instances to have been formerly common, and which is still heard. Near it is Borrogeo, borgar-gjá, 'fort creek'. Borrobol is 'fort-stead'; there is a broch within about a mile of it. Burragaig Bay in Durness appears to be borg-vík, 'fort-bay'. There is also Loch Borralaidh, from borg-hlið, 'fort-slope'. In Assynt is Loch Borrolan, at Altnacealgach, borgar-land, 'fortland'. The river Borgie is 'fort-river'.

Dalr, dale, is found terminally in many names. Armadale in Farr, is 'Arm dale' or 'Bay dale'. Mudale, G. Muthadail, 1570 Mowdaill; 1601 Mowadale, is possibly móðadalr, 'muddy-river dale'. Strathalladale, a hybrid, is helga-dalr, 'holy dale'; the personal name Helgi is also possible. Trantlemore and Trantlebeg, 1527 Trountal, contain the name Thrond, the full genitive of which appears in Trotternish, Skye, G. Trondairnis, Throndar-nes. Langdale is simply Longdale. Rimsdale, 1630 Rimbisdale, and Achrimsdale are from *rymr*, roaring, 'roaring dale'.

Scalmasdale in Kildonan is hard to dissociate from Skálmardalr, 'sword-dale'; 'cloven dale', in Iceland. Skelabosdale is skelabólstaðr-dalr, 'shell-stead dale'. Strathskinsdale is from *skinn*, skin, cf Skinnet in Caithness. Oulmsdale is the present equivalent of Ullipsdale, 'Ulfr's dale'. Keoldale, G. Cealdail, 1559 Kauldale is possibly Kaldi-dalr, 'Cold-dale'. Torrisdale is 'Thorir's dale'. Astle or Asdail in Dornoch is in 1222 Askesdale, 1275 Haskesdale, meaning 'Ashdale'. Swordale, G. Suardail, 1275 Swerdel, is 'sward-dale'. Ospisdale is probably for Ospak's dale; Spinningdale, G. Spainigdail (long *n*), 1464 Spanigidill,1467 Spainzidell,1546 Spangzedaill. It has been referred to *spöng*, gen. *spangar*, 'a spangle', which would, however, result in Spangadail. The second syllable *ig* is doubtless vík, 'a bay'; the first may be spann, 'a pail' or 'measure', possibly with reference to the shape of the small bay on which Spinningdale stands. Migdale, G. Migean, 1275 Miggeweth, 1561 Mygdaill, an obscure name. Helmsdale is known from the Sagas to be Hjalmund's dale.

Ey, an island: Boursa is búrs-ey, 'bower-isle'. Soyea, sauða-ey, 'sheep-isle'. Handa, sand-ey, 'sand-isle', with *s* aspirated. Calbha Bheag and Calbha Mhór, 'calf-isle', a name commonly applied to small islands standing off the shore. Howga of 1570 is in 1601 Haga, now Hoan. Oldaney, G. Alltanaidh, though applied to the island is really a mainland name, and probably Gaelic; the island is Eilean Alltanaidh, the Isle of Oldaney. It is supposed to represent Jura of Ferchar Leighich's charter of 1386; dýr-ey; 'deer isle'.

Erg, shieling; borrowed from O.G. áirge; now àirigh. The classical instance is *Asgrim's ergin* (*Orkneyinga Saga*), which is now Askary, in Caithness. In Sutherland it is rather common terminally as -*ary*. Fiscary, in Tongue, is 'fish-shieling', and about a mile from it is *Ach-an-iasgaich*, 'fishing-field'. Toscary, from *tosk*, a tooth, tusk, means 'tooth-shieling'. Scottarie comes from *skot*, a shot; 'shot-shieling', cf skot-bakki, shot-bank, i.e. butt. Modsary probably contains a contracted form of a personal name, e.g. Mötull, and so with Kedsary, which may be Ketill's shieling. Halmadary, famed for the legend of *Tuiteam Halmadairigh*[1], is most likely 'Hjalmund's shieling'.

1 TGSI, vol 20, p 99.

Sleasdary, in Creich, is doubtful. Creag Thorairigh is 'the rock of Thori's shieling'. Scourie, G. Sgobhairigh, is probably from *skógr*, a shaw, wood; 'shaw-shieling'.

Fjall, a hill, fell, has in several cases been replaced terminally by G. *beinn*, as has happened elsewhere, e.g. Goatfell is in G. Gaodabheinn; so Blaven, 'blue-fell', and others. In Sutherland Sulven, G. Sulabheinn, is for Sula-fjall, 'pillar-hill'. Fashven, G. Faisbheinn, with its tapering peak, is hvass-fjall, 'pointed fell'. Sgribhisbheinn is not clear as to its first part; perhaps it contains *sgriða*, a landslip, scree. Foinaven, G. Foinnebheinn, may be pure Gaelic, meaning 'wart-hill', from its peaks. On the other hand it may represent vind-fjall, 'windy-fell', just as *vindauga*, 'wind-eye', becomes *fuinneog, uinneag*, window. It has been thought that *fjall* has also been replaced by G. *meall*, lump, in Farrmheall, as for Fær-fjall, 'sheep-fell'; but the name is more probably pure Gaelic meaning 'projecting lump'; cf Farrlary. At least four hills in Sutherland are called Maovally, G. Maobhalaidh with old people, now becoming Mao'alaidh; 1564 Movell. All these present the same rounded, semi-elliptical appearance, and I take them to be from maga-fjall, 'maw-fell' or 'paunch-fell'; the aspirated *g* would be sounded *v* as in Borve above. Another name which recurs three or four times is Saval, G. Sàbhail. There is a Saval near Lairg, and in Assynt are Saval Beag and Saval Mor, with a gap between called *Bealach eadar dha Shàbhail*. Eastward is *Lurg an t-Sàbhail*. Sàbhail seems to be a Gaelic form of há-fjall, 'high-fell'. Norse initial *h* before a vowel is usually treated in Gaelic as if it were an aspirated *t*; thus há-bakki, 'high-bank', becomes in Lewis Tàbac. But this *h* might equally well be taken to stand for aspirated *s*, and of this we have one certain instance in Hjaltland, Shetland, which becomes in Gaelic Sealtainn. It may be noted that Sutherland names happen to present no clear instance of Norse initial *h* becoming *t* in Gaelic. Ben Loyal, west of Loch Loyal, near the Kyle of Tongue, is in G. Beinn Laghal; 1601 Lettirlyoll. As far as phonetics go this may represent laga-fjall, 'law-fell', or laga-völlr, 'law-field'. Another suggestion is leið-fjall or leið-völlr, 'leet-fell' or 'leet-field', i.e. places where certain public meetings were held; but, though this makes good sense, it would become Laoghal, rather than Laghal in modern Gaelic. Ben Arkle, where the deer in Sir Robert Gordon's time had forked tails, is G. Airceil, and is thought to mean 'ark-fell', 'chest-fell', from its shape. It may equally well be Gaelic *airceal*, a hiding place, a name which occurs in Lochbroom. In any case it can hardly be erg-fjall, 'shieling-fell', as has been sometimes suggested. Beinn Smeòrail is 'butter-fell', or 'butter-field', (völlr).

Fjörðr, a firth, appears in Loch Inchard, G. Loch Uinnseard, probably engis-fjörðr, 'meadow-firth', and in Loch Laxford, G. Lusard, 'salmon-firth'. Strath Dionard probably contains the Norse name for the Kyle of Durness, into which it opens, and may be dýn-fjörðr, 'noisy-firth'.

Garðr, a garth, yard, court, occurs as *-gary*, *-chary*: Odhrsgaraidh is 'Ögr's garth'. Ach-cheargary is from *kjarr*, copse; 'field of the garth by the copse'. Griamachary, at the foot of Ben Griam, is 'Grim's garth'. Halligary may be either 'sloping garth' or 'Hallr's garth'.

Gil, a ravine, gully, is so common that only examples can be given. Fresgil, in Durness, may be from *fress*, tomcat; *fraes*, noise, 'noisy gully', has also been suggested. Eirigil, from *eyrr*, means 'gravel-beach gully'. Bàligil, bálagil, is 'bale or flame gully'. Àbigil seems to be à-bæ-gil, 'river-stead gully'. Allt Thàisgil is from háls-gil, 'hause (throat) gully'; cf Gob Thàis in Lewis, and Thàisgil in Gairloch. Achrìdigil, field of Rìdigil, probably rjóta-gil, 'rowting or roaring gully'. Achŭrigil, Rosehall, is not to be compared with Loch Urigil, in Assynt, which has the initial vowel long, and may be from *úrr*, wild ox. The Rosehall Urigil is rather from *urð*, 'a heap of stones'. Achriesgil is from *hrís*, copse; 'field of the copse gully'. Connagil is from *kona*, woman, Sc. quean; cf Cuniside, G. Caonasaid, qvenna-setr, showing the genitive plural. Bréisgil may be explained as breið-àss-gil, 'gully by the broad rocky ridge'. Allt Thòirisgil means 'burn of Thorir's ravine'. Sgrigil is 'scree or landslip gully'; Tràligil, 'thrall's gully'. Réigil, 1601 Raygill is given as Gaelic of Rhifail, and has been given me also as Rifagil. The double form may be explained as rifgil or régil, 'big gully'. Suisgil in Kildonan, G. Sisgil, 1527 Seyisgil, 1545 Suisgill, has been referred to seyðisgil, 'seethe-gil'. With it may be compared Gìsgil, 'gushing gil', from *geysa*, gush, whence *geysir*, gusher. Lastly may be taken Dun Dornadilla in Strathmore, in Gaelic Dùn Dornagil, which may well be Thorna-gil, 'thorn-gully'.

Gjá, a creek, has been taken over into Gaelic as *geodha*, and appears terminally as -*go* or -*geo* in Port Vasgo for hvass-gjá, 'tapering creek'; Lamigo, 'lambs' creek'; Borrogeo, 'fort creek'; Sango, 'sandy creek'; Glaisgeo, (?) 'glass creek', but it may be G. 'green creek'.

Hlíð, a slope, genitive hlíðar, occurs in Swordly, 'sward-slope'. Leathad Darnlaidh is probably 'hillside of the thorny slope'. Tuirsligh is for Thursa-hlið, 'giant's slope'; cf *na Tursaichean* in Lewis, applied to the standing stones. Rudha Armli is 'Cape of the bay slope', cf Armadale, and Borralaidh is 'fort-slope'. Fastly is probably hvass-hlið, 'pointed slope', cf Faishven. Flìrum, a rocky islet off Durness, is probably hlíðar-holm, 'sloping isle'; Rob Donn has *leac Fhlìrum*.

Nes, a headland, cape, occurs only thrice: Melness, 'bent-grass cape'; Unes, 1275 Owenes; 1566 Unis; G. Jùneas; often mentioned in connection with the 'ferry of Unes', now the Little Ferry, *am Port Beag*, at mouth of Loch Fleet. Durness, G. Diùranais, 'deer-cape'; cf Diurinish, Skye, and elsewhere.

Setr, a stead, shieling, appears in Sutherland terminally as -*said*, which becomes in English -*side*. Caonasaid has been noted above; 1601 Kennyside. Linside, G. Lionasaid, is for lín-setr, 'flax-stead'. Loch Staonsaid is from stein-setr, 'stony shieling'; Loch Coulside, G. Cùlasaid, is kúlu-setr, 'knob-stead', from *kúlu*, a rounded hill; cf Culbo, in the Black Isle. Hòrasaid is 'Thori's stead or shieling'. Dionsait may be 'noisy stead', from *dynr*, din. Fealasaid is fjall-setr, 'hill-stead', in English Fallside. Bowside, búsetr, 'dwelling-shieling'. Bracsaid is brekka-setr, 'slope-seat'. Sandset, now Sandside, is 'Sandseat'. Clanside, G. Claonasaid, and Clayside are doubtful.

Skiki, a strip: Arscaig and Ascaig have been mentioned. Overscaig is ofarr-skiki, 'over or upper strip'. Poulouriscaig, G. Pollaorisgaig and Poll-éirisgeig, is from *eyrr*, meaning 'pool or hollow place of the gravel-beach-strip'. Boarscaig is búðar-skiki, 'bothy strip'. Malmsgaig, from *málmr*, sand, with secondary meaning of metal; 'sand-strip, or ore-strip' ; cf Malmö in Sweden, and Málmey, Iceland. Calascaig is 'Kali's strip'; cf Calascaig in Lochbroom. Ramascaig is from *hrafn* or *hramn*, a raven: 'ravens' strip', while Ròmascaig is rauma-skiki, 'giant's or clown's strip'. Truderscaig cannot come from trúðr, a juggler, for ð would drop. It is probably Throndar-skiki, 'boar-strip' or 'Thrond's strip'; cf Trantle, above. Skibbercross, G. Sìobarsgaig; 1360 Sibyrs(k)oc; 1562 Syborskeg, Schiberskek; a difficult name; possibly siðu-búr-skiki, 'side-bower strip'; *siða*, 'a side', is common in Norse names. Gordonbush has been given me in Gaelic as Gar-éisgeig, where *gar* is Gaelic meaning 'copse'; éisgeig may be eyði-skiki, 'waste-strip'.

Völlr, a field, gives Carrol, kjarr-völlr, 'copse-field'. Rossal is hross-völlr, 'horse-field'; its grass is injurious to cows, though harmless to horses. Langwell is lang-völlr, 'long-field', and Sletell, 'even-field', from *sléttr*. Musal, 1560 Moswell, is 'mossy-field'; Marrel, mar-völlr, 'seafield'. Brawl, G. Breithal, is breið-völlr, 'broadfield'.

Some names may be added which do not come under these headings. In addition to the personal names already noted, we have Craig Shomhairle and Airigh Shomhairle, 'Somerled's rock and shieling'. Poll Amhlaibh is 'Olaf's or Anlaf's pool', Druim Manuis, 'Magnus' ridge'; Eilean Eglei is 'Egill's ey or isle'. Dalharrald in Farr contains the common Harold, possibly in this case Earl Harold, who was defeated by King William in 1196. Cyderhall is an interesting name. In 1230 it appears as Sywardhoth; 1275, Sytheraw; and Siddera on Blæu's map; clearly 'Sigurd's how' (*haugr*), the burial-place of Earl Sigurd, who died from the effects of a scratch from the buck-tooth of Mælbrigit, Mormær of Moray, whose head he carried at his saddlebow. Sigurd, says the Saga, was 'laid in how' at Ekkiallsbakki. The Gaelic is *Siara*, which may represent Sýr, a pet form of Sigurðr: the full form would be expected to yield *Siarda* in Gaelic. Asher or Oldshore, G. Àisir was in 1551 Aslar, 1559 Astlair, and has been regarded as a contraction from Asleifarvík, Asleif's bay, where King Hacon touched in 1263. Leac Bhiurn in Strathnaver is 'Björn's flagstone'.

Golspie is in 1330 Goldespy, G. Goi(ll)sbidh; the latter part is *bær*, *býr*, a stead, village; the first part has been referred to *gil*, a ravine, which is impossible; also to *gull*, (older *goll*), gold, which, in default of a personal name, is the most probable explanation. Strathfleet, G. Srath-fleòid, comes from *fljót*, flood, a common stream-name. Eilean Klourig (Clobhraig) on the north coast, is klofar-vík, cleft-bay; the island is cleft right through by a narrow channel. Sandwood in Durness stands for sand-vatn, sand-water, the only instance known to me of *vatn* in Sutherland and the mainland of Ross, whereas it is so common in the Western Isles. Two parishes bear Norse names, Tongue, from *tunga*, a tongue; and Assynt, ascribed to áss-endi, rock-end. The difficulty with the latter is that the initial vowel of Assynt is short in Gaelic. The suffixed article is seen in Merkin, the march (*mörk*), Akran, the acre, Pólin, the *ból* or stead. Syre, G. Saghair, is rather uncertain. If we accept initial *s* of Gaelic as arising from Norse *h*, as was suggested in the case of Saval above, it would represent *hagar*, pasture-lands; on the other hand there is a Saghair in Ireland. Storr in Assynt, G. Stòr, is usually supposed to be from *stór*, big, the latter part of the name having dropped. But the name occurs in the *Orkneyinga Saga* as Staur, and there is another point of the same name in the *Heimskringla*, with suffixed article, Staurinn, both apparently from *staurr*, a stake, point. Ben Hope is from *hóp*, a bay, whence Gaelic òb; as Ben Horn is from *horn*, a horn. Ben Clibreck is in G. Clìbric, and may be klif-brekka, 'cliff-slope' but Gaelic *ì* makes this doubtful; in any case the latter part is *brekka*, a slope. Grumbeg and Grummore are interesting. In 1570 they appear as Grubeg and Grubmore, and farther back in 1551 Gnowb Litil and Mekle, from gnúpr, a peak, common in land-names. Loch Merkland is mörk-land, 'march-land'; it is on the watershed. Strath-vagastie appears to be from vaka-staðr, 'watching-stead'. Heilem, which appears in Rob Donn as Hilleam and Huilleum, is in 1530 Wnlem, 1542 Unlem; 1551 Handlemet; 1601 Hunleam and Houndland, and may be hund-holm, 'hound isle'; it is a mushroom-shaped peninsula. *Fors*, a waterfall, gives Forsinard and Forsinain, upper and lower waterfall respectively. Cape Wrath, G. am Parbh, is from *hvarf*, turning-point, cf hvarfs-gnípa, Cape Farewell, in Greenland. Solmar, in Durness, is sól-heimar, 'bright-ham', Brighton, a name found in Iceland. Ben Armin is from *ármaðr*, gen. *ármanns*, a steward, controller, whence G. ármunn, a hero. The Italian looking Ben Stomino, east of Loch Loyal, is said on good authority to be a mere map-name. It appears on a map of Sutherland dated 1823, and has kept its place since. The Gaelic form is Beinn Staim and Loch Staim lies north of it, apparently from the byname Stami. Druim-basbaidh in Farr probably contains a shortened form of a personal name with the -*by* suffix, seen in Golspie; baðs-bær, 'bath-stead' is possible. Drumhollistan, east of Strath-halladale, is 'the ridge of the holy stone'.

In dealing with the Norse element I have had the advantage of consulting a paper contributed some years ago by Dr A. Macbain to the *Highland News*, of which he kindly permitted me to make use.

Innis in Place-Names

Of the two Gaelic words for 'island', *innis* and *eilean*, the former
is native (Welsh *ynys*), the latter is borrowed from Norse *ey-land*,
appearing in Irish as *oilean*, and in early Irish as *ailén*. The two
words must have had a struggle for existence which would be
interesting to trace. The result of it was a victory for the foreigner.
The only word for island now and for centuries, in common
speech, is *eilean*. Its native rival, however, entered on a new
phase of activity in the sense of river-meadow, the Scots 'haugh',
and as such it forms an important element in our place-names.
Very few islands round our coasts contain *innis*, Inch—Inchkeith,
Inchmay, Inchcolm, Inchaddon, and some small isles in lakes,
chiefly Loch Lomond and Loch Awe almost exhaust the list. On
the west coast, the Hebrides were, indeed, as a whole, known as
Innse-gall, the isles of the strangers, but only two or three islets
retain *innis* as an element. The Orkneys, of old Innse Orc, have
now become *Arcaibh* in Gaelic, a dative plural like *Cataibh*,
Sutherland. Innse Cat, the Cat Isles, are mentioned by old
chroniclers as supplying helpers to the Norse at Clontarf (1014);
their location cannot be determined with certainty. The plural,
na h-Innsean, is specially applied to the Indies, e.g. Anns na
h-Innsean as fhaide thall, In the furthest Indies. But it is in the
sense of 'haugh' that *innis* appears most widely in Scottish
topography. Even in early usage there was probably a tendency
to this meaning. Temporary islands are often formed by flooding,
or by the forking of streams, and from this to 'river-side haugh',
'meadow', the transition is easy. The Inches of Perth form a case
in point. Inchaffray, Insula Missarum, 'Mass Isle', is now an isle no
longer, though it is considered to have been one of old. It may
be noted in passing that *innis* is rendered into the Latin of the
charters, etc, by *insula*, even where it has never meant anything
other than 'haugh', a habit which sometimes has given rise to
needless searchings of antiquarian hearts.

At the beginning of names *innis* is usually easy of recognition,
appearing in English as 'inch'. Even here, however, being from
the nature of the case unaccented, it sometimes gets debased to

i's (ish), e.g. Isteane in the Black Isle is for *an innis dian*, the sheltered haugh. On the east coast this shortening is general, e.g. Inchberry is pronounced in Gaelic *I's a' bhàraidh*. No real difficulty, however, results. In terminal position, coming after a qualifying adjective, noun, or even preposition, *innis* assumes a variety of forms, and is often puzzling. Here also, of course, it is unaccented, the stress accent falling on the qualifying word.

1. It may appear as -*nis* (-nish), e.g. Brecknish, Mucknish, in Gaelic Breacinnis, Dappled Haugh; and Mucinnis, Swine Haugh, respectively. Other examples are, Mornish or Morenish, Big Haugh; Slignish, Shell Haugh; Craignish, Rock Haugh. Here it is apt to be confused by the unwary with Norse *nes*, a cape, thus giving rise to bad hybrids. This difficulty is easily got over if we keep in mind that the qualifying word prefixed to *innis* is always Gaelic; that prefixed to *nes* is always Norse. Thus Mishnish, Minginish, Tresnish, and such must be Norse, because their first parts are Norse.

2. Sometimes it becomes -*i's* (-ish), e.g. in Blarish, for Blàrinnis, Spotted Haugh; cf. Brecknish above. Another example is Shinness, G. *Sinneis* for *seaninnis*, Old Haugh, occurring twice in Sutherland. Also I take it now that Farness in the Black Isle is *Fearninnis* (pron. Fearnais), Alder Haugh. Here old spellings are serviceable. Both these latter places have often been wrongly derived from Norse *nes*; the criterion, apart from old spellings, is whether the first part is Gaelic or Norse.

3. *Innis* seems to appear not infrequently as -*isi* (ishie). Morangie, near Tain, appears in 1487 as Morinchy, in 1507 Morinch, 1618 Morinschie; the modern Gaelic is *Móristidh* with *t* developed. This name, which undoubtedly means Big Haugh (cf Morenish above), gives a clue to the ending in such names as *Caoilisidh*, *Cruoisidh*. They most probably contain the old locative case (*innse*), and mean (in the) Narrow Haugh and (in the) Hard Haugh, respectively.

4. Sometimes, but rarely, it becomes -*age* in the English forms. Connage, near Inverness, is in 1532 Conysche, showing the transition stage: Hound-Haugh. Broomage (Larbert) is cited as

Bruminche in 1458, and may be for *braoninnis*, damp meadow; cf Loch Broom in Ross and in Perth, both in Gaelic *braon*. With these may be compared Dunstaffnage, 1309 Dunstaffynch, 1322 Ardstofniche, 1455 Dunstaffage, Gaelic Dun-sta'inis. This has been derived as Gaelic *Dun is dà innis*, a fort and two isles (the two isles are there), but, apart from accentual difficulties, the old forms make it clear that in this case we are dealing with a Norse name *Stafanes*, Staffpoint. In the spelling of 1322, *Ard* is a reduplication of *nes*, forming the typical legitimate hybrid Point of Staffpoint. Dunstaffnage, again, is the Fort of Staffpoint.

5. In composition with the preposition *fo* used adjectivally, innis gives *Foineis*, sub-meadow, small meadow, or possibly, under-meadow, appearing in English as Foynes, Phoineas, Fynes. This rather difficult name has been explained as from *eas*, a waterfall; *fo an eas*, under the fall; but in point of fact, in two of the three places bearing the name with which I am familiar (Nairn, Beauly, Abriachan), there is no waterfall, and there never was one. For the sense may be compared the common Fowlis, G. Fólais from *fo-ghlais*, sub-stream; also Foyers, Gaelic *Foithir*, in plural *na Foithrichean*, flat land lying under a steep declivity. In Stratherrick there are two or three places of this name, apart from the famous waterfall, which is in Gaelic *Eas na Smùid*, Sprayfall.

Note [on Maolrithe]

In last number [of *The Celtic Review*] Mr J. M. Mackinlay queries whether Maolrithe (*Carmina Gadelica*, vol 1, p285) is 'to be identified with St Maolrise, otherwise St Finlagan, who is believed to have given name to Knock Mulreesh in Islay, near which is his chapel—Cill Fheileagan.'

Maolrithe is none other than Maelruba, the genitive being used as nominative. The pronunciation is seen in Amulree, Maelruba's ford.

Mr Mackinlay also asks if Maolruain is a diminutive of St Maelrubha. It is not. Maolruain is an independent name, occurring twice in the *Martyrology of O'Gorman*. The latter part of the compound is found with extension in the Irish word *ruanad*, a champion, whence the very common Irish name Maolruanaidh.

Whatever 'St Maolrise' may be, Finlagan is a place-name, meaning 'little white hollow', well known in connection with the Lords of the Isles.

Topographical Varia [I]

The following notes deal with some of the more uncommon and puzzling elements in our topography. The two last are new. Points in the others have already been incidentally discussed either by Dr Alexander Macbain[1] or myself.

fo

The preposition *fo*, under, is found in its strictly local sense in *foithir*, under-land, flat land lying under a steep eminence. Hence Foyers (with English plural) and several other places of the same name in Stratherrick, e.g. *am Foithir beag, Foithir Mhic Clò'ain*. On the west coast of Ross-shire it seems to become *faithir*, and is applied to the long-continued terraces formed by the old raised beach. Probably there is here a transference from the flat ground below the terrace to the terrace itself. With regard to Foyers, Macbain says, 'older Foyer, for old Gaelic "*fothir*", good land, evidently "low-lying land".'

With a diminutive force *fo* appears in Phoineas or Foynes for *fo-innis*, 'little haugh', or sometimes, possibly, low haugh, as in a case near Abriachan, on the west side of Loch Ness, where the haugh lies below the steep hillside. There is no doubt of its diminutive force in the common Fowlis (Ross-shire, Aberdeen, Perth, Forfar, Stirling), in Gaelic *Fòlais*, or better *Foghlais*, substream (*fo+glas*), a derivation confirmed by the old spelling Foglais in the Charters of Inchaffray. The old district name Fothreve (Fife and Fothreve) has been explained with probability by, I think, Dr Kuno Meyer, as *fo+treb*, sub-dwelling (cf *treabhar*, houses). The puzzling name Fyrish, the name of a farm and adjacent hill in Ferindonald, Ross-shire, in Gaelic *Foighris* or *Faoighris*, may be for *fo-iris*, under-roost. There is in the face of Fyrish Hill (*Cnoc Foighris*) a remarkable projection or spur of considerable size, surrounded by a deep gully. So sandy is its surface that it long defied the attempts made to plant it, but it now grows timber. It is called in Gaelic *Cnocan Dheilgnigh*, the prickly hillock, no doubt from the briars and whins which grew there of

1 TGSI, vol 25.

old. This sort of projection is often called '*spardan*', roost; but in Glenartney Forest the term *iris* is used, and it is possible that in the name Fyrish we have this element.

lòch

The old adjective *lòch* is glossed *dub*, black, in Cormac's *Glossary*, and is equated by Dr Whitley Stokes with Welsh *llwg*, livid, scurvy. Adamnan in his *Life of Columba* (vol 2, p38) mentions a river in Lochaber 'qui Latine dici potest Nigra Dea', or the Black Goddess, and in the headings of chapters to Book I occurs the name Stagnum Lochdae, lake of the Black Goddess, situated somewhere about the 'dorsal ridge' of Alba. Macbain identifies these with the river Lochy (Inverlochy) and Loch Lochy (G. *Lòchaidh*). The Irish Annals record under the year 728 a battle fought between the armies of Nectan and Angus, king of the Picts: bellum monith carno iuxta stagnum Loogdae; but the location is uncertain. The phonetics of Loogdae look Welsh.

The furthest north instance so far noticed is Inchlochel (*Innis-lòicheil*), in Ross-shire. In Inverness-shire, besides Inverlochy, is Lochletter (G. Lòchleitir), dark hillside, and Macbain notes the river Lochy, 'which acts for a short distance as the boundary of Abernethy parish and Inverness county, and which joins the Avon at Inverlochy near Kirkmichael'. Near Dores is *Camas-lòchaidh*, Lochy Bay, and above the Streens on Findhorn is *Poll-lòchaig*, Pool of the dark spot. In Perthshire there is Glen Lochay with its river Lochay (G. Lòchaidh); also the river Lochy from Loch Bee, joining the Orchy, while near Comrie is Drum-lòchlainn, ridge of the dark flat. In Perthshire we have also Inverlochlarig (*Inbhir-lòchlairig*), the Inver of the black pass. Glenlochy at Glenshee is in Gaelic Gleann-lochsaidh, and therefore requires a different explanation. The Lochty Water in Fife may or may not be connected; the quantity of the vowel cannot now be ascertained. Lastly, in Aberdeenshire, may be noted the parish of Leochel, the old spellings of which (Loychel, c1200) make the pronunciation fairly certain.

ialo-s

This is a common element in Gaulish names and is equated with Welsh *ial*, a clear or open space. It still survives in many French names of places, e.g. Verneuil, Verno-ialos, Alder-space, Alder-glade, where *verno-* is Gaelic *fearna*. Though we cannot produce a *Fearnail* in Scotland, we can exactly parallel the French Mareuil, Maroeuil, Mareil and other such, all from the Gaulish *Maro-ialos*, great-clearing, which with us is Morel, G. *Móirl* in Strathdearn, and Moral in Bal-moral and elsewhere. Similarly Leochel and Inch-lochel, noted above, mean 'dark-clearing'. Muthil, G. *Maothail*, is soft space, and near it there is Dargill, representing G. *Deargail*, red spot, a name which recurs in Ireland as Dargle. So far these are the only instances that I have noted as certain, but it may be suspected that Duthil, G. *Daoghal*, contains the same element, as also Culduthel near Inverness, in Gaelic Cuil-daoghail. The first part is difficult.

coll, call, calltuinn

The hazel, as might be expected, plays a prominent part in our topography, appearing, however, much oftener in the short form *coll* or *call* than in the longer (derived) form *calltuinn*. Perhaps the best known name involving the latter is Barcaldine, G. *Barr-calltuinn* in Argyle. Instances of its use in Sutherland, Ross, or Inverness would be exceedingly difficult to produce; in all these counties *call* and *coll* are the forms regularly found. In common speech, on the other hand, *calltuinn* is universal; the others have grown quite obsolete, and are not recognised by all dictionaries. This, together with their resemblance to *coille*, wood, has caused *coll* and *call* to be practically ignored by many writers. In names where it is possible to verify the Gaelic forms there is no difficulty in distinguishing the sound of *coill*, genitive of *call*, with its long *ll*, from *coille*, where the *ll* is short; but when this is not so, and we have only the forms as taken over into Scots, *ll* regularly becomes *w*, whence much confusion has resulted. The most instructive example is Kilcoy in Ross-shire, in 1294 Culcolly, 1479 Culcowy, later Kilcoy, G. *Cuil-challaigh*, a derivative of *call*, meaning 'Nook of the Hazel Wood'[1]. Here the process is plainly seen in operation, and the old record spelling can be checked by the present-day Gaelic form. The same element is seen in *Bealach Collaigh*, Wyvis. Cowie is rather a common name; old spellings, when they are available, show Colly, Collie, or such, and it is to be inferred that all the Cowies were Hazel woods. Similarly our northern Tolly, Tollie, G. *Tollaigh* (from *toll*, hole) becomes in Scots Towie (derived wrongly from *tulach*, a hill, with reversion of meaning).

Coll becomes in Scots cow, whence Duncow, Hazel Fort, in Dumfriesshire, just as *poll* becomes pow, applied to sluggish streams. *Coille*, wood, may also become cow on occasion, as in Cowcaddens, the old spellings of which, Kowcawdennis, Kowcaldenis, point to a derivation from *Coille-challtuinn*, Hazel wood.

The treatment of *calltuinn* is seen from a Perthshire example. Near Comrie is the pretty little spot of Cowden, in old spellings Coldon, the present-day Gaelic of which is *a' Challtuinn*, the Hazel Wood. This settles the meaning of the various Cowdens, including Cowdenbeath, with its differentia implying that this particular Cowden belongs to the parish of Beath. The same element is most probably seen in the famed Cowdenknowes in Berwickshire, old spellings of which are Couldenknowes, 1610; Coldingknowes, 1827.[2] The hybrid form in this case presents no more difficulty than such a term as 'the Moor of Rannoch', and the name is doubly interesting as occurring in Berwickshire. Of course, Coldingham, Bede's Urbs Coludi, is no relation.

Ibert and Offerance

Ibert occurs as a place-name once in Perthshire and twice in Stirlingshire. A Retour of 1640 records 'gleba vocata the Ibert

1 PNRC, p143.
2 *Place-Names of Scotland*, J. B. Johnston.

ecclesiae de Monzie' (the glebe called *the* Ibert belonging to the church of Monzie), and another of 1648 has 'the glebe and kirkland of the viccar of Monzievaird beside the water of Turret, with teynd sheaves of the said glebe called Ibur'. The Ibert still survives upon the map, not, however, beside the water of Turret, but beside the Shaggie Burn, a little way to the north of Monzie Parish Church. In Stirlingshire, Thomas Buchannane was served heir in 1621 to his father John Buchannane of Ibert in 'the church lands of Ibert in the parish of Drymmen', and the name still appears close to the church of Drymen. The other Stirlingshire Ibert was apparently close to the church of Balfron, and appears on record in 1666 as belonging to the Earl of Glencairn. The fact of the connection of these names with Gaelic *iobart*, an offering, is more obvious than the exact manner of it, and there has arisen not unnaturally the usual 'Druidical' theorising—these, it is imagined, were places where sacrifice was offered. The exact significance and point of the name will, however, be apparent from certain phrases in the Book of Deer. There we have, for instance, 'dórat *inedbáirt* dóib úácloic intiprat goníce chlóic pette meic garnáit', 'he gave *in offering* to them from the Stone of the Well to the Stone of the Farm of Garnat's son'. Again, 'Domnall mac meic dubbacin robáith nahúle edbarta rodrostan, Domnall, son of Mac Dubbacin, dedicated (lit. drowned) all the offerings to Drostan'. There are two other instances of similar phraseology. Thus it will be seen that *iobart* was a regular old Gaelic term for an offering made to the Church. The place itself was the *iobart*, and so we have an interesting addition to the Scottish names of places derived from the Celtic Church. It will be noted that two of the three Iberts above mentioned are definitely stated to be Church lands, while the third was near a church.

Iobart means 'an offering', the church collection is still called 'the offeral' in the Highlands, and we shall now proceed to show that the curious place-names Offerance, Offeris are exact parallels of the Iberts. The places of this name, like the Iberts, are confined to Perth and Stirling. They are confined, in fact, to the Menteith neighbourhood, which was dominated by Inchmahome. Near the

Lake of Menteith occur such names as Arnclerich, Arnvicar, Arnprior, and there on the fringe of Flanders Moss (A' Mhòine Fhlànrasach), north of the Kirk of Buchlyvie occurs the name Offerance, in its various divisions of Offerance of Glartur, Over Easter Offerance and Nether Easter Offerance, while at the west end of the Moss is Offerance, north of the Peel of Gartfarren. Offerance of Leckie formed part of Scheirgartane (Ret. 1609 etc), presumably meaning West Gartan. It appears on the map as Offers in Perthshire, in an angle of the Forth, on the south edge of Blair Drummond Moss, and north of the Kirk of Gargunnock. The *Old Statistical Account of the Parish of Callander*, by the Rev James Robertson, contains an interesting note on the etymologies of the parish names, among which is mentioned Offerans, lying, if we may judge from the order followed in the list, between Duncraggan and Lanrick at the west end of Loch Vennachar. 'In Gaelic,' says Mr Robertson, it is '*Oir-roinn*, the side of the point. This name is generally given to places at the side of a river, whether it either runs into a lake or falls into another river.' This description applies well to the land in question, and as in a Retour of 1596 there appears '*lie offeres de Lanark*' in the lordship of Stragartnay we may conclude that this is the place in question. But either the name covered more ground than this, or there was another place of the same name similarly situated at the west end of Loch Achray, for the name of the meadow at the bridge there on the road to Aberfoyle was given me last August[1] as *an t-Oirrinn*, and the rock westwards of it (part of the Trossachs) as *Creag an Oirrinn*[2].

If the minister's derivation is bad, his Gaelic is honest. Oirrinn is manifestly the Gaelic form of Offeran, Latin *offerendum*, whence E. Ir. *oifrend*, Gaelic *aifrionn*, the offering of the Mass,

---

1 In course of an investigation of the names of Perthshire, in which I was helped by the Carnegie Trustees, whose liberality I desire gratefully to acknowledge.

2 My informant was Parlan Macfarlan, who possesses a unique knowledge of the names and traditions of the country between Callander and Loch Lomondside.

pronounced often *aoirinn* (*ao* short). The question arises whether *oirinn* is merely a dialectic variation of *aifrionn*, retaining the original initial vowel, or whether it is not an independent loan of local origin from the same source. The difference in gender (*aifrionn*, fem., *oirinn*, mas.) does not count, the word having been originally neuter. In any case the Gaelic form of Offerance goes to show that the name is to be regarded as parallel to Ibert, and not a mere translation of it.

It has been already noted that the church collection is in the Highlands still called 'the offeral'. It may be added that in E. Ross (once a stronghold of the Celtic Church) the past generation were in the habit of applying the term *iobart* colloquially to any unkempt 'ill-guided' creature, whether beast or body. Was this a sinister reminiscence of the usual condition of animals presented to the Church? If so, then we may regard the *bonna-sia* of the offeral as the legitimate successor of the starveling iobart! 'Cha do chuir mi-fhein ann riamh ach am bonna-sia,' said an elder of my acquaintance. ['I myself never put in more than the halfpenny.']

Topographical Varia [II]

tros

Old Welsh *tros*, across, modern Welsh *traws*, is paralleled in several Perthshire names. To the south of Loch Rannoch is *Troscraig*, Cross-rock, applied to a rock which lies athwart the general run of its neighbours. The same base with extensions is seen in *na Tròisichean*, the Trossachs, i.e. the places lying athwart, between Loch Katrine and Loch Achray. This exactly describes the Trossachs, which fill the gap at the end of Loch Katrine so completely that Loch Katrine's waters have to seek a way for themselves between the Trossachs and the foot of Ben Venue. The curious name Throsk in Stirlingshire, situated near the Forth, may be a derivative of *tros* as *crosg*, a cross place, is from *crois* or rather *cross*, a cross. With this again may be compared the great hill *Trosgaich* at the north end of Loch Lomond, overlooking *Làirig Airnein*, Arnan's crossing; Trosgaich, crossing place, has been transferred from the *làirig* or crossing, to the hill above it. But the old meaning still lingers, for a good authority of his own accord declined to say definitely whether Trosgaich is the name of the hill or not rather of the pass.

Tros may be old Pictish. On the other hand it may be Strathclyde Welsh. Loch Lomond itself is in Welsh Llyn Llumonwy, Lake of Lumon-water, which seems to be plain Welsh for Beacon-water, and *llumon* being borrowed from Latin *lumen*, as its phonetics show, is at any rate not a native Pictish term. The probability is that the name was given by the Strathclyde Britons from beacon fires on Ben Lomond. Gaelic has taken over the name as Loch Laoiminn, in north Gaelic *Loch Laomuinn*, with phonetics influenced by the personal and hero name *Laomuinn* (Norse Law-man) with which it has no real connection. With Ben Lomond may be compared the Welsh Plynlimmon, for Pumlumon. Two or three miles beyond Trosgaich, as one goes up Glenfalloch, is *Clach nam Breatan*, the Britons' stone, a great roughly oblong slab about ten feet long, standing at an angle of about 30° on a cairn of moraine matter. The stone is not visible from the public road, except, I think, at one particular point, but may be readily located by leaving the road at a point a little over a mile beyond Glenfalloch farm (properly Clachnambreatan farm) before one comes to the Falls of Falloch, and, keeping to the left, crossing the railway line above the powder magazine, which latter will serve as a guide when to leave the public road. There are many stones on the hillside, but Clach nam Breatan is too conspicuous to be missed or mistaken. It is well to be thus minute, for it is too probable that in a few years it might be impossible to identify it from local information.

There are several other names in the Menteith district which might reasonably be claimed as Strathclyde Welsh, but these may be reserved for discussion at some other time.

esc, 'Ισκα

The old Irish *esc*, water, Ptolemy's 'Ισκα, whence the river names Exe, Esk, Welsh Usg, appears in Irish in the term Murrisc, a sea-fen, sea-swamp, and in *easgaidh*, a quagmire. Hence, also, our Gaelic *easgann*, Old Irish *escung*, fen-snake (*ung*, Latin *anguis*[1]). The derivative *easgaidh* seems to be obsolete in Scottish Gaelic, but it appears in at least two northern place-names. The eastern part of the present farm of Clashnabuiack, Alness, Ross-shire, was formerly a distinct holding, containing a swampy hollow now drained, and called in Gaelic *Pollaisgidh*, for *poll+easgaidh*, meaning fen-hollow. The other instance occurs at the west end of Loch Ruthven, at the head of Strathnairn, where there is a low-lying farm, much of it once swampy, called Aberskye (accented on first syllable), in Gaelic *Abairsgidh*. Here *abar* is the term seen also in Loch-aber, Irish *abar*, marshy land, now *eabar*, mud, in spoken Scottish Gaelic. Thus Aberskye means mud-fen. The contraction of *Abareasgaidh* into *Abairsgidh* is due to the stress on the first part of the compound. Esky Loch[2] is probably a third instance; but more should be forthcoming.

1 Macbain's *Etymological Dictionary.*
2 W. J. N. Liddall's *Place-Names of Fife and Kinross.*

benn

The primary meaning of *benn* is 'horn', hence 'peak', and in Ireland the bens are peaked hills. With us in Scotland the term, in the oblique form *beinn*, is extended to apply to any hill without regard to shape, though traces of the old usage are common. The diminutive *binnean* always denotes a peaked hill, sometimes by no means diminutive in size. The Binnean in Glendochart is 3,821 feet in height. The adjective *beannach* always means 'peaked', and is applied to a variety of things, including lochs: Loch Beannach, horned loch, is a common name, usually mistranslated. The classical instance is Lacus Bēnācus (Bennācus) in the north of Italy, now Lago di Garda, so called from its running to a horn. The same word with extension is found in Loch Vennachar, Gael. *Loch Bheannchair*, practically the horned loch, or rather loch of the horn-shaped place. In Ross-shire we have the duplicate *Loch Bheannacharan*, with still another extension. It may be noted that *cròc*, antler, is used in a way exactly similar; *Loch Cròcach*, antlered loch; *Lochan na Cròice*, lochlet of the antler. In all these instances the horn is horizontal, not vertical. The vertical meaning is seen, however, in Benly, Gaelic *Binniligh*, a pointed hill at Abriachan, Inverness, from *benn+lach*, place of the horn or peak. A more recondite case is found in Ross-shire in the hill-name *Benndealt*, which was long obscure to me. The hill consists of a ridge dipping towards the middle and having a distinct peak at each end. When one remembers that the Ross-shire Gaelic for saddle is *dialt* (not *diollaid*) the meaning is plainly seen to be 'peak-saddle'. The numerous places called Benchar, Banchor, Bangor, Banchory, are all of the same derivation, but whether the horn in these is horizontal or vertical requires local knowledge in each particular case to determine.

mion; gàg

The adjective *mion*, small (Latin *min-or*), occurs very seldom in names of places. It is seen in Minard on Loch Fyne, *mion+àird*, small cape, and in the *Mionchnoc*, the little hill, to the west of Fyrish, Novar. On Gordon of Straloch's Map (1641-8) appears 'Mountains ... Minigeg' in the Struan neighbourhood, and the Grampian range here is still called *Monadh Mion-gaig*, the mountain range of 'Minigeg'. Here the second element is *gàg*, a cleft, the whole meaning 'little cleft', as distinguished from the various other names involving *gàg* in that wild region. Best known of these is Gaick, in Gaelic *Gàig* (locative case), of sinister reputation. There are also *Garbhgag*, rough cleft, *Singaig*, old cleft, and *Mungaig*, this last involving *mun*, which is probably of same root as *monadh*. The latter two names, and also Miongaig, have the short indefinite or 'sporadic' vowel sound between the two parts of the compound. The use of *gàg* in this district is one of the many instances of the fondness of special localities for special terms. There may be added *Baile na Gàig*, near Dochgarroch, Inverness, a cosy stead, with a cleft in the ridge immediately behind it, also the stream *Faragaig*, Stratherrick.

ith, iodh, ithir

In Old Irish the generic term for corn is *ith*, genitive *etho*. One of the plains of Ireland, cleared by the people of Partholon (some eight generations after the Flood, say the legends) was Mag Ita or Mag Ioth, thus giving corn-growing in Ireland a high antiquity. The word is obsolete with us, except in the compound *iodhlann* (*iodh+lann*), a corn-yard. It occurs, however, in a few names of places, best known of which is Tiree, 'Tir-iodh iosal an eòrna', low-lying Tiree of the barley, famed for its fertility even in the sixth century, when it was tilled by Columban monks. Adamnan Latinises it as Ethica Insula and its sea as Ethicum Pelagus, showing, I suppose, that in his time the Gaelic of it was Tir-etho.

From *ith* is formed *ithir*, corn-land, and I venture to think that to this we may look for the derivation of the names Strathyre and

Stronyre at the head of Loch Lubnaig. Stronyre is a promontory, flat and fertile, by the loch side, forming part of the farm of Laggan. In Gaelic it is *Sròn-eadhair*, and Strathyre is *Srath-eadhair*, though here the *th* of *srath* is in pronunciation rather made to go with the second part, whence a local explanation as 'Strath of the tether' (teadhair) with reference to the windings of the quiet *Balbhaig* which flows through it. But the pronunciation of *Sròn-eadhair* gives the key to the right division, and I think that the names mean Point and Strath of the corn-land. I venture further to identify Strathyre with the place mentioned in the *Annals of Ulster*, under date 653: 'Bellum *Sratho Ethairt* ubi Duncath mac Conaing cecidit', the battle of Strath-ethart, in which fell Duncan, son of Conang. Conang was son of Aedan, King of Dalriada, who died in 621 AD.

Monzie, in Strathearn, appears on record c 1230 as Mugedha; 1268, Monyhge; 1282, Mothyethe; 1283, Muyhe; and the modern Gaelic is *Magh-eadh*. This, as has been pointed out in an appendix to the recently published *Charters of Inchaffray Abbey*, may be explained with tolerable certainty as 'Plain of Corn', a parallel to the Irish Magh Ioth. It will be noted how closely the modern Gaelic form coincides with the oldest charter spelling; the spelling of 1283 is really a very fair phonetic attempt at the same sound, and of value as showing that the Gaelic then was exactly what it is now. The puzzling *n*, which appears both in the English form and in the spelling of 1268, is explained by Professor Mackinnon as the ancient *n-* after neuters, *magh* (Gaulish *magos mages-*) having been originally neuter. Very similar is the case of the adjacent Monzievaird, which appears in the Inchaffray Charters as 1203, Monewarde; 1234, 1239, Moytheuard; 1265, Monyvard; while the present day Gaelic is *Magh-bhàrd*. If it is curious that the old *n* should be represented in the charter spellings of these names, it is still more curious that it has stuck in their modern Englished forms. Yet these are only examples of a large class of names where very ancient forms are preserved after the manner of fossils in modern English. Lovat, for instance, which is doubtless Pictish (root *lov*, wash), is never heard in

Gaelic speech; it is always *A' Mhor'oich*, 'the sea-plain', possibly a translation made when the meaning of the Pictish Lovat was still understood. Balkeith, near Tain, is in Gaelic *Baile na Coille*, also very possibly a translation from the Pictish. The modern Gaelic of Daviot near Inverness is *Deimhidh*, which Dr Macbain happily identified as to derivation with the Welsh Demetae, now Dyfed. From about 1203 onwards, Daviot appears on record as Deveth; the Aberdeen Daviot appears in early documents as Davyoth. Here and in many other cases we have the curious phenomenon of a sort of double nomenclature, the present day Gaelic and the English forms, the former showing the usual regular phonetic changes, the latter preserving fossilised a very old pronunciation. These English forms have been explained as revivals; but this theory, while it may explain some instances, seems to be on the whole inadequate, and the whole subject deserves consideration.

Topographical Varia–III

fortair, gwerthyr, verterae

In the *Antonine Itinerary* and elsewhere mention is made of a place of the Brigantes, called Verterae, identified as to site with the modern Brough-under-Stanmore in Westmoreland. As early Celtic initial *v* becomes in Welsh *gw*, Verterae has been equated by Sir John Rhys with Welsh *gwerthyr*, a fortress. In Gaelic, on the other hand, early initial *v* becomes *f*, e.g. Gaulish *vernos*, alder; Welsh *gwern*; Gaelic *fearna*. I have learned recently from Mr Duncan Campbell, late editor of the *Northern Chronicle*, a Glenlyon man, that one of the ancient round forts in Glenlyon is called in Gaelic *an Fhortair*. In Glenisla parish, Forfarshire, on the right bank of the Isla, stands an ancient castle of the Ogilvies, named Forter, in Gaelic Fortair, while Forthar occurs in Kettle parish, Fife. There seems to be no doubt that in this *fortair* we have the Gaelic form of the old Verterae, meaning fortress. (Of course, notwithstanding the similarity in sound between fort, fortress, and fortair, there is no connection etymologically, the two first being derived from Latin *fortis*, strong.) From these, again, we cannot dissociate Fortingal, the Englished form of Gaelic *Fartairchill*, spelled Forterkil in 1240. The last syllable of Fartairchill may be considered doubtful, but there is no reason why it should not be simply *cill*, church, the meaning of the compound being Forter Church, or Church near the Forter. On this supposition Fartairchill is a Picto-Gaelic hybrid, of a type, however, which is natural and legitimate.

I have several times pointed out the tendency of certain terms to become as it were 'epidemic' in certain districts. There is no clear instance known to me of *fortair* occurring north of Spey. In Banff- and Aberdeen-shires, however, three or four places spelled Fortre appear on record, and in South Pictland *fortair* actually gave the name of the great district of Fortrenn, an oblique case of a nominative Foirtriu (cf Eriu, Erenn, Ireland), meaning the district of Forts. The men of Fortrenn, as has

93

been pointed out by Sir John Rhys, were of old the Verturiones, the folk of the Forts. 'The designation Verturiones,' says Professor Rhys, 'admits of being explained by reference to the military works built in their midst by Agricola and Severus.' It is perhaps more likely that the name is due to the fort-building propensities of the natives themselves; certainly the district is rich enough in Celtic forts to justify the title.

céith, keith, cēto-n

The Old-Celtic *cēto-n*, wood, becomes in modern Welsh *coed*, e.g., Argoed, On-wood, Woodside; Lichfield, in Welsh Llwyd coed, Grey wood, started from Lēto-cēton. Several continental names (see Holder) show the same element. In Gaelic phonetics it should become *ciath*, genitive *céith*, just as *lētos*, grey, becomes *liath*, genitive *léith*. I think it is possible to explain some, at least, of our Keith names by reference to this old word, and it is at any rate worth while to consider them. Balmakeith, near Nairn, is certainly *not* to be so explained, for the Gaelic form of it is Baile MacDhàidh, Davidson's Stead. Balkeith, near Tain, is in Gaelic at the present moment Baile na Coille, Wood-stead, which, as I pointed out long ago[1], looks uncommonly like a translation from the Pictish. With regard to the others of which the Gaelic forms are known, it is to be noted that all are in the genitive case. We have (1) Dalkeith, in 1142 Dalkied, in Gaelic Dail-chéith; (2) Inchkeith, Gaelic Innis-chéith; (3) Keith, in Banffshire, Gaelic Baile-chéith; (4) Dun-chéith, a hill, in the parish of Dores, Inverness, meaning Plateau, Isle, Town and Fort of the wood respectively. In at least one instance of frequent occurrence we appear to have *cēton* in composition. Cormac in his Glossary explains *salchuait* as 'willow wood', for, says he, *cóit* in Welsh means wood. This would give a primitive *salicēton*, which is represented in Scotland by the common *Saileachaidh*, Sallachy, Scots Sauchie-burn. We have probably

---

1 PNRC, p34, where I have referred to Welsh *gwydd*, which seems less likely.

another case in the stream-name Orchy, Glen-orchy, Gaelic *Urchaidh*, representing a primitive **are-cētia*, On-wood stream, River by the Woodside. It must be said that on the Perthshire side Orchy is *Urchadh*; 'Gleann-urcha nam badan,' says John MacGregor (1801); 'Glen Orchy of Woodclumps'. But I do not think that the difference in ending is fatal, and *nam badan* is significant.

As has been indicated above, *keith* in Anglicised forms of Celtic names is by no means always of the same origin. Indeed no sound in such forms needs closer watching than *th*, for *th* in Anglicised names may represent quite a variety of things, e.g. Gaelic *th*, *dh*, *t* slender, *t* broad, *bh* and *ch*. Thus the *keith* of Inverkeithing (see next note) is entirely different from that in Dalkeith.

cethin

The three following names appear to contain the same root:

Inbhir-cheitein, Inverkeithing.
Loch Ceiteirein, Loch Katrine.
Allt and Gleann Ceiteirlinn (Ceitlein on maps), off Glen Etive.

With *ceitein* of the first may be compared Welsh *cethin* dun, dusky; cf Welsh Bryncethin, Dark Hill. The Keithing is opposed to the Peffer as dark to bright. It is not necessary to insist on referring 'dark' and 'bright' in stream names to the actual colour of the water; exposure, or the presence or absence of thick wood were doubtless among the circumstances that originally determined the name.

---

1 I do not know whether Welsh *cethern*, fiends, furies, is connected with *cethin*, dusky. If it is genuine Welsh it might be possible to translate Loch Katrine 'Loch of the Fiends' (Goblins). This, of course, at once suggests connection with Coire nan Uruisgean, the Goblin Corry, a pleasant speculation, if we could be reasonably sure of it, for of old this corry was the great feature of Loch Katrine.

In *Ceiteirein*[1], Katrine, we seem to have an extension of the root ceit, meaning the dark or gloomy place, with reference to its thickly wooded shores.

Ceiteirlinn seems of similar formation, *ceiteir* +?*loinn*, locative of *lann*. The glen is narrow and deep with a northwest exposure.

All these seem to be thoroughly Pictish names. There are several other names that closely resemble them and may be connected, e.g. Catrine in Ayrshire, Caterline, Kincardineshire; Caterthun in Forfarshire.

eag

Eag, a notch, common in names of places, is as a rule easily recognised. In two instances, at least, the Anglicised form carries *n* of the Gaelic article in front, thus becoming Nigg[1]. Lately I came across an instance of its use certain enough, though by no means clear at first sight. In the parish of Duthil, to the east of Sloc-muic, there is a moor called on maps Forrigen, in Gaelic Foirigean (close *o*). The clue to this puzzling combination lies in the fact that the plain of Forrigen lies at the foot of a series of ridges containing many gullies and clefts, collectively called in Gaelic *na h-eagan*, the notches. The first part *for*, is simply our old friend *foter* (from *fo*, under), shortened into *for* (*far*) though aspiration of the *t*, as happens wherever we can get hold of it in Gaelic. Thus Forrigen means 'Under, at the foot of, the Notches'.

Foter or fother becomes *far*[2], as well as *for*, through the tendency to change an old *o* into *a*, of which many examples could be given. Keeping this in view, we shall readily see that Farragon Hill, south of Loch Tummel in Perthshire, is the same as Forrigen, and if further proof is required, reference to the map will show *Beinn Eagach*, the notched hill, a little to the north-east

---

1 PNRC, p50.
2 Cf Fodderletter, in Gaelic *Farleitir*; Fettercairn, as I am informed, is still called by old people *Farcairn* in English.

of it. Farragon Hill is the hill of Farragon, and Farragon itself is the moor under Beinn Eagach.

air: ur

The preposition *air*, on, before, is in Old Celtic *are*, which appears in such words as Are-morica, the district by the sea, and the British Are-cluta, Cluta-side, mentioned as the birthplace of Gildas. With us it appears in composition as *air* (*ear*) or *ur*, e.g. earball or urball (*air + ball*), a tail, urlar (*air + làr*), a floor. So also in place-names.

Erchless, near Beauly, is in Gaelic *Earghlais*, 'on the river Glass', which describes its situation exactly. We may compare Are-cluta above.

Urchany, Beauly, near a small stream, and Urchany, Nairn, are both for *air-canach*, on the white stream or white place[1]. For Canach as a stream name, cf Glencannich and Welsh Aber-canaid.

Urray, in Ross-shire, Gaelic *Urrath*, is for *air + ràth*, near the fort or earthwork, and in Gaul there is Are-dūnon with similar meaning.

Urquhart occurs in Ross, Inverness, Moray and Fife. The Inverness Urquhart appears in Adamnan's *Life of Columba* in the form Airchartdan, in present-day Gaelic *Urchardain*, and has been satisfactorily explained by Macbain as *air + cardden*, Welsh for wood, brake; on-wood, woodside, synonymous with Argoed above-mentioned.

Erchite, near Inverness, is in Gaelic *Earchoid*, the second part of which is difficult, and may be compared with *Blàr-choighde*, Blairwhyte, in the Black Isle.

Orchil, in Perthshire, is in Gaelic *Urchoill*, with same meaning as Urquhart, Woodside. There is also Errichel, near Aberfeldy. It is to be noted that so far as the second part of these goes, the names may be comparatively modern Gaelic or old Pictish: the

---

1 Cf TGSI, vol 25, p83.

word for wood (Welsh *celli*, grove, Gaelic *coille*, wood) being common to both branches of Celtic.

Urrard, in Perthshire, is similarly for *air + àrd*, On-height, or On-point.

Orchy has been already noted.

Topographical Varia–IV

[Note—The stress accent is indicated by a point placed immediately before the stressed syllable.]

ath, ate

The Gaelic prefix *ath* in the modern language corresponds in meaning to Latin *re-*, again, back[1]. In the earlier stages of the language it is used (1) to denote repetition, reiteration, restoration; (2) as an intensive prefix; (3) as Latin *ex-*, often with a depreciative meaning. Examples of these three uses are given by Dr Kuno Meyer[2]. The Gaulish form of *ath* is *ate*, often with intensive force, as in Ate-merus, very merry (Gaelic, *mear*); At-eula, very skilled (Gaelic, *eòl-ach*)[3]. An Irish Ogam inscription has the name Ate-glan, very pure. This prefix, in its various applications, occurs in a few of our place-names, of which some examples may be given with certainty:–

(1) Atholl, in Gaelic •Atholl, •Athall. The old forms are Athotla (Book of Deer), Athfoithle (Irish Annals), and such. Dr Macbain, in his notes to Skene's *Highlanders of Scotland* (p413), rightly derives the name as 'Ath-Fhodla, Second Ireland', i.e. New Ireland. Fodla was one of the names for Ireland, and also that of one of the three mythical queens, really goddesses, of the country. The name may be explained as from a primitive *Vo-dil-a, Little dear one. The stock derivation of Atholl from *àth*, ford, would require the stress accent to fall on the second part of the compound, giving Ath•fhoille, and is therefore manifestly impossible. If we may suppose the name Ath-Fodla to have been given by the first Gaelic settlers of Atholl in fond remembrance of their native land, an interesting parallel may be found on English soil. At Glastonbury, in Somersetshire, there is known to have existed a very ancient Irish settlement and monastery. In Irish records it is referred to as 'Glastimper nan Gaidheal', Glastonbury

---

1 Cf Macbain's *Etym. Dict.*
2 Kuno Meyer, *Contributions to Irish Lexicography.*
3 Holder

of the Gael. In his recent book[1] Mr Edmund McClure says: 'King Edgar granted certain privileges to Glastonbury in 971, according to *Cart. Sax.*, vol 3, p574, in which certain places in the islands (*in insulis*, i.e. in the low insulated lands near the Abbey) are mentioned, among them *"Bekeria*, which is called *Parva Ybernia*," little Ireland.' Bekeria is obviously Bec Eriu. It is now called Bickery. Eriu was another of the Tuatha De Danaan queens, as well as a name for Ireland; doubtless, like Fodla, a local tutelary goddess. To judge by the frequency of her association with rivers, both in Ireland and Scotland, she was specially a goddess of waters.

(2) As an example of the depreciative sense of *ath* may be taken Loch Ashie and Drum Ashie (Drumossie Moor of Burns), near Inverness. The Gaelic is Loch and Druim •Ath(a)isidh, and reference [see p76] to the examples of *innis* in place-names which I collected in vol 3 p241 of the *Celtic Review* (Cruoisidh, Breacaisidh, etc), will make it clear that Ath(a)isidh is the genitive case of Athinnis, a poor or disused meadow, viz •Athinnse, where *innse* in the unaccented syllable is degraded to *i'se, isidh*. For the meaning, compare *athgort*, a disused field; *athlaech*, a dotard; *athrí*, a deposed king; *athlongport*, a disused camp[2]. The meaning suits the place. Inverness folk-etymology makes Ashie one of the numerous band of Danish princes who went about getting themselves killed in places where they had no business to be, such being, presumably, the most obvious way of commemorating their names, unknown to history otherwise.

(3) The intensive use of *ath*, noted at the outset as going back to Gaulish times, and closely allied to the notion of repetition, is well seen in Loch •Athfhinn, Beinn •Athfhinn[3], Inbhir •Athfhinn,

---

1 *British Place-Names in their Historical Setting*, p205.

2 Kuno Meyer, *Contributions to Irish Lexicography*.

3 The following verse, in a song by Archibald Stewart, a native of Glen Aven, deserves quoting in this connection:

'Gu Beinn Athfhinn nan stùc
Nam feadan 's nan lùb
Far an loisgear am fùdar gorm.'

Thos. Sinton, *The Poetry of Badenoch*.

Abhainn •Athfhinn, Englished Loch Aven or Loch A'an, etc. The
River Aven falls into Spey at Ballindalloch. There is a good deal
of local tradition with regard to it, a resumé of which was given
me by Mr John Mathieson of HM Ordnance Survey. Athfhinn, says
tradition, was the wife of Fionn, and lived at Bog-luachrach
opposite Inchrory Lodge. At that time the stream was called 'Uisge
bàn nan clachan sleamhain', Fair water of the slippery stones.
Athfhinn fell in and was drowned. Then said Fionn:

> 'Uisge bhàin nan clachan sleamhain!
> 'S an deach mo bhean a bhàthadh;
> 'S e Athfhinn a bheir mi air an abhainn.'

> 'Fair water of the slippery stones!
> Wherein my wife was drowned,
> Aven I will name the river.'

Since that time no one can be drowned in Aven till it meets the
Alnack, near Tomintoul. So far tradition. The Aven is famed for
the clearness of its water; the fish can be seen hanging in every
pool.

> 'The water of Aven runs so clear
> It would wile a man of a hundred year.'

In fact, *Athfhinn* means simply 'the very clear or bright one',
representing a primitive *Ate-vinda, with which may be compared
for meaning Belisama, 'most bright one', now the Ribble, both
river-goddesses to start with. *Uisge bàn*, Fair Water, echoes the old
name. The legend of Fionn's wife may be a reminiscence of the
primitive river-goddess; the goddesses of certain rivers have by
no means yet passed out of recollection.

(4) The river-name Affric, of Glen Affric, has been derived by
Dr Macbain from •*Ath-bhreac*, which he explained as 'somewhat
speckled'. On the analogy of Aven, it is more probably 'very
speckled'. The term was in use of old as a female proper name;
as applied to the river it was primarily the name of the local water
nymph or river-goddess.

*eadar, *enter, inter*

To define a locality as lying between two given points is a simple and obvious method of fixing situation, which was so extensively used in Gaelic place-names that anything like a complete list of names in which *eadar*, 'between', occurs would be difficult to compile and tedious to read. On the Continent, though Endlicher's glossary of Gaulish terms gives *inter ambes*: *inter rivos*, the old *inter, enter* seems to have been very sparingly used on Celtic ground; at least Holder gives only Inter-catia, occurring twice in Spain, nor is there any recorded instance of its use in ancient Britain.

Both in Gaul and in Britain the stock name for a confluence was Condāte, and that, or a derivative of it, was used to denote the land included by converging streams. In ancient Italy, Interamna, 'between waters', 'Mesopotamia', was not uncommonly so used. In Scotland, as in Ireland, *eadar* is usually, though not always, found in combination with words that imply water—e.g. abhainn, dobhar, allt, caolas, for the obvious reason that water, in stream or loch, forms the clearest of limits. With us, too, as in Ireland, *eadar* is regularly, if not indeed invariably, followed by *dà*, two. Names involving a monosyllabic preposition have the stress accent on the preposition. Our only preposition of more than one syllable is *eadar* itself, and it usually conforms to this rule when the noun following *dà* is a monosyllable; when the noun is not a monosyllable, the principal stress accent falls on the final element of the compound. Further, in these compounds, whether monosyllabic or not, under the influence of the stress accent, the *d* of *dà* is assimilated to the *r* of *eadar*, and the resulting sound is *rr*, as in nàdu*rr*a for nàdu*r*da, and such. Some examples will illustrate all these points:

> Loch eadar dà Shàbhal, Loch between two Savals (hills), pronounced Loch eadra Shàbhal (Sutherland).
>
> Loch Dochfour, between Loch Ness and the river Ness, is in Gaelic an Eadarloch.

Eadar dà abhainn (•Eadra•abhainn), between two rivers, viz., Meadie Burn and the Burn of Strath Dubh (Suth.).

Eadar dà Chalda (•Eadra•Chalda), between two Caldas, Norse for Coldwater (Suth.).

Cnoc eadar dà allt, Hill between two burns (Suth.).

Eadar dà chaolas, Eddra•chiles, between two Kyles (Suth.).

Cnoc dubh eadar da allt a' chlaiginn, Black hill between two 'skull'[1] burns (Ross).

Eadardun, •Edderton, between forts. If *dà* ever occurred here, all trace of it is lost in the Gaelic pronunciation (Ross).

•Edra•dour (obsolete, now Redcastle), between two rivulets (Ross).

Eadar dà Charrann (•Eadra•Charrann, now in English New Kelso), between two Carrons; situated in a circular bend of the River Carron (W. Ross).

Eadrais •Ettridge (Glentruim), explained by Dr Macbain as between two falls, *eas* (Inverness).

Eadar dà fhaodhail (Eadra fhaodhail, in English Ard•roil), between two fords (Lewis).

Eadar dà leacach (•Eadra•leacach), between two slopes (L. Katrine).

Eadar dà dhobhar (Eadra dhobhar, •Edra•dour), between two rivulets (Perth).

Eadar dà ghobhal (Eadra ghobhal, •Edra•goul), between two forks (Loch Tay side). The district between Call•ellochan and Acharn.

Eadar dà dhoimhnid (Eadra dhoimhnid, •Edra•dynate), between two ravines (Strath Tay).

Eadar dà Mhucaidh (Eadra Mhucaidh, •Edra•mucky), between two swine-burns (Strath Tay).

Beinn Eadar dà loch, corruptly now in Gaelic •Meadarloch, •Benderloch, hill between two lochs (Argyll).

•Eadarlinn, between two pools (Loch Awe).

---

1 *Claigionn* here means a skull-shaped hill.

In beith edarda alterin, the birch between two ravines (Book of Deer).

Some names beginning with *eadar* are obscure as to meaning. Such are, near Altas in Sutherland, Cnoc •Eadarmaigh, near Muir of Ord in Ross, Ach•edersan, Gaelic Achd-eadarsan; Inver•edrie, Gaelic Inbhir-eadrain, Glenshee; and Beinn •Eadarainn in Skye.

fonn

Fonn, 'land', borrowed into Gaelic from Latin *fundus*, 'a farm', occurs several times in Perthshire. Fin•castle is in Gaelic Fonn a' Chaisteil, 'the castle land'. The castle in question was a prehistoric one, of the broch type, like the Glenlyon 'castles'. The Tay basin, from Ballinluig (and possibly lower) to Beinn a' Chaisteil, at the very head of Glenlyon on the watershed between Argyll and Perth, contains many sites of round towers, all called in Gaelic Caistealan nam Fiann, 'Castles of the Fiann'[1]. These, though not all conforming exactly in dimensions or structure to the northern broch, are all of the broch type, and it is rather extraordinary that they have never, so far as known to me, been seriously examined since Pennant's time. They are exceedingly ruinous, and it is often difficult to get complete measurements. The best-preserved specimen is that near Creag a' Chaisteil, the Castle Rock, near Fortingal Hotel, which still shows a few feet of Cyclopean masonry all round. An old man, who had been a mason to trade remarked to me last autumn, 'Thug mi fhein an t-uamhas chlach as', 'I took an enormous quantity of stones out of it myself'. With Fincastle cf Fin•dynate (Strathtay), G. fonn dhoimhneid, 'Land near the ravine'.

Fon•ab, Gaelic Fonn an Aba, 'the Abbot's land', in Atholl, was so called, it is said, because it belonged to the Abbot of Dunkeld. In Atholl also there is Fon•vic, Gaelic Fonn a' Bhuic, or Fonn a' Bhuig. It is difficult in Atholl to distinguish *c* from *g*, but 'Land near the Bog' is more probable than 'Buck's land'.

---

1 Caistealan nam Fiann, cf Castella Brigantum, Juvenal, *Sat.*, 14, 196. The sons of Usnech had *fianbhothan*, hunting lodges, in Alba.

Fonn occurs terminally in •Gealuinn (geal-fhuinn), in Glenlyon, and in Kiniegallin, Gaelic Cinn a' Ghealuinn, Tigh Ghealuinn, near Duneaves, Fortingal, a locative of •gealfhonn, 'white land'. Similarly in Glenlyon we have Camas Bhracuinn, from •breacfhonn, 'dappled land'. Breac in Perthshire, and elsewhere, often becomes brac, e.g. Ben Vraggie, Gaelic Beinn Bhracaidh, 'the dappled hill'. It may be noted that Gealuinn in Glenlyon is not far from Dail Chiarlaich, 'Dale of the swarthy place'.

Brannradh

The historic pass of Brander, on Loch Awe-side, is in Gaelic called *am Brannradh*. The name is rare, but not unique, for between Portmaluag in Lismore and the little isle of Eriskay there is a tidal rock, known as *am Brannradh*, which is dangerous to navigation, and which boatmen take good care to avoid. The term, Dr A. Carmichael tells me, is still known in the spoken language in the sense of hindrance, obstruction. The older form is *brannrad*, explained as trap or snare, a meaning which applies well to the pass and to the sea-rock. It would be interesting to know of other instances of its use.

comraich, tearmann, teagarmachd

The privilege of sanctuary once enjoyed by certain churches within a definite radius, though it must have been an important feature in the eyes of the community, has left fewer traces in the names of places than might have been expected. This is no doubt partly owing to disuse, but we may suspect that the rarity of such terms is really less than it appears, and that careful investigation on the ground would lead to some amplification of the scanty survivals noted below. The commonest term for a girth or sanctuary is *comraich*, which appears twice on the mainland of Ross. A' Chomraich, or, more definitely, Comraich Ma Ruibhe, Malruba's Girth, is the Gaelic name of the parish of Applecross. The more famous girth of Tain, connected with St Duthac, is commemorated in Clais na Comraich, the Girth Hollow, a name now almost obsolete, applied to a hollow on the western boundary, near which one of the girth crosses stood of old[1]. In the western isles, there are two instances in North Uist, and one in South Uist. Comraich na h-Eaglais, the Kirk Girth, in North Uist, was connected with the church of Kilmuir, dedicated to the Virgin Mary. The other North Uist instance is Comraich na Trianaid, Trinity Girth, at Trinity Temple (Teampull na Trianaid), Carinish. The ford near it, between North Uist and Benbecula, is Faodhail na Comraich, the Girth Ford, and a channel therein is Sruthan na Comraich, the Girth Streamlet. The South Uist instance is interesting as being non-ecclesiastical. The land assigned to bards had the privileges of an *immunitas* as well as the land assigned to clerics, hence at Staoligearry, which was the official residence of the famous MacMhuirich family, hereditary bards to Clanranald, we have Comraich nam Bard, the Bards' Girth. These Uist instances I owe to Dr A. Carmichael. Dr Joyce in his *Irish Names of Places* makes no mention of *comraich*; the regular Irish term, which is of frequent occurrence, is *tearmann*, borrowed from late Latin *termo, termon-is*, akin to *terminus*, a limit, boundary. That this word was known and used in Scottish Gaelic appears from its mention in *A' Chomhachag*, verse 4 (Mackenzie's *Beauties*), where the aged owl, on being recommended to make confession, replies:

> 'Cha d'rinn mise braid no breugan,
> Cladh no tearmann, a bhristeadh.'

> 'I have neither stolen nor lied,
> Graveyard or girth I have not broken.'

But I have come across only two cases of its use with us. Clach an Tearmainn (locally Tearmaid), the Girth Stone, is at Colonsay. 'Right in the middle of the strand,' says Professor Mackinnon, 'that separates Colonsay and Oronsay, and covered by the sea for twelve hours of the twenty-four, is Clach an Tearmainn, marking

1 See PNRC.

the limit to which the sanctuary rights of Oronsay Priory reached. The base of the structure, strongly built with stone and lime, is still entire, but the cross has disappeared.' It will be noted that the local genitive case of tearmann is *tearmaid*. This explains the name Termit which appears on record in connection with Petty, Inverness. This place, which according to the records belonged to the minister of Petty, was situated, I am informed, where the mansion of Holme-Rose now stands. Termit is obviously a locative of tearmann.

There is a third term of, I think, the same meaning, that deserves attention. On the north side of the Tay, beyond Aberfeldy, between the parish church of Dull and Tirinie, is the farm of Teagarmachd. Opposite to it there used to be a ford in the river called Ath na Teagarmachd, and a small island near it is Eilean na Teagarmachd, showing the word to be a noun feminine. This, together with its ending, familiar in such terms as Tòisigheachd, Thanedom; Baranachd, a barony; Siorramachd, sheriffdom, etc, proves it to be a Gaelic term once well understood, though its meaning is now to seek. Stripping off the suffix -*achd*, we get *teagarm* as the business part of the word, to be referred to *teagair*, to shelter, based on which there must apparently have been a noun *teagairm*, shelter (cf *goir*, to cry; *gairm*, a cry). This would give *teagarmachd* the meaning of shelter-place, or sanctuary, the conclusion being that here we have the name of the ancient girth of Dull.

It is, I think, inconceivable that the above instances nearly exhaust the cases where one or other of the terms mentioned occur. Dr Carmichael tells me that there was, as is to be expected, a girth in Lismore, one of the boundaries of which was Clach an Ealadh. This, as I have already noted (*Celtic Review*, vol 5, p289), is the Irish *elad*, rendered by Dr Kuno Meyer as tomb. There should be other instances yet to be discovered both in the isles and on the mainland of Scotland.

Connel, Congal

The salt-water cataract of Connel, on Loch Etive, is known in Gaelic as Sruth na Con'aill, the *n* of Con'aill being long, with the peculiar lingering sound that indicates original contact with a consonant now lost by aspiration. The word is to be referred to Ir. congal (fem.), a conflict, 'sruth na conghail' yielding the appropriate meaning of 'current of the conflict'. Final slender *l* is apt to be doubled in unstressed syllables. The *Highland Society Dict.* gives '*coingheall*, a whirlpool', and refers to Connel as 'a' choingheall Lathurnach', the Lorne whirlpool. This meaning, which is a natural extension of the original, is countenanced by the following extract[1] from a writer of the early part of the seventeenth century: 'This ferrie called Gonnell when the sea aither ebbs or flows, cryes so vehementlie that it will be heard far off in sundrie parts, at the least one myll or thereby, And when folk doeth goe over that ferrie the boatt or scoutt[2] doeth goe up verie high and otherwhiles doun verie low, that these which are in the boat, will think themselves likelie to be drowned in the sea, And the cause thereof is that there are Connalls and rocks in that ferrie.'

fas, foss

In Old Irish *foss* is an abstract noun, meaning residence, remaining, rest, generally taken as cognate with Greek ἄστυ, a town. In modern Gaelic it is represented by *fois*, rest. In an Old-Irish Metrical Rule occurs 'foss oc etlai', translated by Professor Strachan 'continuance in penitence'. A MS of the eighteenth century reads 'fas'. 'The poem,' says Strachan, 'can hardly be put later than 800AD.' The Old Irish phrase *i fus* is translated by Windisch 'zu Hause', at home. In composition, it appears in foslongport or faslongport, a permanent encampment; fosmullach, the rest-top, i.e. top on which one rests, e.g.

1 *Geog. Coll.*, vol 2, p151.
2 (?) sgoth, from Norse skúta.

fosmullach Sleibe Fuait. It is also recognised as the terminal element of Welsh *ar-os*, to stay. This word, or more probably its Pictish cognate, appears in our names of places as *fas*, a noun not abstract but concrete, denoting a level piece of ground suitable for resting; the sort of place, for instance, where an old-time drover would rest his charge for the night. Examples of this usage are:–

Fas na Clèithe, Station of the Hurdle, at the head of Loch Roe, Sutherland.

Fas a' Cheannaiche, The Merchant's Rest, in Glenstrathfarrar, Inverness-shire. Here a travelling merchant, or pedlar, was murdered. He may have been on his way to or from Lùb nan Ceannaichean at Patt, near the west end of Loch Monar, just where the Gedloch burn enters the loch. Here a fair was wont to be held, at which the people of east and west met and exchanged commodities.

Fas na Coille, Fasna●kyle, Woodside Rest, in Glen Affric.

Fas, in English Foss, in Strathtummel, Perthshire. The upland of Foss, however, on the skirts of Schiehallion, is in Gaelic Bràigh Fasaidh, and an old spelling of Foss is Fossache[1]. This indicates confusion between *fas* and *fasadh*, a term discussed below.

Fas na Cloiche, Fasna●cloich, Resting-place by the Stone, in Appin, Argyll.

Fas-an-darroch, near Dinnet, Deeside, close to an old highway that crossed the Dee.

Allt an Fhaslaghairt (Rob Donn) in Sutherland; i.e. fas-longphort.

Fas-caple, Gaelic Fas a' Chapuill, Kirkhill, Invernessshire; cf for meaning Marcfhasaidh.

There must be more instances—probably a good many more—of *fas* on the mainland of Scotland, discoverable by minute investigation, but I have heard of none in the Western Isles. There

1 Also Fossach and Fosseiche, Robertson's *Index of Missing Charters.*

can be no doubt that this is the element that appears terminally in Pictish names such as Altas, Duffus, pronounced in Gaelic Alltais, Dubhais, respectively, etc, and indeed Dr Macbain practically, though not explicitly, recognised this long ago[1].

In O'Davoren's *Glossary*, edited by Dr Whitley Stokes, there is: dunadh .i. sluaghadh no nert no fas no faslongport; where Stokes translates the gloss: a hosting, or strength, or growth, or encampment. Here we are dealing surely not with *fās*, growth, but with *fas* in a sense somewhat similar to that which it has above.

fasadh, fossad

Old Irish *fossad* (*vo-sta-to[2]) is an adjective meaning firm, stable, stout. Its Welsh equivalent is gwastad, level, plain, smooth; Breton goustad. In composition it appears in fossadlár, a firm level; Welsh gwastadlawr; e.g. fosadhlár Fernmuighe[3], the firm plain of Fernmoy; fosadhlar longpuirt, the firm level of an encampment; as also in fossadmullach, the firm top (cf fosmullach above). On the latter Windisch remarks[4]: 'These originally denote the summit of the hill, on which one halts, rests, makes stay (cf fosadh firáluinn a mullach in chnuic), then, generally, the highest peak, the summit.' In Welsh we also find gwastadfa, a level place, where -fa represents old Celtic magos, a plain, Gaelic magh.

Fossad is also a noun, meaning rest, station, place of residence, and in modern Irish fasadh is still so used.

In Scottish place-names the corresponding *fasadh* is regularly used not as an adjective but as a noun masculine, with one

1 With the ending of Alltais, etc. may be compared Holder's restorations *Bebro-vaston, Beverst, Beaver-stead; *Divo-vaston, Diest; *Novio-vaston, Naoust, Newstead. Also Vasta, Vastense, Vastinum.

The Cymric equivalent perhaps appears in Gwas-moric, a place of old near Carlisle (cf McClure—*British Place Names*, pp137, 138).

2 So Victor Henry; others connect with root of *suidhe*, seat, cf *cobsud*, firm.

3 Todd Lecture, Series XVI, Dr Kuno Meyer.

4 *Tain Bó Cualnge*, p608.

exception to be noted below. In meaning, *fasadh* can scarcely be differentiated from *fas*; and, as was noted above, the two seem to be confused, just as in Irish we have fossmullach and fossadmullach with the same meaning. In the following examples, Ross-shire instances are omitted, as they have been dealt with in *Place-Names of Ross and Cromarty*:–

Fasadh an t-seanna Chlaidh, Station of the old Graveyard, Loch Roe, Sutherland.

•Cromsac, i.e. an Cromfhasadh, the Curved Station, in Armadale, Sutherland; cf Cromasag in Ross-shire.

Tigh an Fhasaidh, Tean•assie, House of the Resting-place, Beauly.

Fasadh an Fhithich, the Raven's Rest. This and the four following are in Glenmoriston, Inverness-shire.

Am Fasadh, the Rest; between Allt Saidhe and Creag Eun.

Fasadh nam Feannag, the Hoodies' Rest, at Achadh nan Conbhairean.

Fasadh a' Ghille Bhioraich, the Sharp-featured Lad's Rest. I do not know its story.

Fasadh an Dìg Ruaidh, Red Ditch Rest. (Dìg should be feminine, and perhaps my informant erred.)

Dabhach an Fhasaidh, Dochan•assie, the Davach of the Rest, at the south-west end of Loch Lochy.

Am Fasadh Fearna, Fassie•fern, the Alderwood Rest, on the northern shore of upper Loch Eil.

•Marcassie for Marcfhasaidh in Morayshire, Horse Rest; cf Glen Marxie in Ross; Gaelic, Gleann Marcfhasaidh.

•Fossoway, Kinross, old spelling Fossedmege, the exact equivalent of Welsh gwastadfa, level place, noted above. In this instance *fossad* is used adjectivally. Cf fossadmullach, fossadlar.

Am Fasadh, a level bit of land near where the Allt Mór (the Wester Bunloit burn) falls into Loch Ness. It is at the foot of one of the steepest and longest braes on the road between Rùsgaich and Caisteal na Sròine—Urquhart Castle.

Am Fasadh, near Foxhole School, Kiltarlity.

Am Fasadh, at the parish march, west of Bridge of Oich, north
side.

Allt an Fhasaidh, on the south side of the Strontian river, with
Dail an Fhasaidh by its side.

Fasadh Bradaig, presumably somewhere in Lochaber (Munro's
Gaelic Grammar, 2nd ed., p223):

Rudha an Fhasaidh (on maps Rudh' an Aiseid) in Eigg. This is
the only fasadh noted in the Western Isles so far. The last
five instances are from the Rev C. M. Robertson.

It is remarkable that Dr Joyce makes no mention of fasadh as an
element in Irish names of places, nor does Rev P. Power in his
highly intensive study of the *Place-Names of Decies*. It does not
seem to occur widely in the Western Isles, but I have no doubt
that the above list could be considerably extended from the
mainland.

Invernahyle

Inverna•hyle in Argyll is in Gaelic Inbhir na h-Aidhle. In Ireland
we have Gleann na h-Aidhle[1], meaning Glen of the Adze, no
doubt from some adze-shaped physical feature. Inverna•hyle
means the estuary of the adze; cf Inber Scéne, river-mouth of the
knife, the Old Irish name for the estuary of the Kenmare river, 'a
most appropriate designation for an estuary that cuts inland like
a pointed knife or dagger. An equally descriptive name is that for
the mouth of the River Bann, which in Old-Irish is called Inber
Túaige, the axe-shaped estuary.'[2]

All these are good examples of the *Irish* method of naming
estuaries and glens from some physical feature or other
circumstance. The Pictish method, on the other hand, which is the
one generally prevalent north of Forth and Clyde, is to name
estuary, glen or strath, and loch after the stream connected with
them. This latter is also the Welsh practice.

1 *Place-Names of Decies*, p334
2 Kuno Meyer in *Eriu*, vol 2, p86

Topographical Varia—V

dubron dobhar

The term *dubron*, water, if we judge by its survivals in French names of places, must have been common in ancient Gaul. It appears in the modern names Dovern, water, Douvres (repeatedly), waters, and in several compounds, more or less disguised, such as Bondoufle, Verdouble[1], the latter of which is mentioned by Pliny as Vernodubrum, i.e. alder-water, or, as we should put it in modern Gaelic, an t-alltan fearna, Gaulish *vernos* becoming *fearna* in Gaelic. Doeveren, in Gelderland, was of old Dubridun from a still older Dubrodunon, water-fort. The river Douro in Spain and Portugal (called in Spanish Duero), is in Latin Durius, and therefore cannot be connected with *dubron*.

Dover, in England, is in French Douvres, representing an Old Celtic locative plural Dubris, at the waters, which actually appears on record more than once. The reference is not to the waters of the English Channel, but to the waters of two small brooks which enter the sea at, or near, Dover harbour[2].

In modern Welsh *dubron* becomes *dwfr*, common in stream names; Cornish *dowr*; Breton *dour*. In Old Irish it was *dobor*, Gaelic *dobhar*, now obsolete in the spoken language, but preserved in compounds, and in many stream and place-names. The oldest Scottish instance occurs in Adamnan's *Life of Columba*, written before AD700, where Columba is recorded to have baptized an aged chief in Skye named Artbranan, 'and the river of the place in which he received baptism is to this very day called by the inhabitants after his name Dobur Artbranani'. This interesting name appears to have been lost. The stream in question was probably quite a little burn.

Dobhar appears at least twice in combination with the preposition *eadar*, between, in the names Edirdovar, now Redcastle, in Ross-shire on the Beauly Firth, and Eddradour in Perthshire. In both cases the 'waters' in question are mere

---

1 see Holder *s.v.* Dubru.
2 *British Place Names in their Historical Setting*, p108.

streamlets. It appears also in the two Aberdours (Banff and Fife), and in Aberchirder (Banff), *Ciardhobhar, Swart Water.

Terminally *dobhar* occurs in Aberarder (Strathnairn and Loch Laggan), outflow of the high water. The Loch Laggan stream-name without the 'aber' is seen in Coire Ardobhair, high-water corry, and in Uinneag Ardobhair, high-water window. Auchterarder means high-water upland. Fe-arder, Deeside, near Balmoral is the bog-channel (*fèith*) of the high water. The popular explanation of the rivers Leader and Adder as grey water and long water respectively is more than doubtful in view of very old spellings which give no countenance to the idea. The common stream-name Calder, in Gaelic *Caladar*, may represent Caladobhar, calling water, from the root *cal*, cry, call, which gives rise to the Balquhidder Calair, notorious for its noise[1]. Dr Macbain, however, always preferred to explain Calder as from a primitive *Calentora, calling water.

Two very interesting cases in which *dobhar* occurs in composition have, I believe, not been hitherto noted. The first is Duror, Argyll, which appears in Macfarlane's *Geographical Collections* and elsewhere[2] as Durgour, Durgoure, Durrour, Dorgowar. This spelling points to the confusion—common in old records—between *gh* and *dh*, the two sounds being in this position identical. Other record spellings are Durwoin 1476; Duroune 1478; Durgune 1493, Durgwyn 1520.[2] In still older records, of which the originals are now unfortunately lost, noted in Robertson's *Index to Missing Charters*, Duror appears as Durdoman, Durdomon. Here there is obvious confusion between final *n* and final *r* (a confusion easily parallelled), while in Robertson's spellings *m* has been written or printed for *w*, also an error easily made. Durdoman, therefore, should be amended to Durdowar, and so on with the others, giving an old *Dùrdhobhar*, representing a primitive *Dūro-dubron. In modern Gaelic *dùr* means dull, stubborn; in the older language it meant hard; used

1 Caldour near Kelso is Caledofre.—*Monastic Annals of Teviotdale*
2 RMS and *Orig. Paroch.*

also in O. Ir. as a noun meaning 'daingean', a fortress. In Gaulish names *dūros* is exceedingly common (see Holder), and its neuter form *dūron* meant a fortress. In Britain Duro-brivae, the name of two Roman stations, now Castor and Rochester, is taken to mean 'the bridges at the fort'. Thus Duror may mean either Hard-water (i.e. Rocky-water) or Fort-water. That the name is primarily that of a stream is indicated by modern usage, which still speaks of Abhainn Dùroir and Glen Duror. The district is referred to as Dùror na h-Apann, Duror of Appin. The name is Pictish doubtless.

The other instance referred to is Morar, on the west coast of Inverness-shire. The name Morar applies to a large district divided by Loch Morar into North Morar and South Morar. The waters of Loch Morar fall into the sea by way of Abhainn Mórar, a stream only a few furlongs in length. It is this stream, however, which has given its name first to the loch, then to the district. The ancient spellings (fourteenth and fifteenth centuries) are Moreobyr, Mordhowar, Mordhowor, Moreovyr, Morowore, which, taken together, clearly indicate *Mórdhobhar*, great-water. In both Duror and Morar the total disappearance of *dh* after *r* is the normal thing, cf Inbhir (Dh)ùbhghlais, Inbhir (Dh)uinnid, Obar (Dh)eathain, Inveruglas, Inverinate, Aberdeen. In Gaelic literature the spelling of Morar has been affected through folk-etymology. In the Book of Clanranald[1] there occur the curious forms 'do mhorshrón', 'Tigherna Mhóiróin'. In *Gillies's Collection*, pp287, 289, there is 'Eas Mhor-oir', which is sufficiently correct, but John Mackenzie in the *Beauties* writes 'Eas Mor-thir', p160, and elsewhere he adopts the same spelling. This confusion with *mórthir*, mainland, appears also in Fàilte na Mórthir[2], "S ann a tha 'n othail air bodaich na Mórthir', the name of a pipe tune. Morar is not now, so far as I know, accompanied by the article, but it is just possible that the feminine forms are so far justified in that *dobhar*, originally neuter, may have been treated as

---

1 *Reliquiæ Celticæ*, vol 2, pp180, 214.
2 *Beauties*, p125.

feminine in Scottish Gaelic. As to that, however, no certain data seem to exist.

The diminutive *dobhrag*, feminine in form, according to modern usage[1], occurs as the name of several brooks or brooklets, e.g. Dobhrag between Shandwick and Arabella in Easter Ross, now a mere ditch; and Dobhrag, the Gaelic form of the Aldourie Burn, Dores. The local rhyme is

> Durus is Darus is Dobhrag.
>
> Dores Dares and Dowrag[2].

Parallel to *dobhrag* is *dobhran*, masculine in form[3]. Above Achterneed, Strathpeffer, are Dobhran and Creag Dhobhrain, where *dobhran* means 'a wet place', i.e. a place where the water from the hillside is apt to collect. (Cf braonan, a damp place, from braon.) I recall no streamlet here, though there may, of course, have been one. With this goes Beinn Dobhrain in Argyll. It is hard to say whether *dobhran* is here a stream-name or a place-name. Not far from it is Inveroran, at the spot where a small burn, Allt Orain (for Allt Dōbhrain), falls into Loch Tealla. Inveroran is for Inbhir Dhobhrain, the *dh* disappearing after *r* as in Morar, Duror, etc above. In the same region near Crianlarich (Gaelic Crithionnlaraich, Aspen-site) is Inverardran, where the mountain stream from Coire Ardrain enters the Dochart. In 1377 Inverardran appears as Inverhardgowrane[4]. Here *g* stands for *dh* exactly as in Durgour above, with which allowance we have an excellent

---

1 In the old language this ending was used also to form masculine diminutives.

2 Another rhyme runs:—
   Mil' eadar Durus is Darus,
   Mil' eadar Darus is Dà.
   A mile between Dores and Dares,
   A mile between Dares and Dā.

3 In common speech dōbhran means 'otter', in which sense it is not uncommon in place-names, but is used with the article, e.g. Rudha 'n dō(bh)rain, 'otter point' (Colonsay), lag an dō(bh)rain, 'otter hollow' (Iona).

4 RMS.

phonetic spelling of Inbhir Arddhobhrain, Inver of the high streamlet.

From the above it will be seen that *dubron*, with its various modern forms, is found over the whole Celtic area, continental and insular.

The forms •Duror from •Dūrdhobhar; •Morar from •Mórdhobhar; •Arder from •Arddhobhar; Inbhir •Ardrain from Inbhir •Arddhobhrain are instructive examples of the influence of the powerful stress accent in Gaelic.

mig

Mig appears as the base of many names in Pictland. Behind Bonar in Sutherland is Migdale, in the thirteenth century Miggevet and Miggeweth, now in Gaelic Migein, with an un-Gaelic *g*, like that of English pig. The precipitous rocky hill on the north side of Loch Migdale is Creag Mhigein. It is quite possible that those three—Migdale, Miggevet or Miggeweth and Migein—were once independent names of different places in the basin of Loch Migdale. Migvie in Stratherrick is in Gaelic Migeaghaidh. It lies low on the south side of Loch Garth. There are also Dal•migavie in Strathdearn, in Gaelic Dail Mhigeaghaidh, and Creag Mhigeachaidh (Macbain) behind Feshie Bridge and Laggan-lia in Badenoch. In Aberdeenshire there is the parish of Migvie and Tarland, in 1183 Migeueth, 1200 Migaveth, clearly the same to start with as the Sutherland Miggeweth. Another Migvie occurs in Lochlee parish, Forfarshire. In Aberdeenshire Midstrath (Birse) was in 1170 Migstrath; 1511 Megstrath, still Migstra in vernacular Scots—a boggy strath. Midmar in the same county was written Migmar down to 1500 at least, and is still pronounced so in Gaelic. The three divisions of Marr are Bràigh Mharr, Braemar; Crò Mharr, Cromar; and Mig Mharr. Strathmiglo in Fife was in 1200 Stradimigglock. Meigle, Perthshire, was of old Migdele and Miggil, now Migeil in Gaelic. Near Comrie as one goes to Glenartney is Miggar, in Gaelic Migear, and in Glenlyon there is •Meggernie, in Gaelic

Migearnaidh. Other instances, of which, however, neither the Gaelic forms nor the old spellings are available, are Creag Meggen, in Glenmuick, Aberdeenshire (cf Creag Mhigein above); Craigie Meg in Glen Prosen, Forfarshire; Craig Mekie in Glen Isla; Megget Water flowing into St Mary's Loch, whence Yarrow issues, both Old British names.

As to the meaning of this frequently occurring base, Macbain, dealing with Creag Mhigeachaidh in Badenoch, referred to *mig*, *meig*, the bleating of a goat. But this explanation, though phonetically admissible, does not suit the localities, nor yet the nature of the compounds, e.g. Mig Mar, Migstrath. The fact is that *mig* is the Pictish for a bog. In Wales we have Kenvig, 'a ridge above a bog', from Welsh *mig*, bog, which appears in migwern (for mig-gwern), a boggy meadow; migwyn (for mig-gwyn), cotton grass, canach; mign, a bog, quagmire. In Old Welsh there occur Gueith Meicen and Rit Meigen[1] battle of the bog, ford of the bog. The battle of Meicen was fought in 633AD, and in the Saxon Chronicles is called the battle of Haethfelth, Heathfield, practically a translation of the British name. Of the places noted above, all that I know by inspection, and all of which I have information, are naturally boggy or marshy. With regard to the occurrence of such names as Creag Mhigein, Creag Mhigeachaidh, etc, it is to be noted that they are exact parallels to Creag Dhobhrain, mentioned under *dobhran* above, that is to say, the meaning is Rock of Miggen, etc; the rock is called after the boggy place near its foot.

In Migear, the base *mig* is extended by the suffix -*ar*, as in Dollar.

Migearnaidh may be an exact parallel to Welsh migwern, pl. migwernydd, a marshy meadow, which describes the place; or it may show the extensions -*ar-n-ach*.

Miglo, old Miglock, may show the sufflx -*lach*, as in G. teaghlach, W. teulu.

---

1 Sir E. Anwyl, 'Wales and the Britons of the North', *Celtic Review*, vol 4, pp127,260.

The extension seen in Mig-vie, Mig-o-vie, Mig-eaghaidh, or Mig-eachaidh, Migg-e-weth is puzzling, partly on account of the apparent variation in the Gaelic pronunciation as compared with the old spellings, and partly because it is difficult to say what value should be attached to the -*th* or -*t* of these old forms. The Gaelic *gh* sound as against the modern and record *v* may be due in part to the fact that *gh* (and *dh*) were at one time frequently sounded *v* in Gaelic, as they still are in certain words in certain districts (e.g. dia*dh*aidh, trua*gh*an, mu dhei*gh*inn). In dealing with a Pictish word Gaelic speakers would be apt to treat the *v* as a *gh*, and level it up to *gh* by analogy. With regard to the *th* of the old forms, if it was really meant for *th* and not for *ch*, it may perhaps represent the faint sound of final *gh* (now silent). We shall probably be right in comparing Migovie with Multovie, Muckovie, Rovie, Arcavie, •Rinavie, all Gaelicised Pictish names, involving the old *magos*, plain, which in the short form -*ma*, mutated into -*fa*, meaning place, spot, is a favourite Cymric ending, occurring also not uncommonly in Irish names such as Fearnmhagh, Farney, alder plain[1].

Baile Bhaodan

The old parish church of Ardchattan stood on an eminence behind the Priory 'in a pleasant place where the sun uses daily to ryse upone, when it ryseth upone one pairt of the countrie, and this is called Kilbedan'[2]. Its well-built walls and gables are still standing except the south wall, which is ruinous. It is often referred to as a chapel, but it was in reality a fairly large church, the parish church of Ardchattan. Old references to it are 'the kirk of Balliebodane in Bendaraloch', 1603; Ballebadin and Bendraloche, 1631, 1632; Ballibodan or Kilbodan in Bendaraloch, 1697.[3] At the present day it is always Baile

---

1 The modern Welsh plural of names in *fa* of this meaning is -*fëydd*, which would give Miggeweth exactly, but in old Welsh the form is -*feu*, e.g. aerfa, battlefield, pl. aerfeu.

2 *Geog. Coll.,* vol 2, p153 (*circa* 1650).

3 *Orig. Paroch.,* vol 2, p148.

Bhaodan, never Cill Bhaodan. Near the church, in the side of a ravine to the east of it, and approached by an alley of arching branches, is a well, said to have been called Tobar Bhaodan, and once reputed holy. In Glen Salach, between Loch Etive and Loch Creran, about a mile eastward of the church, there was a stone called Suidhe Bhaodan, now blasted in pieces[1]. Baodan is the modern Gaelic form of Baedan, of old a very common name among the Gael of Dalriada and of Ireland, and borne by kings and saints. An old tract on the Scots of Dalriada[2] records that a chieftain of Lorn, Fergus Salach, son of Lorn mór, had five sons, one of whom was Baedan 'v tigi leis', i.e. he was head of five houses. By a curious coincidence, the Ardchattan district is now and has been from time immemorial divided into five principal steads, viz Achnaba, Ardachy, Inneon, Ardchattan and Inveresragan. Although the matter hardly admits of proof, it is not altogether fanciful to suppose that Baile Bhaodan may have been the headquarters of this Lorn petty headman the son of Fergus Salach, who may have turned cleric. The name was common: the fact that there appear on record Kilbedan in Morvern, 1509, and Kilbadan Ardgour, 1536, is clear proof that it was borne by a saint, whether that saint was the son of Fergus or not. To prevent confusion, it should be mentioned that the Kinelvadon, i.e. Cineal Bhaodan, whose habitat was Morvern, appear to have been named after Baedan mac Echach mhic Muredach mhic Loairn mhóir, i.e. a great-grandson of the eponym of Cineal Loairn. The other Baedan, dealt with above, was Baedan mac Fergusa Salaig mhic Loairn mhoir, i.e. a grandson of Lorn.

Cosmo Innes in the *Origines Parochiales*, following the *New Statistical Account* of Ardchattan, states that the parish church was dedicated to St Modan. Dr Skene in his second volume follows Cosmo Innes in the same error, and Dr Story following

---

1 The same fate has overtaken Suidhe Chrèunan, a block of stone behind Kilchrenan (Cill Chrèunan) on Loch Awe.

2 Skene, *Chronicles of the Picts and Scots*, p513.

Skene dilates with poetic fervour on the connection of St Modan with Ardchattan. There is not a scrap of evidence for such connection other than the unsupported statement of the *New Statistical Account*, which is based on a misspelling, viz Bal Mhaodan for Baile Bhaodan. The Modan myth is a figment of a class unfortunately too common. The surprising thing is that Cosmo Innes and Skene should have countenanced it in defiance of the records which they knew so well. But apart from the evidence of the records, Modan is in Irish Muadan, which could by no possibility become Maodan in Scottish Gaelic.

Dùn Bhallaire

This is the name of the lofty rock beside Ledaig, Benderloch, which has been tortured by folk etymologists into Dùn Bhaile an Righ. The hoax is fairly old. It was not, however, originated by Pennant, who visited the place on 10th August 1772, and observed 'a range of low hills, at whose western extremity is an entrenchment called Dun-valirè'. The first edition of Anderson's *Guide* (1834) says 'this ridge is called Dun Bhail an Righ, the hill of the king's town'. Cosmo Innes in the *Origines Parochiales* incautiously accepts this statement, and further breaks up Pennant's spelling into Dun-val-i-re, apparently to support the fictitious etymology of the *Guide*. The myth thus accredited and advertised was further spread and popularised by Smith in his book on *Loch Etive and the Sons of Uisneach*, and by others, till it has now become almost an article of faith. At Ledaig one is told that the name is Dun Bhaile an Righ. 'Did not the King of Scotland once live close by in Dùn Mac Snitheachan? No, that is not what they really call it among themselves—they call it Dun Bhallaire. But it *ought* to be Dun Bhaile an Righ—learned men have said so!' It is hardly necessary to point out that the broad *ll* and the stress accent on the first syllable of *Ballaire* are fatal to this pleasant theory. The bona fide present Gaelic pronunciation is exactly that of Pennant's time.

The most probable, if prosaic, explanation is from *ballaire*, a cormorant, 'Cormorant Dùn', and the name may be compared with Beinn Trìleachan, 'Ben of the Oyster-catchers', on the north side of Loch Etive, about half way between Bunawe and the head of the loch.

Topographical Varia–VI

-nt- terminal

Dr Joyce in his invaluable work on *Irish Names of Places*[1] has noted that 'the letter *d* is often added on to the end of words, sometimes with a collective meaning, sometimes with scarcely any meaning at all'. He gives as examples Kealid from *caol*, narrow; Croaghat from *cruach*, a stack; the stream names Buanaid, the lasting river; Dianaid, in English Burn Dennet, the strong or swift stream; and the lake name Lough Oorid, from *uar*, cold. In dealing with the place-names of Badenoch, Dr Macbain compared with the above examples Bialaid, from *beul* (northern *bial*), mouth, and also Ràth-d, in English Raitt, Raitts, Roth(ie), from *ràth*, a circular earthwork.

This termination, while not exactly common, is found with us both in names of places, and especially in names of streams. It is also found elsewhere in the language, in such words as *farmad*, *nàmhaid*, *coimhead*, where we often find that a final post-vocalic *d* is to be explained as arising from a primitive post-vocalic -*nt*[2]. And as the laws of speech that apply to the ordinary language must be taken as applying equally to Celtic names of places, we may look for a similar explanation here also. Reference to Holder's *Altceltischer Sprachschatz* will show numerous examples of names ending in -ant-, -ent-, -ont, which were in fact old participial endings exactly parallel to the Latin and Greek participial endings of the active voice. Thus we have Dru-entia, a river-name with which Dr Macbain compared as to root the Badenoch Druie, and Gaelic *drùdhadh*, oozing; Derv-entio, the river Derwent, Oak Stream, Welsh *derw*, oak; and others, with which may also be compared the Latin Dig-entia, that flowed by Horace's villa.

Some of our Scottish names of places may, I venture to think, be profitably considered from this point of view.

1 Vol 2, p15.
2 See MacBain's *Etym. Dict.*

Drum•derfit, in the Black Isle, has been dealt with in part in *Place Names of Ross and Cromarty*. The modern Gaelic form is *Druima-diar*, locally explained as Ridge of Tears, the second part being plainly a contraction (and probably a modification in Gaelic) of a Pictish and obscure name. The old spelling Drumdervat, taken in connection with the modern Englished form Drum-derfit, points to a primitive *Derventon or *Dervention, meaning Place of Oaks, the name given to the oakclad hollow at the foot of the ridge.

Ailsa Craig in the Firth of Clyde is in Gaelic *Creag Ealasaid*, or *Ealasaid a' Chuain*, the latter being apparently the older designation, dating from a time when *cuan* was still used in its original sense of harbour or inlet. In the modern language Ealasaid means Elizabeth, but the connection of this mighty rock with a name of such a meaning is rather hopeless. The real origin is more likely to be found in the Old Irish *ail*, rock, with extensions, and an exact parallel is provided by the Gaulish name Alisontia (for Alixontia), meaning the rocky place, which in Gaelic gives Ealasaid, just as O. Ir. *ailech* gives Gaelic *eileach*, as in na h-Eileacha Naomha, the holy stone-houses, now usually, but erroneously, referred to as Eilean nan Naomh, or such like. Compare also Craig-ellachie.

From *torc*, boar, Welsh *twrch*, comes *Dùn Turcaid* in Stratherrick. Do'ach Dhùin Turcaid, the davach of Dunturket, lay to the east of the river Fechlin. I had this information from John Cameron, Inchanlennie, in September 1906, since when Macfarlane's *Geographical Collections* have been published (1907). Therein[1] is stated: 'a myl be east Dalnakappul is Dun-Turket upon the east bank of Faechloyn'. Remains of the Dùn are said to exist, but I failed to find the site (somewhere near Loch nan Losgann).

With the same formation as Turcaid, we have Tarvit and Scots-tarvit in Fife, based on *tarbh*, bull, Welsh *taru*, Gaulish *tarvos*,

1 Vol 2, p656.

which, with different extensions, is seen in Tarvie, Tarves, Tarland (=tarbhlann).

Another example of similar type is *Abhainn Conait*, the river Conait, the principal left bank tributary of the Lyon, based on the root of *cù*, dog.

Treasaid in Rannoch is based on O. Ir. *tres*, conflict; Welsh *tres*, toil, stroke. It may echo an ancient battle, and is to be compared with the Sutherland *Treasaididh*, Tressady.

Another place-name of this type is Lovat, for which significantly enough no Gaelic exists other than *a' Mhor'oich*, the sea plain. The root is that of Latin *lav-are*, wash; *lutum*, mud; Gael. *loth*, mud. The site of Lovat is by the shore of the Beauly Firth. The Gaelic name is a sort of translation of the old Pictish.

Glenlivet, in Gaelic *Gleann Lìbheit*, is named after its river, the Livet. The root is *līv-*, shine, glitter; Gaelic *lì*, splendour; Welsh, *lliw*, colour; and Lìbheit comes from a primitive *Līv-entia*, the Glittering one, the name of a goddess doubtless. From the same root, with the common stream and goddess ending -*ŏnā* comes *Liv-ŏnā, whence *Lìobhunn*, the Lyon of Glen Lyon.

Glenturret in Perthshire, mentioned in Robert Burns's song 'Blithe, blithe and merry was she', is called after the Turret, in Gaelic *Turaid*, which gives its name also to Loch Turret. There is another, and less known, Turret and Glen Turret near Roy Bridge in Lochaber, and a third appears on the map on the southern flank of Mt Battock, Kincardineshire. The name has of course been equated with *turaid*, a turret, which is quite a late loan from English, and could have nothing to do with an ancient stream-name. The root is that seen in *turadh*, cessation of rain; *tur*, dry; and the clue to the meaning is to be found in Irish *turloch*, dry loch, i.e. a loch that dries up in summer. A similar idea is seen in the expression 'eilean tioram'[1], dry island, i.e. an island to which one can walk at low tide. On this analogy we should expect the Turrets to be small streams which shrink much in summer, which

---

1 *Tioram* and *tur* are both ultimately from the same root.

they do. The primitive form of *Turaid* was *Tur-entia, meaning the 'drying one', another goddess name.

Streams are not uncommonly called after trees, as for instance the Derwent, already mentioned, from the oak. In Scotland we have the Fernate of Glen Fernate in Athole. Fernate is in Gaelic *Fearnaid*, from *fearna*, alder, Gaulish *vernos*, and represents an old *Vern-entia or such, an exact parallel to Derv-entio.

Gleann Geunaid, in Kirkmichael parish, Perthshire, called in English Glen Derby, has a stream Geunaid. On the analogy of *breun, feur, feun* (from *breg-no-, *veg-ro-, *veg-no- respectively), *geunaid* should arise from a root *geg, given by Whitley Stokes with the meaning 'wie eine Gans schreien', to cry like a goose, giving a primitive *gegnos, goose, whence O. Ir. *gén, genitive *géoin. Thus we may take Geunaid as meaning 'goose stream'. Mr Kenneth Macleod informs me that the glen is a regular stage in the flight of geese from east to west, and that the name is understood locally to have some connection with geese.

The Mossat is a tributary of the Don. It is to be referred to the root of Gaelic *mosach* or *musach*, nasty; Welsh *mws*, effluvia, rank, and may perhaps be compared as to meaning with *Breunag*, from *breun*, rotten, a stream of Stratherrick, that joins Fechlin at Whitebridge[1]. With Mossat goes *Musadaidh*, also in Stratherrick, standing to each other in the same relation as Treasaid to Treasaididh.

Inverdovet in Fife appears in old records as Inverdufatha. Dovet looks like a derivative of *dubh*, Welsh *du*, black.

The Kintail *Duinnid*, with Inver-inate at its mouth, is based on Gaelic *donn*, brown, Welsh *dwn*, dun, dusky. It postulates a primitive *Donnentia.

In the south of Scotland this ending occurs in several river-names. It is probably that of the Teviot, written of old Tefeged. The Megget, which flows into St. Mary's Loch, is based on *mig*, bog, dealt with in No. V of these papers [see p117]. There is

---

1 The name *Breunag* is probably accounted for by the circumstance that there are, as I was informed, some sulphurous springs near the stream.

another Megget in the same region, a tributary of the southern Esk, with a place Megdale on its course.

The Armit is a tributary of Gala Water. It looks as if from Armentio, which actually occurs as an ancient Celtic river-name in Holder, without indication as to place. With it may be compared *Abhainn Armaidh* in Stratherrick, that notable stronghold of Pictish names.

Besides the above I have on my list such names as Res•tennot, Kennet, Moffat, Glen Bucket (in Gaelic *Gleann Buichead*), Dinnet, Tynet Burn (Banff), all more or less difficult names, some of them at least involving the termination above discussed and illustrated. In my opinion, all these names are extremely old, and I take them to belong to the Old British stratum. It is true that coming to us, as they have come, through Gaelic, they show a Gaelic veneer. They have been made to conform to Gaelic phonetics in the same way as loans from Latin and Old Norse have been made to conform. But their formation postulates an origin in the period of old insular Celtic, when the Celtic of Scotland was of the same type as the Gaulish of the first century BC. They belong to a time far more remote than the oldest literary remains of Gaelic or Welsh, and are in short Old British or Pictish. In other words they belong to the period before Gaelic was spoken in Scotland.

braon

The Gaelic *braon* is given by the dictionaries as meaning 'a drop, rain'. The Irish is *bróen*, with same meaning. In Scottish topography the term, in its simple form or with extensions, occurs over a wide range, and usage clearly indicates its meaning here to be 'wet place'. No name involving *braon* is used with the article, so far as I know.

Braon is found simply in *Abhainn Braon*, in Ross-shire, rising in *Lochaidh Bhraoin*, and flowing through *Gleann Braoin* into the salt water *Loch Bhraoin* (Englished Broom). Similarly in Perthshire, near Pitlochry, are *Loch Braon* and *Abhainn Braon*, in

English Loch Broom and River Broom. Fairburn, near Strathpeffer, is *Farrabraoin*, and below it and nearer the Conon is *Braon*. At the head of Strathnairn is *Braon*, in English Brin, a low flat, still in part wet, and formerly liable to flooding from a stream which is now banked.

With extension -*ach*, locative -*aigh*, we get *Cuil-bhraonaigh*, Culbirnie (sometimes spelled Kilburnie), near Beauly, meaning Dampnook, or, possibly, nook of the damp place. This gives the clue to Birnie, best known as the name of a Morayshire parish which appears in early documents as Brennach. The difficult Gaelic *ao* sound troubled the scribes. They represent it sometimes as *o*, sometimes by *a*, oftenest perhaps by *e*. Thus Cill Bhaodan, in Lorne, appears on record as Kilbodane, Kilbadan, Kilbedan; Loch Raonasa, Lochranza, appears as Lochransay and Lochrenasay; Loch Broom, Ross, as Loghbren. Brennach, therefore, may safely be taken to represent *Braonach*, locative Braonaigh, whence in modern Scots vernacular Birnie, meaning '(at) damp place' (cf also Fair*burn*, above). The site of the Kirk of Birnie is close by the river Lossie. The alleged dedication to St Brendan has no support in fact, so far as known to me, nor does Lachlan Shaw, the historian of Moray, make any such suggestion[1]. With this goes Birnie in the Garioch, spelled in Macfarlane's *Geographical Collections* Brinie, Brinnie. Birness, near Ellon, was in 1392 Brenes[2], where the ending -*es* is probably that seen in Alt-as, Gedd-es, etc. The other alternative, *innis*, a haugh, reduced to *is*, is less likely, for in the fourteenth century *innis* would almost certainly have left more trace of itself.

Braonan, little wet place, is the name of a spot in central Ross-shire, close by the river that flows into Loch Moir, and some miles to the west of Kildermorie. The ancient spellings of Birnam, on the Tay near Dunkeld, Brenan, Brynnan, at once make it clear that we are dealing with the same name. It should be possible still

---

1 Kilbirnie, in Ayrshire, is on a different footing, for St Brinnan's Fair was held there (*Orig. Paroch.*), and kil- (church) is prefixed.
2 Johnston's *Place Names of Scotland*.

to get the Gaelic pronunciation of Birnam, but so far I have not heard it.

Broomage, in Stirlingshire, Bruminche 1458 (Johnston), may be for *braon-innis*, damp haugh; compare *braon* into *broom* above, and for *innis* into *-age*, cf Coninnis into Connage; English rubbish into rubbage. *Innis a' Bhraoin*, Englished Inchbrine, occurs in Mr W. Mackay's *Urquhart and Glenmoriston*, p582.

Prefixed Nouns Used as Adjectives

This usage is a survival of the custom which prevailed in the oldest stage of Celtic, as seen in Gaulish, of placing the qualifying part of a compound noun first, whether the qualifying part happens to be noun or adjective, e.g. *Gabromagos*, steed-plain. In the older stages of Gaelic the same practice is common, but it fell out of fashion with the growth of the tendency to place the adjectival part after the noun, which is so distinctive of the modern language. English, on the other hand, and other Teutonic languages which habitually place the adjective in front of the noun have no difficulty at the present day in freely forming compounds in which nouns serving as adjectives stand first. Take, for instance, 'apple-tree', *'abalcrann'*: the former is natural and regular to our ears, the latter, even in modern spelling *ubhalchrann* is felt to be archaic, and we should use *crann ubhal* instead. It is only in compounds of old standing grown familiar by constant usage that modern Gaelic tolerates the ancient order, e.g. *iodhlann*, corn-enclosure; *banais* (i.e. ban-féis), woman-feast, wedding; *ceannmhag*, headrig, endrig; and I think that in all such cases it may be said that the ordinary speakers have little, if any, consciousness of the constituent elements. The prefixed adjective proper is similarly retained in old and familiar expressions, e.g. *seanfhacal*, old-word, proverb; a few adjectives (*deagh, sàr, droch*) are always prefixed, while *sean*, old, varies as to position. In place names the number of adjectives found prefixed is larger, referring chiefly to size, colour, or shape, but with the unvarying restriction that they are adjectives of one syllable[1].

Subjoined are instances of nouns prefixed with adjectival force. All, of course, have the stress accent on the first syllable. It is to be noted that in several cases the prefixed noun is dissyllabic. I add the article in the few cases where it is used.

Am Bannath, Bonar, 'bottom-ford'.

Beala'drum, Belladrum (Beauly), 'fordmouth-ridge'.

Benndealt, 'peak-saddle' (see *Celtic Review*, vol 5, p340) [see p89].

Calagart (Loch Katrine), 'harbour-field'.

Calasraid, Callander, 'harbour-street', 'ferry-street'.

Carnsgeir (Loch Broom), 'cairn-skerry'.

Catinnis (Dalmally), 'wildcat-mead'.

Ceannchnoc, Kenknock (Inverness-shire, Glen Lyon and Glen Lochay), 'head-hill'.

Ceanndoire, in Barra-cheanndoire, Barrachandar (Taynuilt), 'head-copse'. The full name means 'headcopse ridge'.

Ceanndoir in Loch Ceanndoir, now Loch Kinnord (Aberdeenshire), 'head-water' (possibly, but less probably, 'head-copse').

Ceanndrum, Kendrum (Balquhidder), 'head-ridge'.

Colldrum in Kingoldrum (Forfar), 'hazel-ridge'. The Gaelic of Kingoldrum, got by Mr F. C. Diack from an aged woman in Braemar who had the traditional Gaelic form of many Forfar names, is *Cionn-coll-druim* 'at hazel-ridge head'.

an Conbhacan, 'the dog-hook' or 'dog-bend', locally 'dog-tetherstick'; the name of a stone idol still extant in Glen Lyon.

Conchra (Lochalsh and Glendaruel), 'dog-pen', 'wolf-trap'?

1 The older language was freer in this respect, and it would be interesting to determine at what period the restriction began to operate. I have never found a clear instance of a disyllabic adjective being prefixed in our Gaelic names of places.

Conchraig (Creich, Aberdeenshire, Strathearn, and *passim*), 'dog-rock'.

Conghleann, Conaglen (Kilmallie), 'dog-glen', 'wolf-glen'.

Conghlais (Tyndrum and Banff), 'dog-water'.

Coninnis[1] (Dalmally), 'dog-haugh'. *Connage* (Inverness) is the same word Englished.

Craiginnis, Craignish, 'rock-haugh'.

Dairsie (Fifeshire), of old Deruasyn, Dervasyn, 'oakstance'. Cf Dulsie.

an Damhath, Dava (Grantown-on-Spey), 'stag-ford', 'oxford'.

Deirea'camas, Derricambus (Glen Lyon), 'hind-loop', 'last-loop'. It stands on the last bend made by the Lyon before entering the Pass of Lyon.

Dealganros, •Delginross, •Dalcross (Inverness, Strathearn, and Glentilt), 'prickle-point', or 'prickle-wood'.

Dulfhasaidh, Dulsie; *Drochaid Dhulfhasaidh*, Dulsie Bridge on Findhorn, 'plateau-stance'. Cf Dairsie.

Dùnrath, •Downreay (Caithness), 'strong-fort'.

Easdoir' in Craggan-estar (Loch Tay), 'waterfall copse', or 'gully-copse'. In Perthshire, at the present day eas means usually a steep, rough gully with water flowing through it. A waterfall is *spùt*. In this particular case there is a steep gully with two waterfalls and a rapid within a few yards of the 'craggan'. The gully still possesses a *doire* of natural wood.

Eigintoll (Ross-shire), 'stress-hollow', a small corry very difficult of access.

Farnaway (Muir of Ord), *fearnmhagh*, 'alder plain'; the name of an old division of Ross, now obsolete.

Fartairchill, •Fortingal, 'fortress-church', with reference to the ancient round tower on the rock above Balnacraig near the church of Fortingal.

1 Cf Condere (*v.* Condoire) i. doire nan con, i. doire a mbítis eoin allta prius et in eo lupe habitabant: (a grove in which wild dogs were wont to be formerly and she-wolves dwelt therein).—Hogan, *Onomasticon, s.v.*

Feurloch, Feurlochan (Ross and *passim*), 'grass-loch', 'grass-lochlet'.

Lasantulaich (Rannoch), 'fire-knoll'?

Migeaghaigh, Migeachaigh, Migovie, Migvie (Stratherrick, Strathdearn, Aberdeenshire, etc), 'bogplain', see *Celtic Review,* vol 7, p365 [see p117]

Mucinnis, Ardmucknish (Lorne), 'swine-meadow'.

Mucomhaigh, •Muckovie (Inverness), 'swine-plain'.

Muighinnis, •Moyness (Nairn), 'plain-mead'. So *Mag Innis* in Ireland (Hogan).

Multomhaigh, •Multovie (Alness), 'wedder-plain'.

Sliginnis, Slignish (Ardnamurchan), 'shell-mead'.

Taranaich, •Darnaway (Forres), '?-plain'. Lachlan Shaw says: 'In Irish Taranich, probably from Taran or Tarnach, i.e. thunder, because there Jupiter Taranis may have been anciently worshipped'. The Gaelic form as given above was got by me independently from Mr J. Mackintosh, Ardclach, in November of 1906. It is well known.

Tarbhlann, •Tarland (Aberdeen), 'bull-field'[1].

Tollachadh (the site of Kildermorie Lodge, Ross-shire), 'hole-field'. The OS Map thoughtfully improves the name of the hill immediately north of it to '*Meall Toll a' Choin*', really *Meall Tollachaidh*.

---

1 Restored form.

Some Place-Names in the Cairngorm Region

At the request of the Editor [of the *Cairngorm Club Journal*], who has provided me with a copy of the July issue, I have undertaken to write a few notes on this subject, which is naturally of interest to the members of the Club. It would not be very difficult, if the thing were gone about in the right way, to form an approximately complete list of the names within the Club's sphere of operations, in alphabetical order, in orthodox Gaelic spelling, and with authoritative interpretation of their meanings. For this there is one condition necessary, and that is that the names, so far as possible, shall be checked from the mouths of Gaelic speakers native to the surrounding districts, especially Badenoch and Braemar. This is not a piece of work that can be done by any chance man who can read and write Gaelic; it is work for an expert, and one who would do it with authority is the Rev C. M. Robertson, UF Church, Kilchoman, Islay. If the Cairngorm Club can persuade Mr Robertson to spend a summer holiday in Braemar and Badenoch, it will have done a good work. Once the data have been secured, the process of interpretation would not, I believe, in this particular case offer much difficulty. At present, however, there are by no means sufficient data as to the true forms of the names, and it should be obvious that a discussion that does not start from firm data is futile. Yet this, if I may say so with respect, is exactly the character of the discussions in the number before me. The one thing needful, the native pronunciation in Gaelic, is the one thing that nobody thinks of ascertaining.

The name of the pass from Badenoch to Braemar is a case in point. All Gaelic speakers who have the native tradition call it *Làirig Dhrù*, and there is no doubt whatever that the name is connected with the stream Druie, at its Badenoch end. It seemed good, however, to some Ordnance Survey man to write it down not as it was, but as he thought it ought to be, and so we got the official *Làirig Ghruamach*, as we got thousands of 'official' names besides. Dr Macbain, our greatest authority on Gaelic philology, compared the river Druie with the Gaulish stream Druentia, and would connect both with the root of Gaelic *drùdhadh*, oozing, soaking. Those who follow Dr Macbain will not, as a rule, find themselves far wrong.

The *Beinn Iutharn* problem proceeds on the same lines: data not ascertained. Here, however, the question is complicated by dialect. The native pronunciation is difficult to reproduce, but may be written *Beinn (Fh)iùbharainn*, which is dialectic for *Beinn Fhaobharainn*, based on *faobhar*, edge. The dialectic peculiarity is that both in Braemar and on the south side of the Grampians, *faobhar* is palatalised into *fyaobhar*, which becomes in common speech *fiùbhar*. The same sort of palatalisation is heard in the dialectic pronunciation of 'smooth' as 'smyooth'. *Faobhar na beinne*, the edge of the hill, is a well-known Gaelic expression, applied to the sloping part of the outline or sky-line of a hill, as opposed to the flat outline or sky-line of the top, which is *fàire*. The termination in *Beinn Fhiùbharainn* is not clear; it may be *roinn*, a point, spit, yielding the meaning 'edge-point'.

Allt na Bienne is truly an impossible form for Scottish Gaelic, whatever it might be for a possible French variety. On the other hand, it does not follow that *Allt na Beinne* is right, though it is unquestionably good Gaelic. The question here again is—What do the Gaelic people call the stream? The best authority available to me assures me that it is called *Beanaidh* (Bennie) simply, without the addition of *allt* or *abhainn*. If so, the name belongs to the large class of stream names with the ending *(a)idh*, common in the North and East of Scotland—that is, in Pictland —e.g. Tromie, Geldie, Divie. The root may be that of old Irish *ben-im*, I smite.

Burn o' Vat is a correct translation of *Allt na Dabhaich*, which is the original. The term *dabhach* (davoch) was applied to any large vat, but it is familiar to me only as applied to the vat used in connection with distilling, especially of a private nature. There is another *Allt na Dabhaich* at Dunvallary, Ledaig. The secondary use of *dabhach*, as applied in Scotland to a measure of land, is well known.

Cairntoul has been often discussed. It is surely simply *Carn an t-sabhail*, Barn-cairn. What and where is the barn? *Carn Sabhail* in Ross means Cairn of Barns (plural) and it is noted for its grass. But among the Cairngorms, the term *sabhal* is used to denote, fancifully, wild rocks—e.g. *Sabhalan* Bynack, the barns of Bynack. I think Cairntable, in Galloway, is the same as Cairntoul, but whether the barn was real or metaphorical, I do not know here either.

The Devil's Point is known to be a euphemistic translation of *Bod an Deamhain*. To judge from the place-names, the Devil had quite a connection in Aberdeenshire—e.g. Bogenjohn, for *Bog an Deamhain*, the Devil's morass; and other places which I refrain from naming.

In Braeriach, 'brae' is *bràigh*, upper part; seen in Braemar, Braemoray and many other instances, followed: by a genitive case—'upper part of Mar', and so on. Here, however, it is qualified by the adjective *riabhach*, brindled, the name meaning 'the brindled upland'.

Derry is known in Gaelic as *an Doire*, the copse. The old name of Londonderry in Ireland is *Doire Calgaich*, Calgach's (=Calgacus) oak-copse, mentioned in Adamnan's *Life of Columba* (c700AD) as Roboretum Calgaci. But *doire* now means any kind of copse, not oak only. There is another Derry on the north side of Loch Earn, Perthshire, also *an Doire* in Gaelic.

Of Loch Etchachan I can say nothing, for I do not know whether the initial vowel is long or short as the word is pronounced in Gaelic.

Loch Avon takes its name from the stream that issues from it, and this is well named *Athfhinn*, the very white one, from the clearness of its water. Avon elsewhere usually represents *abhainn*, a river, but not here.

Loch Callater is in Gaelic pronounced *Loch Caladair*, and *Caladar* becomes in Scotch Cawdor. It is a stream name, a compound of *cal*, call, and *dobhar*, water. It ought to be a sounding stream, like the *Calair* of Balquhidder. The idea of 'calling' is quite common in river names. Any one who has fished a pool below a little rapid at dead of night knows how the stream talks.

The same idea is seen in Lochnagar, in Gaelic *Loch na Gàire*, the loch of the outcry, with reference to the howling of the wind among the rocks. It is hardly necessary to say that now the name has been transferred from loch to mountain.

Glen Giusachan, or in Gaelic spelling *Giùthsachan*, means Glen of the little fir wood, the term *giuthsachan* being a diminutive of *giuthsach*, a fir wood, seen in *Cinn a' Ghiùthsaich*, Kingussie, 'at Firwood Head'.

The name Corriemuillie occurs twice in Ross-shire as well as in Aberdeenshire. It means 'Mill Corry', from *muileann*, mas. or fem., a mill; genitive, *muilne*, fem. The mills in question would have been, doubtless, of the old type with horizontal wheel connected directly by a rigid vertical shaft with the millstone above it; in fact, a water-driven quern This kind of mill is still in active use in Lewis, where I saw one last year.

I have taken the above place-names at random from the July number of the *Journal*.

Place-Names of Strathdearn

These notes are based on material collected in the course of two months spent in Strathdearn in the autumn of 1919, when I had the opportunity of seeing the places and of hearing the names pronounced in their native Gaelic form.

Strathdearn is the valley of the river Findhorn above the Streens. Findhorn Bridge stands about 1,000 feet above sea-level: the Coigs, near the head of the strath, are nearly 300 feet higher. The course of the river is from south-west to north-east; consequently both sides of the strath get their fair share of sun— there is no *deisear* or *tuaithear*.

Certain negative aspects of this district deserve mention. One of these is the lack of prehistoric structures. So far as I could see, Strathdearn possesses no ancient forts and no ancient burial cairns of any size. There are, however, numerous small tumuli which may contain burials. There are also hut-circles, of which I saw some half-dozen in the lower part of the strath near Tom Beag. Another thing notably lacking is traces of the Celtic Church. I found no saint's name commemorated, no holy well, no ecclesiastical place-name of any kind. These are rather unusual features in a Gaelic district of this size.

The list of names which I submit could no doubt be expanded, but it contains all, or nearly all, the names of any importance, and I have put them in alphabetical order.

Ach(adh) nan Dailthean, Field of the Dales, is to be compared with Loch nan Dailthean in Gairloch. In both cases there is a distinct stress on the second syllable of *dailthean*, and the a is open. The place is between Milltown and Ruthven.

Ach(adh) an t-Sabhail, Field of the Barn; the name of the home-farm of Kyllachy.

Allt a' Mhuilinn, the Mill-burn; west of Beannchar Uaine. Some relics of the mill are still to be seen. It was near the junction of the burn with the Findhorn.

Allt Còsach, the Burn of Recesses or Clefts. It flows past the smithy on the south side of Findhorn Bridge, close to the public road, and at this part it has cut out a pretty little ravine. There is no cave here or elsewhere on its course, so far as I know.

Aldnakilie; according to Macfarlane, Inner Inn (Invereen) is 'upon the water of Aldnakilie running out of Glen na Moy'. This would make 'Aldnakilie' another name for the stream known as Fionntag.

Allt na Frìthe, the Burn of the Deer-forest, now anglicised as Freeburn. 'Le Free', the Forest, appears on record in 1507 RMS.

Allt na h-Iolairig, Elrick Burn, joins Findhorn some way above Coignafearn. *Iolairig* is the dialectic form of the more correct *Eileirig*, which is the Gaelic pronunciation in Perthshire. The nature and purpose of the *Eileirig* or Elrick are well known. It was a confined pass, natural or artificial, through which deer were driven so that they might be shot by the nobles and gentry. Each of the latter had a position assigned him, referred to in 'Oran na Comhachaig' as *tom sealga*, corresponding to the Irish term *dumha sealga*, hunting knoll or station. The origin of the word has been much discussed, but it was, I think, finally settled by myself some years ago. In the *Book of Deer* it is recorded that Malcolum son of Mael-Bríghde gave the *elerc* to the old monastery of Deer (Malcolum mac Moilbrigte dorat ind elerc). The *elerc* is now Elrick in the parish of Old Deer. This, however, is not the oldest form of the word. In the Milan Glosses, ascribed to the first half of the ninth century (i.e. about 250 years earlier than the entry in question could have been made), we find in *erelcaib* as a gloss to explain *in insidiis*, in ambush (Ml. 28, c.1). Another of the same body of glosses runs: 'ba hi temul dugníth Saul cona muntair intleda 7 *erelca* fri Duaid' (it was in darkness that Saul with his people used to make snares and *ambushes* against David) (Ml. 30, a.3). These are, so far as I know, the only instances of the occurrence of the word *erelc* in literature, but they suffice. *Erelc* means an ambush, and it is clear that in the *elerc* of the *Book of Deer* we have a later form which has undergone metathesis (compare Old Irish *bélre*, later *bérla*, speech). As to the modern form *eleirig*, it is clear that the final syllable has developed out of the indefinite vowel sound heard between *r* and *g* in, for instance, *deirg*, *leirg*. The correct form would be *eileirg*. One would naturally expect to find instances of the term preserved in Irish place-names, but Dr Joyce mentions none, and the Reverend P. Power tells me that he has never met a case of it. This may be accounted for by the fact that in ancient Ireland this particular method of deer-hunting or deer-slaying was not used; the Irish either chased the deer with hounds or trapped them in pitfalls (*cuithe*) with a spear firmly fixed in a wooden stock (*reap*) in the bottom, point upwards (Joyce, *Social Hist. of Ancient Ireland*, vol 2, pp467-69). We may infer that the *eileirg* method was either adopted by the Gael in Scotland from the earlier inhabitants or developed independently. It occurs with us freely in Galloway, and there is one instance in Roxburgh, near the head of Borthwick Water. It occurs also in Forfar, Kincardine and Aberdeen shires, and is common in Perthshire. The furthest north instances known to me are Elrick near Loch Ruthven in Strathnairn and Elrick south of Loch Affric. (See further *Aoibhinn an Obair an t-Sealg, Celtic Review*, vol 9).

Allt Ruighe Reubhan, the Burn of Reubhan's Slope; Reubhan may be a proper name or nickname, with which may perhaps be compared *Caol crodha mac Rèibhinn* (*Rel. Celt.*, vol 1, p346). It comes down at Coire Mhóruigh.

Allt Shrath Nìn, the Strathnoon Burn.

Aodann Chat, Edinchat; Face of the Sheepcote (*cata*) is the local explanation, which is doubtless correct; near Inverbrough.

Ardachaidh, Highfield; the high-lying farm NE of Coire Mhóruigh.

Bad Iarrtaigh, perhaps Iarrtach's Clump, from a proper name based on *iarr*, ask, seek. It is between Coire Mhóruigh and Dalarossie.

Badfyne 1508 RMS, Balfyne 1507 RMS.

Baile a' Bhràghad, Stead of the Upland; Balvraid, at the junction of the waters of Gleann Seileach, Gleann Circe, and Bruachag.

Baile a' Mhuilinn, Mill-town, on Fionntag: referred to as the mill of Sligache 1634 RMS.

Baile a' Mhuilinn, Mill-town, on Bruachag, near Balvraid.

Baile nam Bodach, Carls' Stead: now Dell of Moirle.

Baile nan Gordanach, the Gordons' Stead.

Beannchar, Banquharry Estir and Westir 1507 RMS. The latter probably corresponded to what is now called Beannchar Uaine, Banchoruan of OSM.

As has been pointed out by Dr Joyce and others, Beannchar is a derivative of *beann*, a horn, a peak. The second part is the noun *cor*, a cast, a setting, and the word means literally Horn-cast, Horn-set. Words of similar formation are common, e.g., Irish *cleth-chor*, 'a wattle-setting', a palisade, fence; *buachur*, 'a cow-cast', a cow's dung; *ur-char*, 'an on-cast', a throw, shot. There are many places that bear this name, or modification of it, in Ireland and Scotland, and the reason of its application has to be considered separately in each case. Dr Joyce considers that in Ireland it is usually applied to places where there is a peaked hill or a collection of peaks, i.e. the 'horn' is vertical. In Scotland the same may apply in certain cases, but it is with us undoubtedly a favourite term to denote horned lakes or horned parts of streams. There are instances to show that the application of the Celtic terms for 'horn' in this way is very old. The best known example is Lacus Bēnācus, 'the horned lake', in the north of Italy, now called Lago di Garda, where Bēnācus stands for Bennācus, our Gaelic *beannach*, horned, peaked. Several of our Highland lakes are called Loch Beannach. Similarly we find Loch Cròcach, Antlered Loch, in Sutherland. Another early Celtic word for 'horn' was *cornu*, cognate with Latin *cornu*, and the second century geographer Ptolemy records Cornācon, on a bend of the Danube, now Sotin. The Danube makes a sharp hornlike bend there, and Cornācon means 'Horn-place'. Returning now to *beannchar*, 'horn-cast', we find it occurring in the names of three considerable lochs— (1) Loch Vennachar, in Gaelic *Loch Bheannchair*, and spelled formerly Lochbannochquhar, Lochbanquhar (Ret.), Loch Banchar, Loch Bennachar (*Geog. Coll.*); (2) Loch Beanncharan at the head of Strathconon, a diminutive form; (3) Loch Beanncharan in Glen Strathfarrar, also diminutive. All three are horn-shaped, with long tapering ends. Next take the case of streams. Reference to the map will show that the Strathdearn Beannchar, on the OSM 'Banchor', is a little below Garbole, on the opposite or right bank of Findhorn. Here the river makes a right-angled bend to the north-west, then a similar bend to the north-east, runs in this direction for about half a mile, and then makes a right-angled bend to the south and another to the north-east. The result is a striking resemblance to a broad brow garnished with two short upstanding horns, and there can be no doubt that this is the Beannchar. There are somewhat similar horn-like bends on the Don near Corbanchory and Edinbanchory. At Banchory in Perthshire there is a striking collection of horn-like bends of the river Isla, and the parish is well named Bendochy, i.e. *Beannachaidh*, Horn-place. Bannachra (Banachran, Macfarlane) in Glen Fruin, Dumbartonshire, is at a succession of sharp bends of the river. At Tulaich Bheannchair, Tullybanchor, near Comrie, the river Earn shows similar features. At Banchory Ternan on the Dee, the river forms two broad sweeping symmetrical horns. On Findhorn, again, there is another Beannchar, Banchor, above Dulsie Bridge; the horn-like bend of the river is at Wester Dulsie, a little to the east of the place now called Banchor. There was a place called Benchar on the river Ness; 'the salmon fishings upon the lake and water of Ness, appertaining to the lands of Beandcher, with their pertinents, lying within the castle lands of Inverness and sheriffdom thereof'. The name may have referred to the broad bend of the Ness below Dochgarroch, which resembles that of the Findhorn at Beannchar, near Garbole. The Beannchar of Glenbanchor, near Newtonmore, probably relates to a feature of the river Calder, but I do not know the exact position of the place so called. There are two other instances of the name, Banchory Devenick in Kincardineshire and Banchor NNW of Kinghorn in Fife. In the latter case there is a long narrow outcrop of rock, now covered with grass, which forms quite a notable feature, and which is doubtless the 'horn-cast'. The church of Banchory Devenick, says an account dated 1725, stands just on the south side of the river Dee, one mile distant from the bridge of Dee (Macfarlane). This fixes the site of the place: it is just at a bend of the river which forms two pronounced horns that spread symmetrically from a somewhat narrow forehead.

The result of this examination is that of the fourteen or fifteen instances noted, only one is not connected with water, and all the others are at or near horn-like projections of water. Sometimes there is only one horn; often there are two, spreading from a forehead or base.

A word may be said on the form Banchory. It is to be noted that the Strathdearn Beannchar is spelled Banquhary in 1507. Similarly Banchor near Kinghorn appears formerly as Banchrie (Ret.). The explanation that occurs to me is that *beannchar* was with us declined like *cathair*, gen. *cathrach*, dat. acc. *cathraigh*, and that Banchory represents an old *Beannchraigh*, locative-dative. We may compare *urchair*, which contains the same element, gen. *urchrach*.

Bruachag, the High-banked Stream, is the name of the burn which enters Findhorn at Inverbrough. Compare the river Bruachag at Kinlochewe.

Ceann na Coille, Wood-end, above Mid Morile.

a' Chlach Sgoilte, the Cloven Stone, where the Findhorn rises.

a' Chluain, Clune; Cloanemoir 1507 RMS, the Meadow. In Ireland, says Dr Joyce, 'its exact meaning is a fertile piece of land surrounded by a bog or marsh, or by a bog on one side, and water on the other'. Our Cluain is certainly a fertile piece of land, by the side of the Findhorn, but there is no sign of a bog. Behind it is Coire na Cluanach.

a' Chor Mhór, the Big rounded Hill, near Corrybrough. *Cor* in this sense is common in Ireland but rare in Scotland; it is masculine, and our instance is in the dative or locative case.

an Cnocan Dubh, Knockandoo, the Black Hillock, now used as the name of the farm above Clune.

Cóig na Fearna, Cognefairne 1634 RMS, Fifth of the Alder.

Cóig na Fionndarnaich, Cognofintrache 1639 RMS; Cognifintrache 1634 RMS, explained by Dr Macbain as Fifth of the 'Bronze Place' (Fionndruinich). It may be from *fionndarnach*, rank grass.

Cóig na Sgàlan, Cogneskellane 1639 RMS; Cognescaller 1634 RMS, Fifth of the Huts or Tents.

Cóig na Sìthe, Cogneschie 1634 RMS, Fifth of the Fairy Hill.

Cóig a' Mhuilinn, Fifth of the Mill: I could not identify it.

The saying with regard to the Cóigs is well known: Tha cóig choigimh an Eirinn agus tha cóig chóigimh an Srath-Eireann, ach is fhearr aon chóigimh an Eirinn na cóig chóigimh an Srath-Eireann [see pp222-23]. The Cóigs form a compact little community at a height of well over 1,200 feet above sea level. At this height the crops are late and liable to damage from frost, but in September of 1919 I observed a first-rate crop of fruit of various kinds in the garden of Cóig na Fearna, all fully ripe. Strathdearn is not the only place in Scotland that has five Cóigs: there are, or were, five in Strathallan also.

Coileachaigh, Kyllachy; Cullochquhoy 1507 RMS; Kellachie 1616 RMS, Place of Grouse Cocks; based on *coileach*. Dr Macbain at one time considered it to be dative plural, *coileachaibh*, a locative like Gallaibh, Caithness; Cataibh, Sutherland, but the sound of the final syllable is against this, and in his last paper he wrote Coileachaigh. He probably regarded it as locative of a nominative in -*ach*, which termination has in some cases a collective force.

Coille na Tulaich, Wood of the Hill, near Tullochclury. Here as usual in our place-names, *tulach* is feminine, as it is in Irish. In composition it is often obscured, e.g. Lochan na Fuar'laich (Fuarthulaich), Loch na Breac-laich, etc.

Coire Mhóruigh, Corrievorrie; Corriworache 1616 RMS; probably Corry of the big Reach or Hill-slope. Its burn is Allt Ruighe Reubhan, which suggests that there were two 'reaches', one called Ruighe Reubhan, and the other the Mór-ruighe.

Coire na Cluanach, Corry of the Meadow, behind Clune. This genitive of *cluain* is notable as implying an old dative *cluanaigh*, whence the common Cluny. We may compare *cail*, a damp meadow, not uncommon in Perthshire nomenclature, with genitive *calach*, as in Coille na Calach, east of Keltney Burn, Aberfeldy: compare Cail-fhraochaigh, Heathfield, in Kilmuir Easter, Ross-shire. Similarly *cairt*, a charter, a card, has a genitive *cartach*, dative *cartaigh*.

Corrbhruach, Corrybrough; Estir and Westir Correbrouchy 1507 RMS; Ester and Wester Correbruchty 1508 RMS; Steep Bank. The primary meaning of *corr* is tapering to a point, e.g. corr-shleagh, corr-mheur (whence *corrag*), corr-bheann, cuach chorr; secondary meanings are (1) unsteady, (2) steep.

an Dail Bheag, the Little Dale, high up near the head of the Strath.

Dail an Fhraoich, Heather Dale, where Dalmigavie Lodge is.

Dail Bheannchair, Dail of Banchor.

Dail (Dul) Fhearghuis, Dalarossie; in Register of Moray Dullersy, Dolerwsy, Dulergusyn, Dultargusy (for -fargusy), Dalergusy, Dulerus, etc. The church of Dalarossie stands on a fairly wide flat close to Findhorn, and this flat is doubtless the *dol* or *dul* which of old belonged to or was occupied by the Fergus whose name is here preserved. The old genitive of Fergus was Ferguso, Fergusa, whence the final -*ie*. A discussion of the term *dol*, *dul*, will be found in Dr Macbain's paper in vol 25 of our *Transactions* [*of the Gaelic Society of Inverness*]. It is clearly a survival from Old British times, and may perhaps be compared with Gaulish Rigo-dulon.

Dail Mhigeachaidh, Dalmigavie; Dale or Flat of Migavie. Migavie is elsewhere in anglicised spelling Migovie, Migvie. Its base *mig* is common on the east side of Scotland, from Migdale in Sutherland to Strathmiglo in Fifeshire: instances are collected and discussed in a paper in the *Celtic Review*, vol 7 [see p117]. It is, I think, to be compared with Welsh *mign*, a bog, quagmire: *mig-wyn*, white moss on bogs. The second part varies in Gaelic pronunciation, for Migovie in Stratherrick is in Gaelic *Migeaghaidh*, and it is this *gh*, and not *ch*, that is represented by *v* in the anglicised forms. It is probably to be compared with Gaelic *magh*, Welsh *maes*, a plain; *ma*, a place: both from Early Celtic *magos*, a plain. On this supposition Migavie would mean boggy plain, which, to judge from its appearance and situation, would describe what it must have been in olden times.

an Dail Thomach, Daltomach: Dalquhemoche 1507 RMS, the Dale of Hillocks: compare Dail Teamhair, Dale of Taras (i.e. eminences of good prospect), in Glencasley, Sutherland. In our place-names *tom* is often troublesome. In Irish it means a bush or tuft usually; a knoll sometimes. In Welsh *tom*, *tomen*, mean mound. With us, *tom*, on the east side at least, means a rounded eminence for the most part, though we can speak of *tom luachrach*, a clump of rushes. In many cases, e.g. names like *Tom-beithe*, local knowledge is necessary to decide the exact meaning.

Dul mac Gearraidh, Dalmagarry; so Kenneth Mackenzie of Castle Leather, pp208, 209, 211. Old forms are Tullowch Makcarre, RM; Tullichnagairie, 1634 RMS; Tullochmakerrie, 1661 Ret.; Tulloc Smagarre, Macfarlane (obviously for Tulloch Magarrie). These cannot be reconciled with the modern name either in Gaelic or in English, and may refer to an adjacent ridge which may have formed the original site of the stead. The *dul* in this case also is a level haugh by the burnside, rather elevated above it, forming a plateau. As *mac* is genitive plural, it would regularly in the older stages of the language eclipse the following consonant; in other words, *Gearraidh* may well represent *gCearraidh*, thus justifying the early spelling Makcarre, and suggesting a proper name or nickname *Cearrach*; compare *cearrach*, Ir. *cearrbhach*, a gamester, a gambler.

Dulatir, RMS 1507, the Black (i.e. sunless) Slope. I did not know the name in time to try to locate it.

Easgan, Fenny or Boggy Stream, one of the head waters of Findhorn, from *easg*, a marsh, whence *easgach*, a marshy place. 'The river Deveron springes out of Escaiche, in the head of Glenbuickett' (*Antiq. of Aberd. & Banff*, vol 1, p121). Thus both Findhorn and Deveron have a like origin. The rivers Esk of Forfarshire are known in Braemar Gaelic as Uisge Easg, doubtless from the same root, though not necessarily with the same shade of meaning.

Fearann a' Bhothsaich, Vass's Land, some green patches, once cultivated, in the hill pasture of Baile nan Gordanach, conspicuous from the public road that goes by Slochd.

Fionntag, the Little White One, the name of the stream from Loch Moy; compare Gleann Fionntaig and the personal name Fionntan. So Dubhag, the Little Black One, a common burn-name. *Fionn* has the secondary meaning of 'holy, blessed', and if Macfarlane's Aldnakilie stands for Allt na Cille, 'church burn', Fionntag may really mean 'the little holy stream' (see Aldnakilie above).

an Garbuil (anns a' Gharbuil), Garbole; a hardened form of *garbh-bholl*, 'big boll', with reference to the amount of corn seed required to sow the cultivated part of old.

Gleann Circe, Glenkirk; Glen of the Grouse-hen; here as often the singular is used collectively; compare *Cinn-déis*,

Kindeace, from *dias*, an ear of corn, signifying good cornland.

Gleann Màsaran, Glen Mazeran; Invermastreane, 1507 RMS; Inner Mastrachan, Avon Mastrachan, Glen Mastrachan, Macfarlane. Màsaran is obviously a stream name: for *s* from *st* compare Glen Prosen, of old Glen Prostyn, now in Gaelic Gleann Pràsain. It is probably British, and I have met nothing likely to throw light on it.

Gleann Seileach, Willow Glen.

Gleann Tairbhidh or Tarbhaidh, from an old *tarbda*, bullish, bull-like, here probably applied to the stream: *tarbh*, bull, occurs in several ancient stream names, e.g. Abertarff. In Ireland there occurs also Tarbga as a place-name, e.g. cath Tarbgi (Hogan, *Onomasticon*), which would result in Tarbhaigh with us. Compare Tarvie near Garve, and Duntarvie in West Lothian. Other names involving *tarbh* are Tarves, Tarvit, Tarland.

Inbhir Bhruachaig, Inverbrough, where Bruachag joins Findhorn.

Inbhir Fhinn, Invereen; Inverin, 1634 RMS; Inverine, 1661 Retours. Though the farmhouse of Invereen is situated about a mile from the junction of Fionntag with Findhorn, the farm goes right up to the junction, and as there is no other stream near, it seems clear that the 'inver' must be that of Fionntag. It is worth noting that in the Gaelic of this district the term 'inver' is understood to cover not only the spot where one stream joins another, but also the lower reaches of the stream that gives its name to the junction.

Leathdoch Bheannchair, the half-davoch (*leth-dabhach*) of Banchor. From Mr C. Fraser-Mackintosh's notes it appears that there was a Davach of Beannchar, but I could trace only the half-davach.

Leathdoch nan Cóig, the half-davach of the Coigs. The whole davach was known, I think, as the Davach of Sìth-bheinne or Schifyn.

Móir'l and Móir'l Mhór, Morile; Moreweg and Moralemore, 1507 RMS. Dr Macbain refers it to a Pictish (or Old British) Mor-ialon, Large Clearing; Welsh *ial*, open space, and compares Bal-moral. We may compare also Innis Lòicheil, Monar, from *lòch*, black. But it is right to say that this ending occurs in Irish *Deargail*, red spot (Joyce, vol 2), so that though Móir'l may well be Old British it is not necessarily so.

Mórcloinn; Moreclun 1507, 1508 RMS; an obscure compound, apparently *mórc-loinn*; *loinn* is locative of *lann*, an enclosure, a field. The first part cannot be *mór*, for it would be followed by aspiration.

Poll-lòchaig, Pollouchy 1507 RMS; Pallouchy, Pollouchty, 1508 RMS; Pool of the little Black One. Lòchaig is apparently the name of the burn that joins Findhorn here from the north. *Lòch*, black, enters into a number of place-names, though obsolete in the language. Its earliest appearance is in Adamnan's Lochdiae, otherwise Nigra Dea, the Black Goddess, now the river Lochy in Lochaber. The other streams of the same name are (1) Abhainn Lòcha of Gleann Lòcha (Glenlochay), Killin, at the head of Loch Tay; (2) Abhainn Lòcha, from Tyndrum, a tributary of Orchy; (3) The Lochy of Banffshire, a tributary of Avon (*Celtic Review*, vol 5) [see p81].

Preas, Copse, the name of the holding west of Baile nan Gordanach. *Preas* now means a bush, but in place-names the old meaning of copse is usual, if not invariable.

Rathaig Bheag, Raigbeg; Reauchbeg 1507 RMS; Rauchbeg 1508 RMS. The little Rathlet; *ràth* is a circular fortification with earthen walls or ramparts, but it is sometimes applied with us to hut-circles, e.g. Cùil na Ràtha, a small holding near Bonar Bridge, with a hut-circle close to the dwelling-house. I did not see the structure which gives its name to Raigbeg, but as described to me it appeared to be a hut-circle.

Ràthaig Mhór, Raigmore; Rauchmore 1507 1508; the big Rathlet. This structure is on the top of a birchclad knoll in the fields below the farmhouse of Drumbane. It is almost or quite circular, with a diameter of about 33 feet, and is marked by a low turf-covered wall of earth and stones. It has been used as a place of burial, and my informant, Mr Davidson, Findhorn Bridge, judged that the last burial took place nearly a hundred years ago. A small mound within the enclosure may mark a grave. The knoll itself is called *An Sìthean*, the Fairy Seat. Mr Davidson had heard of another burial place situated at or near the mouth of the burn between Clune and Press, which had been swept away by the great flood of 1829. It may be added in connection with the burials in Raigmore, that in Ireland it was not unusual to bury unbaptized children in a Rath.

Ruadhainn, Ruthven; Riven, 1634 RMS; Rowan, 1661 RMS; Rothuan in Stratheren, 1236, RM. The other places of this name in Inverness-shire are Ruthven in Badenoch and Loch Ruthven in Strathnairn, the modern Gaelic forms of all three being identical. There are also Ruthven and Aber-ruthven in Perthshire; Ruthven in Banffshire, in Aberdeenshire (twice), in Forfar, and in Berwickshire. The following are some reliable old spellings, irrespective of the particular Ruthven they apply to: Ecclesia S. Petri de Rothfan, c1224; Rothuan, 1226, 1236; Rothvan; Rothwin, 1247; Rothewen, 1257; Rothewane, 1266; Rothfin, 1270; Rothuen, Rotheuen; Aber-ruadeuien, c1198; Aber-rotheven in Stradherne, c1199; Aber-rothevin, c1200; Aber-rotheuin, c1211; Logyrothman in Mar, c1200. The connection of the first part with Gaelic *ruadh*, red, is obvious. The last syllable *-ven* might represent (1) *beinn*, peak (Blaven, Sulven, Morven, etc); (2) *mèinn*, ore; (3) possibly Welsh *maen*, a stone. At Ruthven near Huntly there is no peak of any description, and the stone of the place is blueish basalt. But the water of the stream that passes this Ruthven is noticeably ruddy, owing to the presence of iron, and the district is full of iron pan and ferruginous deposits. While this is something, more data are required for a definite conclusion.

Sìth-bheinne, Schevin; Schesyn (for Schevyn?), 1506 RMS; Schyphin, 1639 RMS, Fairy Hill of (the) Peak, Pointed Fairy Hill. 'The great davoch of Schevin,' says Dr Fraser-Mackintosh, 'commonly called Coignafearn or the Monalia. runs at the back of the parishes of Alvie, Kingussie, and Laggan' (*Antiq. Notes*, Second Series, p428). Dr Macbain says 'Cùig-na-Sìth, fairy hill, near is the Sìdh-bheinn, the Schiphein of the charters' (TGSI, vol 25).

an Sìthean, the Fairy Hill, on which Rathaig Mhór is.

an t-Sleaghach; Sligache, 1634 RMS; Sleawoche, 1661 Ret.; Sleach, Marfarlane; 'Slyack is E of Fintack lying besyde the milne', *ib.* The meaning is 'the place of the gully or rift', from the root *sleg*, as in *sleagh*, a spear. It is rather a common name, e.g. Sleaghach, Slioch, the mountain near Kinlochewe, whose distinctive feature is the numerous gullies which flute the sides of its truncated cone; Sleaghach near Onich; Sleaghach near Killin, Perthshire; Dùnan na Sleaghaich, Morvern; Sleach, Glengairn, etc.

an Soillsean, the Bright Spot, the name of a little clearing in the wood between the FC Manse and Raigbeg, occupied by cottages.

na Srianaibh, the Streens of Findhorn; the Bridles, dative-locative plural of *srian*, a bridle—a graphic and appropriate name for this remarkable gorge.

Srath Eireann, Strathdearn, is Stratheren c1224 RM. Near Dulsie Bridge on Findhorn is Dùn Eireann, Dunearn: the village of Findhorn at the mouth of the river was Inbhir Eireann, Invererne, but the latter name is now applied to a farm on the right bank some little way up. Cullerne is east by south of Findhorn village, probably for Cùil Eireann, Nook of Earn, while on the left side, opposite Invererne, is Earnhill, for Cnoc Eireann. On record there is 'the land of the prepositura of Invereren', which appears in Scots as 'the Griefschipe', 'the Greivschippe', etc (Ret.); Lachlan Shaw says: 'Below Mundole, on the side of the river, is the Grieship.' Sir Thomas Dick Lauder's map of the Moray

Floods puts the centre of the 'Grieshope' opposite Broom of Moy. What was the exact nature of this 'prepositure' or Grieveship is not clear, to me at least, but it appears to have been connected in some way with the old village of Findhorn, which was swallowed by the sea about 1700.

The Findhorn is in Gaelic now Uisge Eire, formerly doubtless Uisge Eireann; similarly Strathearn in Perthshire is now Srath Eir', for the older Srath Eireann. It has been customary to regard Eire or Finn-Eire as primarily the name of the river, but I have come to think that this supposition is more than doubtful. In the case of Allt Eireann, Auldearn, not very far away, it is clear that we have to do with a stream which is named after a district: Erin appears not infrequently on record in this sense, e.g. 'the church of Eryn with the chapel of Invernarren (Nairn)', in RM. Erin, in fact, was the old name of the parish of Auldearn, and Allt Eireann means 'Erin's Burn', i.e. 'Ireland's Burn'. In the same way, as I believe, the district about the mouth of Findhorn was called Finn-Eire, i.e. White Ireland, with reference to the white sands there, and the river which entered the sea there was called Uisge Finn-Eireann, 'the Water of White Ireland'. In contradistinction we find further east the river Deveron, which from the old forms clearly means 'Black Erin', also, as I think, from the district at its mouth. The inference is that both names were given in consequence of Gaelic settlements, and that neither of them belongs to the oldest stratum of our place-names: the river name Narunn, Nairn, for instance, is very much older. It may be noticed incidentally that the names Cullerne and Earnhill are not readily explained as from a river name; they are easily understood if the district in which they occur was known as Erin. A good instance of similar change of name is the river Orrin in Ross-shire, which I once wrongly thought to belong to the oldest stratum of our names. Orrin really comes from *oifrend*, an offering; its glen is Glenafaryn in Macfarlane, and its junction with the Conon near the church of Urray is

Inverafren in RMS. Here the 'offering' was doubtless a grant of land to the church of Urray, and from this *oifrend* came not only the name of the river Orrin, but also the names Glen Orrin and Inver Orrin. The old name of Orrin is unknown, but the case of the Findhorn is different: its position agrees with that assigned by Ptolemy to the river which he calls Loxa. The superficial resemblance of Loxa and Lossie has caused Skene and others to equate the two, but the Lossie is much too far to the east to suit the position given by Ptolemy, and its name is easily explained from Gaelic.

Strathnoon appears as Easter Straneune and Wester Straneune in 1508 RMS; in Macfarlane it is Stron-eyin; the present Gaelic form is Sra(th)-nìn. The place is on the south side of Findhorn, east of Beannchar: it is not a strath in the ordinary sense, but a holme or haugh by the river side, Easter and Wester Strathnoon being divided by a burn: Both parts are uncertain to me. The first part may be either *sron*, nose, point, or *srath*, for in unstressed position *sron* may become *s(t)ran*, as in Stranraer for Sron Reamhar, 'thick cape'.

Tom-aitinn, Tomatin, is 'knoll of juniper'. I do not know the position of the *tom* which gave rise to the name, but juniper grows on the hillsides to a height of well over 1,000 feet.

Tom-ghealagaidh, on the right bank of Findhorn opposite Ruthven, is a shapely hill of 1,250 feet. The second part, Gealagaidh, occurs as the name of a farm on Dulnan near Carr-Bridge, called in English Gallovie, and means 'the white *agaidh*' with which is to be compared Blàragaidh, Blargie, 'the dappled *agaidh*', in Laggan; Tanagaidh, 'the thin *agaidh*', near Kinlochewe; Agaidh Mhór, Aviemore 'the big *agaidh*', and near it Agaidh an Lochain, 'the *agaidh* of the lochlet'. The meaning of *agaidh* is uncertain. So far as I could make out, there is no special feature about Aviemore, Avielochan, or Gallovie. On the south side of Tom-ghealagaidh a small burn comes through a little gorge with white stones, which are visible from a considerable distance.

Gleann Tanagaidh is a very narrow glen, with steep sides. To these may be added Rogie, near Strathpeffer, in Gaelic Ro'agaidh, meaning apparently 'great *agaidh*'. There is thus some suggestion that *agaidh* may mean something like 'gorge', 'cleft'.

The descriptions in Macfarlane's *Geographical Collections* are as follows:–

Seats in Stra-Erin in Murray

Imprimis is Cognashy or the Elfs fyft part. Cogylewrach is from it half a myl. from that half a myl is Cogy Scallan. half a myl thence Cogywarn. half a myl therfra Dalmegawy. half a myl from that Dalomy. therfrom half a myl is Inner Mastrachan. with Avon Mastrachan cuming from Glen Mastrachan 2 myl long. that burne entereth upon the northsyd of Erin. half a myl from it is Cowlachy. a myl thence Bewnachar Mackay. a. myl therfra Bewnachar Mack Huchion. a myl thence Stron-eyin. a myl therfra Cory-vory. 2 myl thence upon the north syd of the water, Moril Beg. 2 myl thence Raeg-moir, a myl thence Raeg Beg. Upon the north Morilmoir. 2 myl thence on the southsyd of the river Corybroichmoir. half a myl thence Corybroichbeg. a myl thence Pulocheg. upon the northsyd Rowin a myl from the former. a myl therfra Sleach; a myl from that Inner Inn. upon the water of Aldnakilie running out of Glen na moy. a myl thence Innerbruachag with Alt Bruachag. 2 myl thence Frei up fra the water northward. Up in the month Muybeg. Ilan na Muymoir in Loch Muy twa myl long. a myl thence Tulloch Mackerry. 2 myl above it towards the month is Ardnaslanach [*read* Alt-]. Item Lochin na Clach Skuilt a little Loch on the head of Stra Erin 3 myles above Cogy Shy, and 5 myl from Abirchalladyr in Stra Arkeg (Stratherrick).—*Geographical Collections* (Scottish History Society), vol 2, p258.

Stratheiren in Murrey and Lochmuy

Kirk of Muy ... situate on the west syde of Loch Muy ... in it Mackintoish his house scituate ... In this loch are founde trowts called Reedwyns [*read* Reedwyms. i.e. 'red-bellies', i.e. char or *tarrdheargan*] taken only betwix Michelmess and Hallowmess. At the north end of the Loch stands Muymoir, at the west a wood equal in lenth with the Loch, at the south end of both lyes Tulloch cleurr. West of the Loch stands Muybeg and the kirk. Altnaslanach from the Loch NW, and W ½ myle ane wood called Kyle na hiren, just west from it ane other called Craig na en or the birds wood ... Item a third wood called Derirr na cloich or the Scrabblackwood. Item another wood ½ myle above Muybeg called Derirr na Shamprak or the Cleverwoode [*read* Clover-]. ane other wood due S from Muybeg called Liadeirr or Letir the lyart [grey] woode and a bush beneath it, near the south nocke of the Loch called Letyir beg. The other woode which extends the lenth of the Loch is called Letyr Mair.

The water of Fintack runnes out of the Loch SE and upon it is a milne. It runnes into Findorne 14 myles above Tarnowaye. Tulloc Smagarre is W of Fintacke, Slyack is E of Fintack lying besyde the milne. The tounes over against other midwaye twixt the Loch and water.

At the inver of the water NE of Findorne lyes Ruven on the syde of Findorne Water. On that same syde lyes Keancraig a myle beneath Ruven with a great Craige called Craigcrockanor the Steepie craige. ½ myle under it on the same syde lyes Lagriach or the spotted valley. The nethermost town of that part called Bothagan not ¼ myle distant from the other toune.

On the S syde of the water of Findorne which runnes from SW to NE stands Cochlachin 4 myles from Muybegg. above that ¼ myl stands Baalcrokan. and from that 1 myl stands Pollochack or the Lochpoole. a wood interjected twixt the forsaid townes called Dow lettyir, then a wood above called Lettyir gallerie [?Gealagaidh]; Corry bruoch beg or the little bray quarrel a towne standing a myle SW from the last named town and Letyir galerie interjected betwixt the two. ane other called Corry bruoch moir ½ myle from the other; it lyes due south from Findorne.—*Ib.*, p607.

Names of Places around Inverness

The names of places around Inverness are of three kinds, Pictish, Gaelic, and English, or rather Scots. Several of the English names are very old, and go to prove what we know otherwise, that there was a strong English element in Inverness from the twelfth century onwards. Of the Gaelic names, many are still older; others are more recent. Oldest of all are the Pictish names, of which there are about a dozen, more or less, in the following list. We may take it that the Pictish names are at least as old as 700 AD, probably much older.

Abban of Abban Street means a more or less disused river channel; also a backwater (*àban*). The river once went by this route to the sea.

Abriachan—in 1239 Abirhacyn; 1334 Aberbreachy. The first part is *aber*, a Pictish word of the same meaning as Gaelic *inver*, a confluence. It is common on the east and in the midland parts of Scotland, e.g. Aberdeen, confluence of the Don. On the west we have Applecross, which is a contraction of the old name Apor-crossan, and Loch Aber, which means 'loch of the confluences', from the rivers—Lochy, Nevis, etc—which enter the sea there. The latter part is the old name of the stream, perhaps Briachan.

Aird—height or promontory; the Aird in Kiltarlity is in Gaelic *Aird Mhic Shimidh*, Lord Lovat's height, Mac Shimidh, Simon's son, being Lord Lovat's patronymic.

Achpopuli—field of the tent or booth, from *pobull*, *puball*, old genitive *poible*, *puible*, a tent, pavilion. Latin *papilio*, a butterfly; Greek παπυλεῶν, a tent of heavy cloth.

Aldourie—the Dourie burn; the stream is now *Dobhrag* in Gaelic, meaning simply 'streamlet', from *dobhar*, water, burn.

Allanfearn—*an t-àilean fearna*, the alder green.

Altnaskiach—the hawthorn burn.

Ardersier—*Ard na Saor*, promontory or point of the wrights; final *n* of *nan* is lost before *s*. Another possible explanation is from *saothair*, a promontory or passage covered at high water, a term not uncommon on the West Coast.

Ardturlie—*Ard-rolaidh*; an obscure name.

Avoch—*Obhach*, stream-place, from Old Gaelic *ab*, *oub*, later *abh*, a stream; hence also *Loch Obhaich*, Loch Oich, 'loch of stream-place'.

Ballifeary—in 1244 Balnafare as 'town of the watching' (*Baile na Faire*); in the olden times sentinels would be posted here to give timely notice of any hostile visit by the unruly neighbours of the town.

Balloch Hill—the Balloch (*Bealach*) was the old Gaelic name for the 'gap' through which Castle Street now runs. The Balloch Hill is at the top of Castle Street. 'Le Ballocis Hill', 1376.

Balnafettack—*Baile nam Feadag*, Homestead of the Plovers. In names of places Bal- usually means 'homestead', the Scottish 'toun'.

Balnagaick—Homestead of the cleft or opening (*gàg*); there is a gap in the ridge behind it.

Balrobert—Robert's stead; a very old name.

Balvonie—*Baile a' Mhonaidh*, Moor-stead.

Barnhill—formerly also Cott Hill. In the 18th century there were no houses here, only three thatched cots.

Beauly—a name of French origin, *beau lieu* (*bellus locus*), beautiful place; given by the Norman founders of the Priory of Beauly. There is another Beaulieu in Hampshire.

Beaufort—another French name given by the Norman barons, meaning 'beautiful fort'. The Gaelic name for it is Dunie (*Dùnaidh*), which means 'stronghold'. There was a fortress there of old.

Bochrubin—*Both Chrùbin*, Booth of the little Claw, with reference to a claw-like physical feature.

Bogbain—*Am Bog Bàn*, the white bog, so called probably from the white cotton grass which once grew there.

Bona—*Am Bàn Àth*, the white ford; before the river was deepened at its outlet from Loch Ness in forming the Canal, there was a ford where the ferry is now, marked by white shingle.

Broadstone Park—so called from a stone, now buried under the footpath in Kingsmills Road, which was bored to serve perhaps as base for a flagstaff. It probably means 'the *bored* stone'.

Brochnain—*Bruach an Eidhinn*, Ivy bank.

Bught—Old Scots *boucht*, *bought*, a bending, bay, sheep-pen; the same word really is English bow, to bend.

Bunachton—*Both Neachdain*, Nectan's Booth. Nectan was a great Pictish name, whence the surname MacNaughton.

Caiplich—*a' Chaiplich*, the place of horses, i.e. horse pasture. *Capull* is Gaelic for horse; the Romans borrowed it from the Gauls as *caballus*, whence our cavalry, chivalry.

Cameron Barracks—the ridge was formerly called Knockintinnel (*Cnoc an Tionail*), the rallying hill.

Capel Inch—Horse 'inch' or links; an old market stance. Cf Inches, Merkinch.

Castle Street—see Balloch Hill and Doomsdale Street.

Castlehill of Inches—the Gaelic is *Caisteal Stìll*—Castle of the Stripe (of land), of which the English is a corruption.

Castle Heather—so written at least as early as 1758, but the older name was Castle-leather or Leffare, from Gaelic *Lethoir*, a hill side. 'The Lordship of Leffare' is mentioned in 1460.

Clachnacuddin—*Clach nam Cùdainn*, Stone of the Tubs. Women carrying water from the river used to rest their tubs on it. The famous stone is now preserved under the cross on the Exchange.

Clachnaharry—usually taken as for *Clach na h-Aire*, Stone of the Watch; the Gaelic pronunciation, however, is in favour of *Clach na h-Aithrigh(e)*, Stone of Penance, or, of Repentance[1]; compare *Clach a' Pheanais*, Stone of Penance, beside Cill Chaitriona, St Catherine's Chapel, in Colonsay, at

---

1 Mr James Fraser, the writer of the Wardlaw Manuscript, says: 'The battle of Clach-ni-harry, i.e. the Repentance or Pennance Stone, happened June 27, 1378' (p87). The term *aithrighe*, fem., now obsolete in Scottish Gaelic but current in Irish, was evidently well understood in his time; the modern term is *aithreachas*, masc.

which penance was made after confession; the penance would consist in repeating a given number of paternosters, etc.

Cradlehall—so called, it is said, from a sort of lift or elevator used in the house by Edward Caulfield, who was in charge of the roads after General Wade, and lived there.

Craigphadrick—Patrick's Rock. The name is said not to be very old, and to have been given after a tenant who lived near it.

Culcabock—*Cùil na Càbaig*, Nook of the Cheese; the reason of the name is unknown.

Culduthel—*Cùil-daodhail*; *cùil* means 'nook' as above; *duthel* is the same as in the parish name Duthil, the meaning of which is difficult.

Culloden—*Cùil-lodair*; this name, so prominent in Highland history, means Nook of the Marsh. *Cùil*, a nook, is common in place-names round Inverness.

Dalcross—*Dealganros*, formerly Delginross, means Prickly Point, or Prickly Wood, from whins or thorns. Gaelic *ros* usually means 'a point' or 'cape', but it may also mean 'a wood'.

Dares—*Darus*, another form of *dorus*, a door, in the sense of a narrow pass.

Daviot—*Deimhidh*, in 1234 Deveth, a Pictish name meaning 'Strong place', so called most probably from its hill fort, the Dun of Daviot (*Dùn Deimhidh*).

Diriebught, in 1376 Deyrbowchte, commonly said to mean 'The poor's Land'; but it may rather mean 'The poor or barren Land'.

Dochcairn or Davochcairn, Davach of the Cairn. Davach is old Gaelic for a vat, and is still so used, but it was also used as a measure of land, and is very common in that sense all over Pictland. It was, in fact, the standard land-measure.

Dochfour—a Pictish name, means the davach of (good) pasture.

Dochgarroch—means probably the Davach of rough ground; cf the Garioch in Aberdeenshire.

Dochnacraig—Davoch of the Rock.

Dochnalurg—Davach of the Shank, a term often applied to a long thin ridge. All these 'Dochs' are places near Dochfour.

Doomsdale Street—the old name for Castle Street. It led to the place of execution.

Dores—*Durus*, formerly from ancient times spelled Durris, in 1530 Durrys, the same name as Durris in Kincardineshire and Durris-deer in Ayrshire; it is probably for Dubhros, 'dark wood' or 'dark point'.

Drakies—*Dreigidh*, is in 1369 Drakeis; in 1376 Drekechys; another Pictish name; meaning unknown.

Drummond—*Druiminn*, means 'at' or 'on the ridge'. In old writings it is called Drumdevan 'idle ridge', i.e. 'uncultivated ridge'; (*druim diomhain*).

Dunlichity means 'the Dūn or Fort of Flichity', which again means 'wet place'.

Duntelchaig—*Dun t-Seilcheig*, Fort of (the) Snail; viewed from Abriachan this hill looks exactly like a snail. There seems to be no trace of a fort now.

Erchite (Dores)—*Airchoid*, a Pictish name, probably meaning on or near the Clearing; Park-side.

Essich—*Easaich*, Place of Waterfalls.

Foyers—*Foithir*; means 'low-land'; here 'little slope' or 'terrace'. The Falls of Foyers is in Gaelic *Eas na Smùid*, Spray-fall, often, but wrongly, thought to give the name to Loch Ness, as if it were Loch an Easa.

Glenurquhart—a 'glen' is a valley narrower and less level than a 'strath'. Urquhart is a Pictish name meaning copse-side, wood-side; cf Erchite.

Haugh—a very old English, or rather Scottish name, mentioned in William the Lyon's charter of 1180. In 1360 it is written Halc, old Scots *halche*, flat land by a waterside. In English *l* before a consonant becomes silent (Holm, talk, should), but Gaelic-speaking people still use the old form almost exactly—*an Talchan.*

Holm—from English holm, an island in a river. Here again the old form is used in Gaelic, *an Tuilm.* (In borrowing Teutonic words Gaelic regularly changes initial *h* into *t*). Holm here means 'river-meadow'.

Inches—*Na h-Innseagan,* means the meadows (*innis*).

Inverness means the confluence of the Ness (with the sea), i.e. the place at the mouth of the Ness. *Inver* is Gaelic, probably changed from an old *aber.* The River Ness appears in Adamnan's *Life of Columba* as Nesa; the Norse called it Nis, which is the spelling in modern Gaelic (pronounced *Neesh*). Rivers were worshipped as deities by the ancient Celts, and Nesa was most probably a water goddess.

Kessock Ferry takes its name from St Kessock, who was specially connected with Loch Lomond side. There were often small chapels or oratories near ferries, and there may have been one here dedicated to St Kessock.

Kiltarlity—the *Cill* or Church of St Talorgan, a saint with a Pictish name, meaning 'White-brow'. The saint's name was later corrupted into Taraglan.

Kilvean—the *Cill* or Church of St Bean (two syllables).

Kingsmills—a very old English name. A charter of Alexander II (1232) mentions 'our mill at Inverness'. The mill was subsequently granted to the town.

Kinmylies—in the same charter the land of *Kinmyly* is granted by the King to the Bishop of Moray; it is *Cinn a' Mhìlidh,* 'warrior's head', or 'headland'; compare Carmylie in Fife.

Knockintinnel—the rallying hill, the ridge on which the Cameron Barracks now stand.

Knocknageal—*Cnoc nan Giall,* the Hill of the Hostages; probably from some compact there entered into, in which hostages were given as pledge.

Leachkin—*An Leacainn,* the Hillside—a very common name.

Leys—*An Leigheas,* meaning uncertain.

Loch Ardle—the name of an old barony near Inverness revived in recent times.

Loch Ashie—*Loch Athaisidh*, also Drum Ashie, which has become famous in the form of Drummossie. There are idle tales of a Scandinavian Prince 'Ashie' who was killed there. The name probably means 'bare or poor meadow', from *ath-innse*, locative case of *ath-innis*. So Breckishie, dappled meadow, and many other names.

Loch na Shanish—*Loch na Seanis* for *Sean-innse*; means Loch of the Old Meadow.

Longman—An interesting name, thought to mean Ship-flat, which is unlikely to be correct.

Lovat—from *lobh*, rot, with *-id* extension; compare *Both Lobhach* in Glen Fintaig. In Gaelic now it is *a' Mhormhoich*, the Sea-plain.

Maggot—so called from a chapel of St Margaret.

Merkinch—The Horse Meadow (or, in this case, island). When Abban Street was a river channel, the Merkinch was an island, and a common grazing ground for horses.

Midmills—between Kingsmills and the Diriebucht mill.

Millburn—takes its names from the water which worked those mills.

Moray—means the land by the sea-side; the littoral. The province of Moray extended from Spey to the borders of Lochaber. (Early Celtic *Mori-treb-*, 'sea-settlement').

Muckovie—a very ancient name, meaning Swine-field (*mucomhaigh*).

Muirtown—formerly Easter Kinmylies.

Nairn (River)—a Pictish name meaning practically stream The root is the same as Latin nare, to swim, whence the Italian river Nar, and its town Narnia. The name of the town of Nairn is shortened from Invernairn.

Petty—*Peitigh*, a Pictish name, meaning 'Place of Pits'; 'pit' (*peit*) was a Pictish word meaning 'a piece of land', a 'homestead'.

Porterfield—from the Porter of the Castle, who was an important official. Other officials of the great castles besides the porter often held land near the castle, such as the Forester, the Smith, the Mair or Steward the Sergeant, and the Currour or Courier.

Raigmore—*Ràthaig Mhór; Rath*, of which *ràthaig* is a derivative, means a fortified homestead. The original Raigmore is in Strathdearn.

Risaurie—*An Ruigh Samhraidh*, 'the summer pasture land'— where cattle grazed in summer.

Scaniport—Cleft-ferry, i.e. ferry of the cleft; the ferry was on Loch Ness.

Scategate, Scathegate, or Scatisgat—the old name for the road to the sea by Rose Street, probably so called because scat or tax was there levied on fish brought into the burgh for sale. Gate in old Scots means road.

Scorguie—Windy point.

Strathglass—*Srath-ghlais*, a strath is a broad and fairly level valley; *glais* is old Gaelic for 'stream', and is common in stream names.

Tomnahurich—*Tom na h-Iubhraich*, Hillock of the Yew-wood. The oldest form of the word *iubhrach*, a yew wood, is Eborācon, whence also the name York.

Torbreck—*an Torr Breac*, the dappled hill.

Torvean—*Torr Bheathain*, St Bean's hill; cf Kilvean.

The Place-Names of Breadalbane

Breadalbane is the name applied to the district round about Loch Tay and the river basins at the head of the Loch, namely, Glen Lochay and Glen Dochart with Strath Fillan. On the east it may be considered to begin on the south side of the Tay at the burn called Cromalltan, the bent little burn, between Taymouth and Stix, that is to say near the eastern entrance to the grounds of Taymouth Castle. On the north side of Tay, Breadalbane is reckoned to begin at Point of Lyon, Rinn *Liomhunn*, where the River Lyon enters Tay, nearly opposite to Cromalltan. Thence its northern march runs along the top of Drummond Hill to Clach an Tuirc, the boar's stone, by the road side as one goes from Fearnan on Loch Tay to Fortingall. This well-known stone is in the march between the parishes of Fortingall and Kenmore. Thence the march of Breadalbane runs between the farm of Borland and the small farm of Achtar, *Ach-tearra*, the latter being on Garth estate and the former on Breadalbane, and so up to the watershed between Loch Tay and Glen Lyon, running westward along the watershed between Glen Lyon on the north and Glen Lochay on the south, to the county march in the neighbourhood of Tyndrum. On the south side of Loch Tay, Breadalbane is similarly divided from Glen Almond and Strath Earn, while Glen Dochart marches with Balquhidder. The total length from Point of Lyon to Carn Droma (near Tyndrum) is about forty miles, the first half being from Point of Lyon to Killin, and the second from Killin to Carn Droma. The whole region would correspond with the old Lordship of Deisir and Tuathair, the north or sunny side and the south or north-looking side of Loch Tay respectively, including Glen Lochay and Mam Lorne, and in addition the old Lordship of Glen Dochart.

The name Breadalbane never appears in charters or State documents till fairly recent times. It is not found in the printed Retours of Service, which come down to about 1700, nor in the Register of the Great Seal, whose eleven volumes come down to 1668. It was in fact a popular term, not denoting a province or administrative district. According to very old tradition the whole of what is now Perthshire was included in the two ancient provinces of Fotla and Fortriu. At a later period Fortriu (or Fortrenn, which is the genitive case of Fortriu) appears as Strath Earn and Menteith, while Fotla is represented by Atholl and Gowrie. Thus the district of Breadalbane must have formed part either of Strath Earn or of Atholl, and the choice between the two is not in doubt. Breadalbane was part of the old province of Atholl.

The meaning of the name is clear enough. The Gaelic is Bra'id Albann, and *Bra'id* is short for *Bràghaid*, the dative-locative case of *bràighe*, upper part of the chest, very commonly applied to the upland part of a district, as in Bràighe Chat, Braechat, the part of Sutherland round about Lairg, literally 'the upland of Cats', the ancient tribe of Cats who gave their name to Caithness and the south-eastern part of Sutherland; Brae-mar, the upland of the district of Mar; Brae-moray, the upland of Moray; Brae-Lochaber, the upland of Lochaber, and so on. The contraction of *bràghaid* into *bra'id*, with shortening of the vowel *a*, is due to the vigorous stress on *Albann*, the second part of the compound name. This contraction appears in the first instance of the name in Gaelic literature, namely in a poem in the book of the Dean of Lismore, where the writer mentions the MacGregors as 'na fir sin a Bra'id Albann' ('those men from Breadalbane'). As the line must have seven syllables, we must read *Bra'id*, unless indeed we amend it to 'na fir a Bràghaid Albann'. In any case the meaning is 'the upland of Alba'. Here Alba is used in the restricted denotation, pointed out by Skene, of the region east of Druim Alban, between Forth and the Grampians and round by Aberdeen to Moray, the old Pictish part of Kenneth MacAlpin's kingdom. In this connection it is interesting to note that the river Lochay of Glen Lochay is styled in Gaelic *Lòchá Albannach*, Lochay of Alba, as distinguished from the Lochay which flows westward from near Tyndrum, styled *Lòchá Urchaidh*, Lochay of Orchy. The glen of the latter is *Gleann Lòchá Latharna*, Glen Lochay of Lorn.

We may now note such traces of the old Celtic Church as remain in Breadalbane, beginning at the west with Strath Fillan, named after one of the saints called Faolán, meaning 'little wolf'. When, as often happens, there are several saints of the same name, an effective way of distinction and identification is the 'day' recorded as proper to the saint in question, i.e. the day of his death. This was the day on which the saint's festival fell, and as a rule it has been handed down with wonderful fidelity. Sixteen saints bore the name of Faolán, but Faolán of Strath Fillan's day was January 9, according to the Aberdeen Breviary, and this is confirmed by the fact that his fair, Féill Fhaoláin, was held at Killin on that day. This identifies him with Faolán, the saint of Cill Fhaoláin, Kilillan, in Kintail. His mother, Cáintigerna (Kentigerna), was a princess of Leinster, and her death is recorded in the Annals of Ulster at AD734. The Aberdeen Breviary gives the legend, which may be true, how Kentigerna, with her son Faolán and his uncle Comgan, fled from Leinster to Lochalsh, of which church Comgan is patron, while the lady is commemorated by the ancient church of Cill Chaointiorn, on the south side of Loch Duich. The saint of St Fillan's, near the foot of Loch Earn, was a different and much earlier Faolán, whose day was June 20.

That a strath should be named after a saint may sound somewhat strange, but reference to my recent book on our Celtic Place-Names will show that such names are not unknown. The site of St Fillan's Church and of the ancient monastery of Glen Dochart is now called in Gaelic *an Clachán* or *Clachán Shraitheo*, where *Sraitheo* is the local pronunciation of *Sraithibh*, '(at) Straths', the dative-locative plural of *srath*. A lament for Gille-easbuig MacCaluim, a huntsman in Benmore of Glen Dochart, composed by his wife, has—

> 'Thug mi giùlan do Shraithibh
> A rinn mo sgathadh gu truagh;
> Thug mi giùlan an Caorann
> A chaochail mo shnuadh.'

'I brought a burden to Sraithibh (Straths) that wounded me sadly; I brought a burden to Caorann that altered my hue' (Gillies's Collection, p54). That is to say, her husband was buried in

St Fillan's graveyard, where, if I recollect rightly, there are still rowan trees. A poem on the persecution of the MacGregors has—

'Cha d' fhuair mi d' an sgeula
Ach iad bhi 'n dé air na Sraithibh.'

'All that I heard of their story is that they were yesterday in Strath Fillan' (Turner's Collection, p283). Very little is known, to me at least, of the monastery. An important and interesting reference to its abbot occurs in a statute of King David I (AD 1124-53), which sets forth the proceedings with regard to stolen cattle (*de catallo furato*). 'And gif he that is challangyt callis ony man till his warrand in Ergyl quhilk pertenis to Scotland, than sall he cum to the erle of Atholl or to the abbot of Glendochir, and thai sall send wyth hym thar men that sall ber witnes to the forsayd assise' (Acts of Parliament, vol 1, p372 *red*)[1].

This does not necessarily mean that the abbot in King David's time was an ecclesiastic personage: he may very well have been a lay abbot, who possessed the patrimony of the old monastery. It is fairly certain that the Macnab chiefs were descended from the lay abbot of Glen Dochart. An early—if not the earliest—mention of Macnab occurs in the Index to Missing Charters, printed in vol 1 of the Register of the Great Seal of Scotland as under the reign of David II (AD 1328-70): 'to Gilbert Macnab and his heirs whosoever of all and several the lands of Bovain [Bo-vàin, Both mheadhoin] in the lordship of Glendochard.' On February 26 1317-18, King Robert I made a grant to the abbot and convent of Inchaffray of the right of patronage (*ius patronatus*) of the Church of Killin in Glen Dochart, on the condition that the abbot and convent would provide a canon to officiate in the Church of Strathfillan (Strathfulane). In October of the same year the Bishop of Dunkeld, an intimate friend of King Robert, granted the Church of Killin with all its lands, fruits, revenues, to the prior and canons

1 The Latin text is:—'Si calumpniatus aliquem warrantum vocaverit in Ergadia que pertinet ad Scotiam tunc veniat ad comitem Atholie et ad abbatem de Glendocheroch et ipsi mittent cum eo homines qui testentur super dictam assisam.'

of Inchaffray, who should be appointed by the abbot of Inchaffray to serve in the chapel of St Fillan in Glen Dochart (Charters of Inchaffray). The prior of St Fillan's chapel was to be presented by the abbot and convent and instituted by the bishop. The vicarage of Killin was to be served by a canon or by a secular chaplain. Thus St Fillan's chapel or church in Strathfillan, instead of becoming an appanage of Killin as at first proposed, was made into a priory and endowed with the patrimony of the Church of Killin. These second thoughts may well have been prompted, as the Introduction to the Inchaffray Charters suggests, by gratitude to St Fillan, whose armbone (according to Boece) was venerated by Bruce on the night before the battle of Bannockburn[1].

A pool in the river below the old church or priory is known as Linne Fhaoláin. Here lunatics used once to be immersed, but for this and other traditions I must refer to Mr James MacDiarmid's excellent paper in vol 26 of our *Transactions* [*of the Gaelic Society of Inverness*]. St Fillan's relics were in the custody of several men in Glen Dochart styled *deòradh* or *deòr*, anglicized as Dewar, and each of them appears to have held a croft in respect of his custodianship. The keeper of the bell was Deòr a' Bheàrnain (Dewar of the Gapped one), and his croft was at *an Suidhe*, St Fillan's Seat, spelled in English Suie; where there are a cemetery and the remains of a chapel. Another Dewar's croft was connected with Caibeal na Fairge, probably 'chapel of the shrine', the walls of which still stand at Auchlyne. A third was in Acharn, near Killin; the relic preserved here may have been St Fillan's arm. Within the memory of men still living the mill on Dochart at Killin ground no meal on St Fillan's day. East of Killin there are no traces of the saint so far as known to me.

Killin is in Gaelic *Cill fhinn*, and there are at least three other places of the same name, one at Garve, one in Stratherrick, and one beside Loch Freuchie (Loch Fraochaidh) in Glen Quaich, Amulree. The second part *finn* may be the short form of a saint's

---

1 Compare CPNS, p285. The mention of the armbone is in favour of St Fillan of Glen Dochart.)

name in the genitive case—nom., Fionn; gen., Finn; e.g. Findbarr might be reduced to Fionn, and we find both Gillefin and the corresponding Welsh form Gilguyn about 1166 and 1296 respectively in the Holyrood Charters. Another and perhaps more likely explanation is to take *finn* as dative singular feminine, agreeing with *cill*, and to translate the name as 'at white church' or 'holy, blessed church'. In that case Fionnlairig, Finlarig, near by, might be suggested to mean 'holy pass' rather than 'white pass'. The ancient stone font of Killin is now honourably placed within the church, and regularly used at baptisms.

On the north side of Loch Tay, on the farm of Morenish and not far from the loch, is the venerable burial place known as Cladh Da Bhì, 'thy Bì's cemetery'. It stands on a flat, and is surrounded by a modern wall; its interior is much higher than the surface of the ground outside. A little way to the north there is a knoll called Tom a' Chluig, the knoll of the bell: but the bell that once sounded there has disappeared. Cladh Da Bhì was the burial place of the MacDiarmids of Glen Lochay, an old sept, and in particular of those MacDiarmids who were styled *rìoghail*, royal. There were two sections of the Clan MacDiarmid, the one called *rìoghail* and the other *dubh-bhusach*, black-mouthed, and according to tradition none of the latter were allowed to be buried here. Another burial place of the same name is stated on good authority to have been near Stix, close to the eastern entrance to Taymouth grounds, but no trace of it exists now. An interesting tradition relating to the latter is given in *Celtic Place-Names* (p308), and I happened to discover recently that the same tradition is told of Cill Da Bhì, Kildavie, in Kintyre. Da Bhì is a variant of Mo Bhì, my Bì, just as we find Mo Laise and Do Laise, my Laise and thy Laise, but we have no data to identify the saint with certainty.

In his poem entitled 'An Airc,' Alexander MacDonald has the verse—

> 'Ma thàrras tu fear Choire Chunna,
> Na fàg fa chunnart nan tonn e;

Thoir air bòrd a steach an duine ud,
Is buin ris urramach neo-lombais.'

'If you chance on the laird of Coire Chunna,
Leave him not at the mercy of the waves;
Bring that man on board your ship,
And deal with him respectfully and generously.'

Coire Chunna, or as it appears on maps Car-whin, is, or was, the name of a large township to the west of Lawers. I am not sure of the exact position of the corrie itself, but it gets its name from a saint called Cunne or Cunna, who is commemorated in Glen Lyon by the ancient cemetery known as Cladh Chunna, near Invervar. He appears in the Irish Calendars as Do Chunne at Sept 6, but I have met no account of him otherwise.

Opposite Ardeonaig, and between Morenish and Lawers Burn, is Baile na h-Annaid, the stead of the Annat. There is no trace whatever of the ancient church or cell which must have stood here, nor is there even a trace of the burial place to be seen on the surface of the ground. Stone coffins, however, have been found in front of the farmhouse, and Mr Duncan MacDonald, the tenant, when I visited the place, told me that his plough sometimes met them, and that they were also found within his garden. I heard no tradition apart from this. The site is most pleasant, snug and sunny—what an old poet called *buaile gréine*, a fold of sun.

Another and more recent burial place, called Cladh Phobuil, was at the south-east corner of Baile nan Sum, Balnasuim, 'stead of the soums' or soumings, close to the loch side. I have not seen it, but I am told that very little trace of it remains. Cladh Phobuil is probably to be compared with Ir. *teach pobail*, a church or chapel, rather than *pubal*, fem., a hut, tent.

On the left side of the Lawers Burn, just where it enters Loch Tay, is a burial place now in use and well tended, called Cladh Machuim; in Gaelic, Cladh Magh Thuaim, the burial place of the plain of (the) *tuam*. *Tuam* or *tuama* means a grave or place of burial, as in Màiri Nighean Alasdair Ruaidh's 'Cumha do MhacLeòid'—

> 'Gun do chorp a bhith as dùthaich
> Anns an tuama bu dual duit'

'that your body is not within the countryside in the sepulchre of your ancestors'. 'Colum Cille nam feart 's nan tuam', 'Colum Cille of the graves and sepulchres', occurs in *Carmina Gadelica*, vol 1, p248. Thus Cladh Magh Thuaim means 'the burial place of the plain, or flat, of the place of burial'. *Cladh* and *tuam* mean much the same thing, only that strictly speaking *tuam* is a single grave, while *cladh* is a graveyard. Close by the graveyard, but on the right side of the burn, is the old church of Lawers, built in 1669. A great part of the roof still holds good. The timber was taken, as I was told, all the way from the Black Wood of Rannoch across Làirig Chalabha, the pass from Rannoch to Glen Lyon, and thence by Làirig an Lochá to Loch Tay side. In fastening the timbers together no iron was used, but wooden pins only, as may still be seen. A few yards to the west of the church is the two-storeyed old house of Lawers, now roofless.

On the farm of Borland, near Fearnan, there was once a chapel of St Ciaran, which stood on the left side of the road that leads to the farmhouse, and a little way from where it leaves the public road from Fearnan to Fortingall. Its position can still be traced when the field is under young corn by the difference in colour. Between the site of the chapel and the public road by the loch side there is Dail Chiarain, Ciaran's meadow. The font of the old chapel was taken to Taymouth Castle, but Mr Alexander Campbell, now proprietor of Borland, recovered it and placed it with a suitable inscription by the roadside, close to the site of the chapel. Mr Campbell, I may mention, is the eighth Campbell in lineal descent to occupy the farm of Borland, and he and Mr James MacDiarmid are the two most learned and accurate native authorities now living on all that pertains to Breadalbane. In the immediate neighbourhood, but in the parish of Fortingall, there is on the farm of Duneaves a field beside Lyon, called Dail Chiarain, which was probably part of the patrimony of the chapel of Borland. The saint commemorated here is probably Ciaran of Cluain Mac Nois, known as Ciaran mac an t-Saoir, 'son of the artificer, wright, or carpenter'. He died in AD 549.

Close by the site of the chapel on Borland is Clach na Triuthaich, Stone of the Measles, a large stone, somewhat chair-shaped, with a square cavity containing water. On the upper surface of the stone there are faint traces of cup marks. The water in the cavity was held to cure measles. The stone has been described by Rev Hugh Macmillan in *Proceedings of the Scottish Society of Antiquaries*, vol 18, p369. He gives its name as Clach na Cruich (i.e. Cruthaich, Criuthaich), and I was informed that in the district this was an old name for measles. He also describes a stone in the woods of Auchmore at Killin called 'Fuaran na Druidh Chasad', or the 'Well of the Whooping Cough', but of it I failed to find tradition.

The pleasant hamlet of Fearnan was formerly known as Sròn Feàrnain, Point of Fearnan, for the district of Fearnan included much more than the present township. The old village of Stronfearnan, long vanished, stood about the present burial ground, which is known as Cladh na Sròine. It is a small rectangular walled enclosure without any ecclesiastical associations so far as I could learn. It probably dates from the time when St Ciaran's chapel and cemetery on Borland began to be disused.

At the lower end of the loch and near the north side of it is the Isle of Loch Tay, often mentioned in charters and elsewhere. It is little more than an acre in extent, more or less round in shape, and well wooded. Here Sybilla, wife of Alexander I, and natural daughter of Henry I of England, died on June 12, 1122, and here she was buried. It was King Alexander who founded the abbey of Scone, and after his wife's death he granted the Isle to the monks of Scone, and founded thereon the priory of Loch Tay. The history of the priory and of the Isle, so far as known, is sketched by John Christie in his valuable little book, *The Lairds and Lands of Loch Tayside*. It continued to be a religious establishment for over three hundred years, but for a considerable part of that time it appears to have been occupied by nuns. The late Mr Gilbert Christie of Auchlyne, in Glen Dochart, gave me the name of the Isle as Eilean nam Bannaomh, the Isle of the female saints. He was then ninety-five years of age, hale and vigorous of mind. Féill nam Bannaomh, one of the Kenmore fairs, used to be held on July 26.

The old parish church of Kenmore was at Inchadney, at the apex of a small peninsula formed by the Tay just east of the Castle, and on the north side of the river. The sad story of its disuse about 1762, and its subsequent demolition and the desecration of its graveyard, is told by Mr John Christie in the book mentioned. He and others were of opinion that Inchadney contains the name of Aidan, whom he calls the titular saint of Kenmore. This is, however, impossible. Aidan or Aedan is the old Irish spelling of a name which would now be Aodhan, a diminutive of Aodh, familiar in the name MacAoidh, Mackay. Thus, if the name contained Aidan, it would now be in Gaelic Innis Aodhain, whereas it is well known to the older folk as Innis Chailtnidh; the younger speakers tend to make it Innis Chaitnidh or Chaidnidh. Who the real titular saint of Kenmore is I do not know, unless he is Mo Bhì, already mentioned, whose original church is supposed to have been on the south side of Tay, not quite opposite to Inchadney, but further to the east.

On the south side of Loch Tay the only church site is at Ardeonaig, Aird Eódhnaig, formerly on record as Ardewnan. The meaning is 'Adamnan's promontory'. Adamnan, the ninth abbot of Iona, is regularly in Gaelic *Eódhnan* as, for instance, Muileann Eódhnain, Adamnan's Mill, near Bridge of Balgie, in Glen Lyon; Croit Eódhnain, Adamnan's Croft, in Glen Falloch; Tom Eódhnain, Adamnan's Knoll, at Insh in Badenoch. Mr James MacDiarmid relates the tradition how, when St Fillan came to Breadalbane, he was accompanied by Adamnan from Iona, and how, when they came to Carn Droma, they cast lots as to which of them should hold on by Glen Dochart and which should turn to Glen Lyon. Glen Lyon fell to Adamnan, Breadalbane to Fillan. Now, though we need not take this tradition as historical fact, it is not so impossible in point of chronology as some such traditions are. Adamnan died in AD704; Fillan's mother died in AD734. If we suppose her to have been eighty when she died, a little calculation will show that her son may have been about thirty at the time of Adamnan's death. In any case the two saints, Adamnan and Fillan, were contemporary for some considerable part of their lives, and in all probability were known to each other. The church of Ardeonaig is Cill Mo Charmaig, my Cormac's Church. Cormac was a common Irish name, and there is nothing to show which particular Cormac is commemorated here. But as I have suggested elsewhere, he was probably from Iona, and one of Adamnan's monks (CPNS, p149). In Glen Lochay there is Coire Charmaig, which may be named after him as Coire Chunna is named after Cunna whose cemetery is in Glen Lyon. It is worth noting that the glen behind Ardeonaig is called Fionnghleann, meaning probably 'holy glen' rather than 'white glen' or 'bright glen.' The clerics of the early Church showed here their usual good sense in choice of a site, for Ardeonaig is certainly the most attractive, as well as the most central, spot on this side of the loch.

With the possible exception of Coire Charmaig, there are no traces of the old Church in Glen Lochay.

On the west, Breadalbane is bounded by the mountain range, running roughly north and south, which Adamnan calls in Latin Dorsum Britanniæ, Britanniæ Dorsum, Dorsum Britannicum, 'the dorsal ridge of Britain'. In Adamnan's time, and long after it, Alba, which is now the Gaelic name for Scotland, denoted the whole of Britain; there was no special name for Scotland, for the good reason that our Scotland, as distinct from England, did not then exist as a political entity. His Dorsum Britanniæ is a translation of the Gaelic Druim Alban, but as it happens the mountain range so named is confined geographically to that part of Britain or Alba which is now Scotland, and thus we translate the term as 'the backbone, or dorsal ridge, of Scotland'. This range is pierced by several passes, some of which offer no difficulty to travellers. Of these one is the pass from the west to Dalmally and thence either up Glen Orchy and down Glen Lyon, or by way of Tyndrum down Glen Dochart. I am told that of these alternative routes that by way of Glen Orchy and Glen Lyon was the usual one, within the last few centuries at least. The early clerics appear to have used both. Another easy pass is that from the west to Inverness by way of the Great Glen, and this was the way by which Columba came to Inverness. A third is the route now traversed by the railway from Dingwall to Kyle, from which another pass branches off at Achnasheen, leading to Kinlochewe and the sea. A fourth is the pass from Lochinver—or for that matter from Lochbroom—to the valley of the Oykel river, which enters the Dornoch Firth. Both of the latter two were probably traversed by Maelruba of Applecross. The first two go through regions of old and nearly continuous habitation; none of the four or five is nearly so formidable as the high and desolate crossing over Druim-uachdar.

The western limit of Breadalbane was the scene of Robert Bruce's fight with Argyll's men after the battle of Methven in 1306 and the memory of that encounter is preserved by the name Dail an Righ, the king's meadow, by the river side just east of Tyndrum. I have tried to show that the neighbourhood of the small loch that lies west of Tyndrum was the scene of a much earlier battle, which took place in AD729, between Nechtan, king of the Picts, and the Pictish lord from the eastern midlands, Oengus, son of Fergus (CPNS, p401). This battle was fought near a loch called Loch Loogdae, or, as we should say now, Loch Lòchaidh; the name of the Tyndrum loch now is Lochan na Bì, 'the lochlet of pitch-pine', but the stream from it is called Lòchaidh. Further, the battle is named by the Irish authorities, 'bellum Monith Carno', and by the Welsh chronicle, 'bellum montis Carno', i.e. it took place on hill ground distinguished by a cairn or cairns. There seems to be no spot in Scotland north of Forth which satisfies all the conditions except this one which I suggest. In this connection it is of interest to note that the old name for Clifton, just west of Tyndrum, was Achadh nan Tuirighnean, which means 'field of the kings', from an old Irish word for king. I had this from the late Mr Archibald Fletcher of Auchtertyre, in Strath Fillan, a gentleman of the old stock of the Fletchers of Glen Orchy. Of course he had no idea what the name meant. Auchtertyre is in Gaelic *Uachdar thìre*, 'upper part of the land or district', which well describes it. In Strath Tay there is *Iochdar thìre*, 'lower part of the land', made now in English into Eastertyre. There is another Auchtertyre of the same meaning in Lochalsh.

Glen Dochart is named after its river, which is the same as the Renfrewshire river Cart, with prefix *do-*, 'evil'; *cartaim*, I cleanse; Welsh *carthu*, purge; 'ag cartadh a' bhàthaich', 'cleaning out the byre'. Dochart means 'evil-scourer', with reference to its rough rapids near Killin. Similarly we have Gleann Dochartaich, at the head of Loch Maree.

For Lòchá, Lochay, at Killin and Tyndrum, 'black goddess', and for Tatha, O. Ir. Tóe, 'silent one', see CPNS.

Coninnis means 'hound meadow'; it is the same name really as Connage.

Iuich, which might be spelled in Gaelic, Iuthaich, is rather an obscure name; possibly 'yew-place', from Irish *eo*, a yew tree.

Inverhervie is locally taken to mean 'bull's confluence', but the pronunciation, *Inbhir h-eirbhe*, rather suggests eirbhe, a fence or wall, as in Allt na h-eirbhe, Altnaharra, 'burn of the wall'.

Inverhaggernie is in Gaelic, Inbhir Chagarnaidh, meaning, as I suppose, 'confluence of the whispering stream'.

Crianlaraich, at the upper end of Glen Falloch, is Crithionnlaraich, 'aspen-site', with stress, of course, on the first part of the compound. Cf Eigintoll, 'difficulty hole'; etc (noun + noun).

Glen Falloch itself is Gleann Falach, and sometimes supposed to mean 'hidden glen' or 'glen of hiding'. In my opinion the second part is the genitive singular of *fail*, a ring, common in Irish Gaelic. The circumstance to which the name is owing can only be matter of speculation, like Gleann Cochuill, 'glen of the cowl or hood', between Aberfeldy and Strath Braan. Cf Cluain Falach, *Acall.*, l. 4487.

Inverardran is for Inbhir Arddobhrain, confluence of the high streamlet, with reference to its source.

Auchessan is 'field of the little waterfall'.

Coire Sheanain is probably Seanan's Corrie, from a man's name.

Innis Eoghain, Innishewan, is Eoghan's meadow.

Luib is 'loop or green bend'.

Both Uachdar, Bowachter, is 'upper hut'; further along is Both Mheadhoin, Bovain, 'middle hut', from the fourteenth century onwards the seat of Macnab. I could not find out where the third *Both* is. In Glen Lednock, above Comrie, there is another Both Uachdar, made into Bowalker in English, and on maps styled Botnah-Acaire.

Leathad Charraigh, Ledchary, is 'slope of the pillarstone', or 'of the rock'.

Lianghartan apparently means 'flax field'.

Auchlyne, the best farm in Glen Dochart, is in Gaelic, *Achloinne*, which I took to mean 'pleasant field'. The tenant, Mr Gilbert Christie, the venerable man already mentioned, disagreed with this, and would divide the name as *Ath-chloinne*, 'the children's ford', with reference to the drowning of some children in the river. The name, however, is old, and the tale about the children is probably folk-etymology. Further, the full form *Achadh loinne* occurs in the rhyme quoted later on.

Ardchoille, Ardchyle, 'high wood', is a name well known in connection with the MacGregors. It is a cheerful little crofting hamlet, and when I used to frequent Glen Dochart it was the only place where one saw children. From Killin to Innishewan, on the north side of the glen, a distance of eight miles or more, there was only one child, and *he* was adopted.

Craoit Chòis, Croftchose, 'croft of the nook'. Such is the local pronunciation of *croit*, the *aoi* being short.

Creag Nèamhaidh, Craignavie, 'heavenly rock,' is traditionally said to have been a preaching station of St Fillan.

Lix is the English plural of *Lic*, the dative singular of *leac*, a flagstone, also a hard slope, as in Leac Ruaidh at the head of Glen

Roy. The latter is the meaning here. There are Easter, Wester, and Mid Lix; Easter Lix is called Toll Lic. An Argyll man of my acquaintance used to declare that Lix got its name from the fact that a milestone there bore the inscription LIX—a fact which I failed to verify, for a good reason.

The following tale was given me first by Mr Gilbert Christie, who wrote down the Gaelic part of it for me in his house at Auchlyne, and quite lately by Mr Alexander Campbell of Borland. Two Highlanders met in Lower Canada during the French War, and on one asking the other where he came from, the answer was, 'from Glen Dochart'. The other asked him to mention some names to prove it, and he replied [with a list of names of places] as follows:–

> 'Tha Fas a' Ghràig an Leathad a' Charraigh,
> Is Coille Chasaidh an Ardchoille,
> Caibeal na Fairc(e) an Achadh-loinne,
> Tom an Taghain 's Meall na Samhna,
> Lochan nan Arm anns an t-Suidhe,
> Is Tom Ruigh an Innis Eoghain,
> Dail Clachaig am Both Uachdair,
> Is daimh air cruachain Beinne Móire.'

The second man, being asked to prove his connection with the district, replied thus:–

> 'Tha Allt an Tuairneir an Lic Uachdarach—
> Is luath e 'nar théid e 'na shiubhal;
> Ach théid an Righ fo an t-sluasaid,
> Ge luath e, mun ruig a an Suidhe.'

'The Turner's Burn is in Upper Lick—it is full swift when it gets a-going; but the king will go beneath the shovel, for all its swiftness, ere it reaches Suie.' The point of the latter lines is that in order to reach Suie the burn would have to alter its course, and incidentally to do some work against the force of gravitation—the man thus proving knowledge of the ground.

The following are additional names. Names in Glen Dochart are marked (1), Glen Lochay (2), north side of Loch Tay (Deisir Locha Tatha) (3), south side (Tuathair) (4):–

Ach' Chomair (4), field of the confluence, i.e. of the Ardtalnaig and Glen Cloy burns.

Ach'-ianaich (3), field of fowling.

Ach' mór (3), big field.

Ach' riabhach, Achrioch (1), brindled field.

Allt a' Bhealaich, burn of the pass, on Duithnis.

Allt a' Mhinn (3), goat kid's burn.

Allt na Breaclaich (4), for Allt na Breacthulaich, burn of the spotted hill. So Lochan na Fuar'laich, lochlet of the cold hill, behind Rosehall, Sutherland; Dail Chiar'laich, meadow of the swart hill, Glen Lyon. In Older Gaelic *tulach* is feminine.

Allt Dubhchlair (2), burn of the black flat.

Allt M(h)ucaidh (3), swine burn; *mhucaidh* is from *muc*, with the common adjectival suffix *-de*, *-da*, as in *diade*, *diadha*, our *diadhaidh*.

Allt Phadairligh (3), Padderlie's burn, now the western march of Borland. Padairligh was a noted ùruisg [water-demon].

Allt an Tuilbheum (3), burn of the flood-breach, just west of Fearnan; so named from a breach caused by a heavy flood in the old aqueduct or mill lade which slants down the hillside west of Borland farm-house.

Allt an t-Sleaghaich (4), burn of the rifted place; so An Sleaghach, Slioch, on Loch Maree, from its rifted sides.

Am Fichead Sgillinn (4), the twenty pennies, is the designation of a farm in Ardeonaig.

Ard-radnaig (4), is obscure to me.

Ard-talnaig or Ard-talanaig (4), also obscure. 'Height of the castle (talla) of Eonan', offered by J. B. Johnston, is, of course, impossible. There are capes at Ard-radnaig and here. Record forms are Ardentollenie 1536; Ardtollony 1564, 1573 (RMS); Ardeintollene 1630; Ardintollanie 1640 (Ret.).

Ath Bun-deòra, ford of dewar-foot; Ath-chuirn, ford of the cairn; Ath Both-(sh)lànaigh, ford of ... hut; Ath Leathan, broad ford (Kirkton); Ath Léig, marsh ford, from *léag*, a swamp or marsh: an Ath fhiar (dative), the slanting ford; Ath nan Craobh Darach, oak-trees ford; Ath Phadaidh, Patie's ford; an Ath Ruadh (dative), the red ford—all on the river Dochart; unfortunately I have not noted their position.

Ath a' Chairn, Acharn (4), ford of the cairn. Acharn (1), Ach' a' chairn, field of the cairn.

Ath na Cairidh (4), ford of the fish-weir; near Kenmore.

Bad Odhar, Badour (2), the dun spot or clump; mentioned by Donnchadh Bàn.

Bad a' Mhaim, Badvaim (2), spot or clump of the rounded hillock.

Baile an Fhraoich, Balnreich (3), heather stead.

Baile an Fheàrna, Balnearn (3), alder stead.

Baile MacNeachdain, Balmacnaughton (4), MacNaughton's stead. Otherwise An Dà Fhichead Sgillinn, the forty shillings.

Bealach, or in full Bealach nan Laogh, the calves' pass; Taymouth, the seat of MacGregor before it passed to the Campbells. The name is regularly Bealach, not Am Bealach.

Beinn Sheasgarnaich (2), peak of Seasgarnach, i.e. sheltered place, in its lee.

Blàr Liaragain (3), moor of Liaragan, perhaps from *liarag*, some sort of weed; cf Creag Liarag.

Beinn nan Iomairean (2), peak of the rigs or ridges; behind Inverhaggernie, on the Glen Lochay side.

Am Borlainn, A' Bhorlainn, Borland (3), the board-land or mensal land of Robertson of Struan, who had a residence at Fearnan, close by. On Borland are: Garbh Cheathramh, rough quarter; Rinn a' Chroisg, point of the crossing; Croit an Ailein, croft of the meadow (east of Borland farmhouse and north of the farm road); Dail Chiarain, St Ciaran's meadow (at Borland gate); Cladh Chiarain, St Ciaran's graveyard (near the former, but now cultivated).

Both-tuarnaigh (2); meaning uncertain; may be based on *tuar*, food, or, more probably, on *tuathair*, northern aspect.

Bràigh an Trithinn (4), upland of the third part; Middle-third appears on record hereabout. For Sgeir an Trithinn, in Gairloch Bay; see PNRC.

Bràigh a' Bhaile, Braeval (1), upland of the homestead.

Cail Eileachan, Callelochan (4), damp meadow of Eileachan, i.e. little *eileach*, mill-lade; cf Baile an Eilich, in Glen Fincastle. On Cail Eileachan are Leothad a' Chaisteil, slope of the castle; Tom a' Chaisteil, knoll of the castle.

Caisteal an Radhair, castle of the pasture slope, is the name of a fort on the hill-side westward from Ardeonaig.

Ceannchnoc, Kenknock (2), head hill; situated in Glen Lochay as is Ceannchnoc in Glen Lyon, forming a partial barrier about the middle of the glens.

An Ceannmhor, Kenmore, at foot of Loch Tay, 'the bigheaded (place)', the adjective being used as a noun. Tigh Mór a' Cheannmhoir is Kenmore Hotel. Another Ceannmhor, Kenmore, on Loch Fyne, is, if I remember rightly, feminine—A' Cheannmhor. Kenmure in Galloway is the same name, stressed on first part, as are the others.

A' Chail Fhinn, the white meadow, fair meadow (dative), is the name of Glen of Ardtalnaig. Cail, a damp meadow, is not uncommon in Perthshire, e.g. Cail Bhruair and Cail Mhinn (Calvine) in Blair-Atholl; Coille na Calach, wood of the damp meadow, south-east of Coshieville. A northern example is Cail Fhraochaidh, Heathfield, in Kilmuir Easter, Ross-shire.

A' Chaiteag Shìomain, or A' Chaiteag, west of Meall nan Tarmachan, Hill of the Ptarmigan, is so named from its likeness to a round heap of corn, kept in place by a straw rope. This was the explanation given me by Mr James MacDiarmid.

Camus (a') Churaich, Camusurich (4), bay of the curach or coracle.

Càraidh and Muileann Càraidh, Carie (3); probably from *càthar*, mossy ground; i.e. dative-locative of *càthrach*, mossy place.

Cathair an Rìgh, the king's seat, is above Morenish.

Cinn Alla, Kinnell, near Killin, at head of rock or crag (*all*). Kinnoul, near Perth, is the same in Gaelic.

Clach MhicRèill, MacNeil's stone, is a boulder fairly high up on the NW part of Borland. Bàta MhicRèill, MacNeil's Boat, is a ferry below Ballinluig. Tomcrail, near Killiecrankie, is in Gaelic Tom MhicRèill, MacNeil's Knoll—all with change of *n* to *r*.

Claigionn, Clagan (4), (the) skull, from a skull-shaped knoll. Blæu's Atlas has Piercuil, i.e. Peirceall, jaw, east of Acharn Burn.

Claon Labhair Shìos (Ballinluig) and Claon Labhair Shuas (3), slope of Lower and of Upper Lawers.

Cloichearan, shortened Cloichran (4), little causeway or stepping-stones: cf Baile Chloichrigh, Pitlochry.

Coire Charmaig (2), Cormac's Corrie; mentioned by Iain Lom in connection with the fight of Sròn a' Chlachain, and also by William Ross.

Coire Cheathaich (2), corrie of the mist, famed by Donnchadh Bàn. An older name for it appears to have been An Coire Altruim, 'the Nursery', the latter appearing on an old map.

Cragan, Craggan (4), little rock or rocky knoll.

Cragan Easdair, Cragganester (3), little rock of fall-water—*easdobhar*. The stream close by forms a succession of waterfalls.

Cragan an Ruathair (3), little rock of the onset: cf Blàr an Ruathair, Blairnroar, S of Comrie.

Cragan Toll, Craggantoll (3), rock of holes. It has a very large number of interesting cupmarks, the largest number I have ever seen together. Cloich Phollaich, Clochfoldich, in Strath Tay, is named after a cupmarked stone near the farm-house;

see CPNS, p512. There are many stones so marked in the Loch Tay district.

Creag Iubhair (1), yew tree rock.

A' Chreag Loisgte (1), the burnt rock, below Beinn Chaluim, Calum's peak.

Creag Liarag (1), opposite Sloc a' Ghuir in Ben More; cf Liaragan. Below the rock is An Liaran, an old shieling.

Crannaich, Crannich (3), tree-place; so in Strath Conon and in Rosskeen.

Creag a' Mhionaich (3), rock of the entrails, so called from irony water oozing from the rock.

Craoit an Taghain, Croftintygan (3), croft of the marten.

Craoit a' Bhealaich, Croftvellich (3), croft of the pass.

Cromalltan (4), bent little burn; near Styx.

Cùil-tìridh, Kiltyrie (3), nook of parching of corn (*tìreadh*). A spot on this place is locally reckoned the central point of Scotland.

Na Cùiltean (3), the nooks; near Cloichearan; cùilt is common in Perthshire, with *ù* long, shortened in unstressed position. Cults, Aberdeenshire, is the Englished plural. Cùil an t-Seogail, Coilantogle, rye nook, on Loch Vennachar, was of old Cùilt an t-Seogail.

A' Chùilt Raithnich, Cuiltrannich (3), the nook of bracken. For the formation compare An Lòn Roid, the bog myrtle meadow, Boath, Alness; An t-Allt Giuthais, on the way from Garve to Ullapool; 'an leabhar Psalm-so Dhaibhioth', 'this Psalm-book of David' (Robert Kirk).

Cuingleitir, Coiletter (1), defile-slope; a compound of *cong*, a narrow, a strait defile, as in Cuingleum, Coylum. A very narrow-passage leading to a landing place for boats at Gob na Heiste Duirinish, Skye, is called An Cuing; still used in this sense in Lewis Gaelic: M. Ir. *conc*.

Dal-drabhaig, Baldravaig (2); uncertain. Mr James MacDiarmid suggested that *drabhag* may mean 'refuse' (left by the river). Another suggestion is *drabhag*, a slattern, used as a nickname. *Dal* is for older *dul*, a flat, a meadow, not Norse *dalr*.

An Dail, Dall (4), the meadow; 'Baran crìon na Dalach' was a suitor for the hand of Gregor MacGregor's wife; *Bàrd. Ghàidhlig*, pp245, 329. So Baile na Dalach, Balindalloch.

Dail na(n) Gothach (1), on Achriach: *gothach* (from *guth*, voice; genitive *gotha*) is the reed of a bagpipe; here it may mean 'talkative person, gossip, babbler'.

Dewarnafergus Croft (1), croft of the 'dewar' of the *fairge*, a relic of St Fillan, was within the ten-merk land of Auchlyne; Caibeal na Fairge, on Auchlyne, has been mentioned above.

Druim Glas, Drumglas (3), the green ridge.

Dubh Ailean, Duallin (3), black meadow. Owing to the stress on *dubh* (the qualifying term), initial *à* of *àilean* is sometimes shortened. Compare Croit an àilein above.

An Duibhnis (1), the dark or black meadow—*dubh* and *inis*.

Dùn (a') Chroisg, Duncrosk (2), fort of the crossing, i.e. Làirig Bhreislich.

Dùn Mac Tuathail (3), fort of Tuathal's son, the fort on the eastern end of Drummond Hill. The Annals of Ulster record the death of Tuathal. son of Artgus, chief bishop of Fortriu and abbot of Dun Caillenn (Dunkeld) in 865; but as Tuathal was a common personal name, no inference can be drawn. Old Welsh Tudgual.

Eadra-ghobhal, Eddragoul (4), for eadar dà ghobhal, between two forks; lies between Cail Eileachan and Acharn, Loch Tay.

Eadra Mhucaidh, or Eadar 'a Mhucaidh, Edramucky (3), for eadar dà Mhucaidh, between two swine burns. Another stream named simply Muc is at Inbhir Mhuic, Innerwick, Glen Lyon.

Eilean nam Breaban, an artificial islet below Wester Carwhin.

Eilean Dhonnach' Dhuibh (3), Black Duncan's island, below Morenish. This is Sir Duncan Campbell of Glen Orchy, etc, who died in 1631.

Eilean Putachan, an isle near the east march of Finlarig (Christie).

Eilean Reamhainn (?), Eilean Rowan; Ilanran (RMS and Retours); near the junction of Lochay and Dochart, the site of a 'castle' of Macnab (Christie). I give the Gaelic form from memory.

Fearnan (3), alder place, probably reduced from a compound name. It was a thirty-merk land, extending from 'the west march of the Port of Loch Tay to Allt Paderleigh'—Christie. It was long held by Robertson of Struan, who had a house there, the site of which is still seen. His court was held at Tom a' Mhòid, near the house. A house which stands on this site has large portions of the Judge's Seat, Suidhe a' Bhritheimh, built into its walls. Lower down, just east of Tigh an Loan Hotel, is Tom na Croiche, where malefactors were hanged. The burial ground at Fearnan is Cladh na Sròine, burial ground of the point. The old village of Sròn Fearnain, long ago demolished, encircled this cemetery—Christie.

The market stance of Fearnan is supposed to be marked by Clach na Croise, Stone of the Cross, near the fifth milestone from Kenmore. On the shore of the loch, below Clach na Croise, there is a reef of rock called Creag Aimhreit, Rock of Discord; but I have not heard the tradition attached.

Allt Ruadh Fearnain, the red burn of Fearnan, east of the shepherd's house at Balnearn, rises in a well near the top of Borland hill, called Fuaran na Mòna Buidhe, and is noted for its good water. East of An t-Allt Ruadh is Allt na Taibhse, burn of the spectre, in English now 'the Bogle Burn'.

The brae at Fearnan on the road from the north is Bruthach Clach an Sgrìodain, the brae of the stone of the scree.

Fionnghleann (4); being above Ardeonaig and leading thereto, most probably means 'holy glen'; compare Fionnlairig, leading to Cill Fhinn, Killin.

Gleann a' Chlachain (1), glen of the Kirktown; its stream flows by St Fillan's Chapel.

Guala Dhochard (1), shoulder of Dochart; on the road, near Achmore; 'a bad place'.

Innis Bhuidhe (1), yellow isle, from the colour of its mosses, the Macnab burial place, in Dochart, just below the bridge as one enters Killin.

Innis Chaorach (2), at foot of Allt Caorach, probably from *caor*, a torrent.

Lagan Mhóirnis (3), hollow of Morenish.

Làirig Bhreislich (2), pass of rout or confusion, between Duncrosk and Bridge of Balgie.

Làirig Luaidhe (2), pass of lead, from Tir Aigh to Moar in Glen Lyon.

Làirig Mhic Bhàididh (2) MacWattie's pass, at head of Coire Cheathaich.

Làirig nan Lunn (2), pass of the staves, from Ceannchnoc to Pubal in Glen Lyon.

Labhar, Lawers (3), from the name of the stream, 'sounding one'; Welsh, *Llafar*; E. Celt., *Labara*. The divisions of Lawers are Labhar Shios, L. Shuas, and L. na Craoibhe, OSM Lawernacroy.

Leac Bhuidhe (4), Leckbuie, yellow hill-slope.

Leacainn, Leckine (1), hill-slope; dative-locative of *leac*; a cheek, hill-side. So 'the Leachkin', near Inverness.

Leitir Ailein, Letterellen (3), apparently Allan's slope. A *leitir* always slopes towards water, stream or loch; literally 'half-land', i.e. with land on one side; or, as Cormac had it: leitir i. leth-tirim 7 leth-fliuch. This traditional meaning was given me in my boyhood.

Lic, Lix (1); the plural English form is from the threefold division of Lic Iochdrach, L. Uachdrach, and L. Mheadonach, Lower, Upper, and Mid Lic (see pp176-77).

Loch Easan (1), waterfall loch; it is supposed to have a lake-dwelling.

Lochan na Bì (1), lochlet of bog fir; source of Lòchaidh Urchaidh, and of old called Loch Lòchaidh; see CPNS. Blàr na Bì, moor of the bog fir or pitch pine, is in Strath Conon.

Loch na Breaclaich (4), loch of the spotted hill or eminence (see p178).

Loch Iubhair (1), yew loch. The remains of MacGregor's residence are extant on an island in Loch Dochart, the western part of L. Iubhair. Mentioned in a poem to MacGregor in the *Book of the Dean of Lismore*.

Loch Màragan (1), the parent of Inverhaggernie Burn; possibly from *màthair*, mother; the source of Etive is *Màthair* Eite.

Lochan nan Arm (1), lochlet of the weapons; connected traditionally with the battle of Dail Rìgh (King Robert Bruce).

Lùb Churran (2), bend of wild carrots or radishes.

An Lùb Mór (1), the big loop or bend; a large park opposite Crianlarich.

Lurg Lomain(n), Lurglomand (4), shank or projecting spur of loman; *loman dearg* is used around Loch Tay to denote 'the edge of the deep water at the loch side'.

Magh-iarlanaich, plain or field of Iarlanach; probably from *iarlann*, west field.

Marg, a merk-land, common around Loch Tay. Christie has the following, most of which I have heard in Gaelic:– Marg Beag, M. Mór, M. na Crannaig, in Easter Ardeonaig; M. a' Chragain and M. an Easa, in Tirarthur; M. Cruaidh, on west end of Drummond Hill; M. Dubh, Ardeonaig; M. an Luig, in lands of Killin and of Morenish; M. an Tuim, near M. an Luig of Morenish (the Tom appears as Tomb); M. an t-Sruthain, Lawers; M. na Dalach, Dall; M. (a') Ghobhann, Killin; M. a'

Phuill, M. Dubh, M. na h-Atha (merk-land of the kiln), all belonged to Wester Carwhin.

Meall Ghaoirdidh (2); meaning uncertain; also Dail Ghaoirdidh.

Meall Greagh (3), mountain of studs of horses. Here horses used to be pastured in summer. It is east of Ben Lawers.

Mèillear Shìos and Mèillear Shuas, East and West Mèillear (3), the former on OSM, wrongly, Meall Odhar.

Monadh Mór, Monomor (1), big moor or hill land.

Móirnis, Morenish (3), contracted from *mór innis*, big meadow, owing to the stress on *mór*. The same elements result in Móiristi(dh), Morangie, Tain, with developed *t* and *insi*, the old dative of *inis, innis*.

Murlagan (2), contracted from *murbhalgan*, with metathesis of (*bh*)*algan*, the diminutive of *murbhalg*, 'a sea-bag', inlet. This term, primarily connected with the seacoast, has come to be used in inland names on loch and river—in this case the murbhalgan is a bight on the river Lochay. See CPNS, p79, ff.

Am Port, the Port of Loch Tay; there is also Am Port Bàn, the fair haven, near it.

Port an Eilein, Portnellan (1), haven of the island, Loch Iubhair.

An Réidhmhuin, Remony (4), the level brake or copse (*muine*). I have also heard it as in the anglicised form, i.e. Réimonaidh.

Rinn a' Chuilg (3), cape of the sharp point, between the two Morenish burns.

Ruighe a' Bhàird (4), the bard's reach or slope, on the south-east shoulder of Drummond Hill; probably connected with the official Bard of MacGregor at Bealach.

Seanlaraich, Shenlarich (3, 4), old stance or site.

Sgitheag and Baile na Sgitheag, Skiag (4), hawthorn, hawthorn stead.

Sleaghach, Sleoch (4), rifted or gullied place; part of the Macnab lands: also Allt an t-Sleaghaich above.

Sloc a' Ghuir (1), pit of brooding birds; on the west face of Ben More.

Sròn a' Chlachain, above Killin; scene of the battle in June 1646.

Na Stuicean, Na Stuiceannan, Styx, Stix (4), the stocks or stumps, i.e. most probably, of an old wood. There is also Stix at Killin.

An Socach, Succoth (4), the snouted place, a common name for the spit of land between two burns. Also Allt an t-Socaich.

Suidhe, Suie (1), (the) Seat; connected with St Fillan. For other examples see CPNS.

Tigh an Droma, Tyndrum (1), house of the ridge, the ridge being Druim Albann, the dividing range or watershed between the east and the west of Scotland—sometimes confused by modern writers with the range which divides north from south, known from of old as Monadh, now commonly called the Grampians.

Tigh an Fhraoich (1), house of heather, among the heather.

Tigh nam Feart (1), house of the graves; *feart* in place-names usually means 'grave', but the application here is uncertain.

An Tiobairt, the well, at Port Bàn, near Kenmore.

Tir-àidh, Tirai (2), land of good luck, prosperity; the best land in Glen Lochay, as I was told; *àdh*.

Tìr Artuir, Tirarthur (3), Arthur's land; who Arthur was is unknown.

Tom a' Mhòid, at Fearnan—see above.

Tom na Croiche, gallows-mound, at Killin and also in Taymouth Park and at Fearnan. Close to the first is Tom nan Giall, knoll of the hostages; so Cnoc nan Giall (Knocknagael), Inverness.

Tom Breac (3), spotted knoll.

Tom a' Chrochair, Tomcrocher (3), the hangman's knoll.

Tom nan Riadh, knoll of the stripes.

Tom nan Daisean (4), knoll of the ricks (hay or corn).

Tom Mhòrair (3), behind Cùil Tìridh; where Seumas Mór Mac Ghill-Fhionntaig, the last smuggler on Loch Tay side, had a still.

An Tulaich, Tullich (2, 4), the eminence, hill; here dative feminine, as usual in older Gaelic.

Tulaich-cann, Tullichcan (4), the second part (which may be *cannadh*) is uncertain to me.

Tulaich-chùil, Tullichuil (4), hill of or at the back; hind-hill. I have also heard Toll a' Chùil.

I will conclude this rather rambling discourse with a tale of Fionn in Glen Dochart. It is of interest as being one of the few accounts of the death of Fionn, and it agrees with the ancient Irish tales in that it makes Fionn's death due to a leap, sometimes styled in Irish, 'léim baoise', a leap of folly. This then is the tale:– Once on a time a certain man named Taileachd mac Cuilgeadain lived in Eilean Iubhair, near Ben More, in Glen Dochart, and he had a fairy sweetheart.

Now Fionn mac Cumhail got to know of the lady, and he went in to the Isle to see her, and he took pleasure in being with her. But at last Taileachd discovered that Fionn was often meeting his sweetheart, and when he had examined them both concerning the matter, he and Fionn grew so jealous of each other that they were like to fall to blows.

'Nay,' said the lady; 'I will make order for you, and be not angry with each other. The man who wins the victory in a leap, it is he that I will follow with pleasure.'

The warriors then went out to leap. Taileachd leaped from the Isle on to dry ground, and Fionn leaped nimbly after him. Then said Taileachd, 'I would leap the pool backwards, and unless you do the same, I shall have the fame by right.' They both leaped backward, but Taileachd leaped first, and he landed on dry land. But when Fionn leaped after him he sank down to his head. Then Taileachd seized the advantage at Fionn's back, and he swept the head off Fionn ere he could turn round. Taileachd fled for fear of the Fiann, bearing Fionn's head with him, till he reached the head of Loch Laidon (in Rannoch). There, being weary of carrying it, he put the head on a pole on a black knoll at a ford of the river, and that ford was thenceforth called Ath Chinn.

Now, when the Fiann found Fionn's headless body beside the lochan, they raised up their king and their lord, and they buried him behind a knoll, in a grave which is ever since called Cill Fhinn (Killin).

The Fiann were wroth at the wrong and the insult that had been done them, and they went on the track of the head till they found it on a heathery knoll at Ath Chinn. They then put a finger under Fionn's 'tooth of knowledge', and it was revealed to them that Taileachd was hiding in a cave in Ben Alder (north-east of Loch Laidon). There they found him, and put him to the question: 'Taileachd, do you repent of slaying Fionn?' And Taileachd replied, 'I do not repent unless Goll repents of his persecution of Clann Chuilgeadain.' Thereupon the Fiann struck off Taileachd's right hand and then his left hand in requital of the great evil he had wrought, and again they questioned him, 'Taileachd, do you repent of Fionn?' And again Taileachd replied, 'I do not repent, unless Goll repents of his persecution of Clann Chuilgeadain.' The Fiann wrenched and twisted one of his legs from the hip by means of a tough iron tongs, and they pounded the other leg with hard flagstones from the rocky hillside, and again put the question, 'Taileachd, do you repent of what you did to Fionn?' 'By my king,' said Taileachd, 'I do not repent unless Goll repents.' The two eyes in Taileachd's head the Fiann burnt with rough boiling beer. 'Taileachd, do you repent of Fionn?' And Taileachd for the last time answered, 'By my king, I do not repent unless Goll repents of his persecution of Clann Chuilgeadain.' 'We drove our spears through Taileachd's heart and slew him.'

This has all the marks of a very old tale, with one exception, namely, the explanation of Cill Fhinn as 'Fionn's burial place'. *Cill* in the sense of 'burial place' is modern; the old meaning is always 'church'.

I have not met Taileachd's name elsewhere. Clann Chuilgeadain appear in a version of Laoidh nan Ceann, printed in *Leabhar na Féinne* (p16). In this lay Conall Cearnach returns after avenging the death of Cu Chulainn, bringing to Emer, the dead hero's wife, the heads of Cu Chulainn's slayers on a withy (*gad*). Emer asks their names one by one, and Conall answers: 'Who are these six purple-faced, squint-eyed, black-haired heads?' 'These are the heads of six brothers, the children of Cuilgeadan (Clann Chuilgeadain).' In the version preserved by the Dean of Lismore the six brothers are styled correctly *clann Chailitin*, the name by which they are known in the oldest manuscript accounts. It would seem, therefore, that in the tale of Fionn's death *clann Chuilgeadain* may be a corrupt form of *clann Chailitin*, and that the name was transferred from the tale of the death of Cu Chulainn to the later tale of the death of Fionn.

Our version of the tale is to be compared with that given in *Zeitschrift f. Celtische Philologie* vol 1, p462. Here Fionn in his old age determines to test his strength by an attempt to leap across the Boyne at a place which bore the name of *Lèim Fhinn*. There he fell between two rocks, and his brains were dashed out. Fishermen of the Boyne found him, and one of them, named Aicleach, cut off his head, which they took into an empty house. They boiled some fish, and one of them said, 'Give the head a tooth-morsel' (*dant-mír*). This was done, and the head spoke and uttered a rann.

The compilation of Fenian tales entitled 'Acallach na Senórach' (The Conversation of the Ancient Men) contains a poem in which occurs the rann—

'Da cét bliadan co mblàithe ocus tricha gan tlàithe
saegal Finn, ba fata a ré, co torchair 'ga léim bàissi.'

'Two hundred fair years (lit. years with smoothness) and thirty without weakness were the lifespan of Fionn—long was its duration—till he fell in attempting his leap of folly' (line 2537).

Another poem in the same collection has—

'Do marbad Find na Féinne ic tabairt a laech-léime';

'Fionn of the Fiann was killed in performing his warrior-leap' (line 2873).

NOTE.—For much of the above I am indebted to my friends, Mr Alexander Campbell, of Borland, and Mr James MacDiarmid, descended from the Barons of Glen Lochay, both now passed away. I had also the privilege of conversations with the late Mr John MacNaughton, of Lochs. For information on several points I have to thank Mr John Campbell, Borland, and the Rev W. A. Gillies, Kenmore.

Place-Names of Perthshire
The Lyon Basin

Lìomhunn, Lyon, an old British, pre-Gaelic, name, means 'Polisher, Smoother'; in Wales, Afon Llifon—discussed in CPNS, p433.

The point where Lyon enters Tay near the eastern end of Drummond Hill is Rinn Lìomhunn, Point of Lyon. During the summer of 1640 the Earl of Argyll was engaged under the Scottish Parliament in reducing the clans of the North who were against the Covenanters. He had some sort of encounter with the Earl of Atholl near this spot, and seizing him by treachery, as is alleged, sent him prisoner to Stirling. It was somewhat later that Argyll burned the House of Airlie in Angus. Both events are referred to by Iain Lom in his poem on the battle of Ardrennich, near Inveraray, where the Atholl men defeated the Campbells:–

> B'olc a b'fhiach do Dhiùc Atholl
> Dhol an coinne riut *Eardsaidh*;
> An déidh latha Rinn Lìomhunn
> Thug sibh ìocshlaint mar earlais;
> Mheall sibh null thar an abhainn
> Marcus Atholl 's a bhràthair;
> Chuir sibh an làimh an toll-bùth iad,
> Is loisg sibh dùthaich Iarla Iarlaidh.

High up on the south-east side of Drummond Hill there was a small farm of about 28 acres called Ruigh a' Bhaird, the Bard's Slope, a name which suggests that this was the patrimony of the bard attached to the house of Bealach or Taymouth. The prehistoric fort Dun Mac Tuathail is on a spur of the hill looking due east.

Comrie, near the junction of Lyon and Keltney Burn, is Cuimrigh, pronounced exactly the same as Cuimrigh, Comrie, in Strathearn, both being the dative-locative of *comrach*, a confluence, though they might be explained as from Welsh *cymerau*, the plural of *cymer*, a confluence, taken over into Gaelic.

On the left bank of Lyon by the roadside west of Tirinie is a wood called Coille na Calach, the wood of the damp meadow. *Cail*, genitive *calach*, fem., occurs also in a' Chail Fhinn, the white (or fair) meadow on the south side of Loch Tay (dative case); there are also Cail Bhruar, Bruar Meadow, and Cail Mhinn, Calvin, kid's meadow, near Struan. In Ross-shire we have Cail Fhraochaidh, correctly anglicised as Heathfield, in Kilmuir Easter parish.

Above Coille na Calach is Tom an t-Seogail, rye-hillock, on the farm of Tulach a' Bhile, hill of the brae-edge. On Tom an t-Seogail, as I was told by Mr Alexander Campbell of Borland, the chiefs of old used to meet in council.

This brings us to the pleasant spot of Cois a' Bhile, Coshieville, meaning 'near the brae-edge', an idiomatic use of *cois* or *an cois*, seen for instance in '*cois na tuinne*', 'hard by the wave'. Coshieville has an inn and once had a famous market on August 9 (old style), known as Féill Mo-Choid. There is another Cois a' Bhile, Coshieville, at Grandtully, Strath Tay, a snug little hamlet nestling under a brae-edge.

Keltney Burn—a very rocky burn—is Allt Chailtnidh (CPNS p441), a name closely akin to Cailtidh, Kelty, near Callander; akin also to the numerous streams called Caladar, Calder, Cawdor. The root is that seen in O. Ir. *calath*, hard; Welsh *caled*, hard.

On Keltney Burn is the old castle of Garth, Caisteal Ghairt, otherwise known as Caisteal a' Chuilein Chursta, the wicked (cursed) whelp's castle. An Cuilean Cursta is said to mean the Wolf of Badenoch, but it was his son who held land here—the whelp of the old Wolf. From him the Stewarts of this region claim descent. Tigh a' Chuilein Chursta, the wicked whelp's house, i.e. the site of it, is at Eas Ghobhdaidh, below An Cnoc Riabhach on the right bank of Cluny Burn on the estate of Edradynate, Eadar-dà-dhoimhnid, between two ravines. Descendants of the Wolf of Badenoch are buried at Killiechassie chapel close by.

High up on the right side of Keltney Burn is Lìteagan, a name of which I offer no explanation. Here is the first or lowest down of the famous circular forts or castles in the Lyon basin, and on the farm of Lìteagan is Radhar a' Chaisteil, the outfield of the castle. Here also is Reangam for *reang-thom*, a compound of *reanga*, a ridge, and *tom*, a knoll, meaning 'ridged knoll' (see Dinneen, *reang, reanga*).

The Burn comes from Gleann Gobhlandaidh, the first part of which is obviously *gobhal*, a fork; but the rest of the compound is not clear to me. Still higher up, on the eastern flank of Schiehallion, is Tom a' Phubaill, knoll of the tent or booth, where *puball* is masculine. Elsewhere we have *pobal*, fem., genitive *poible*, as in Abhainn Poible, booth-river, in northeast Ross-shire, and Achadh Poible, Ach-populi, tent-field, Abriachan. Tom a' Phubaill was the scene of a battle between the Atholl men and the Campbells of Argyll, in which the former were defeated; it is referred to by Iain Lom:–

> 'S iomadh marcaiche stàtail,
> gar an àir' mi ach cuid diubh,
> Eadar geata bhràigh Acuinn
> gu slios Blàir nam fear luidneach;
> Mur ghabh sud is bràigh Ardail
> agus bràighe Both-chuidir,
> Ghabhadh leigeadh gu stàtail
> an éirig là Tom a' Phubaill.

On the left bank of Lyon, above Keltney Burn, is Blàrais, Blarish, a compound of *blar*, dappled and *innis*, a meadow, contracted to *i's* in unstressed position. Similarly Innis an Dùin, Inchandown, in Ross-shire, is pronounced I's an Dùin, the stress falling on *dùin*. Breacais, Breckish, in Skye, is for *breac-i's*, dappled meadow; Connage is for *con-i's*, hound meadow. Further examples will be found in *The Celtic Review*, vol 3, p239 [see p77]. Somewhere on Blarish moor (air mon Bhlàrais) is a place called Port Ghàidheal; I am not certain of the meaning of port here, nor could I get any one to fix the exact spot so named.

Druim (a') Charraigh, Drumcarry, ridge of the rock, boulder, or standing stone, comes next to Blarish. The farmhouse stands on an elevated plateau, a place of old habitation.

Next is the modern mansion of Garth, west of which is Baile na Creige, Balnacraig, rock stead. On the high bluff behind Balnacraig is An Dùn Geal, one of the most famous of the 'castles' connected in tradition with Fionn mac Cumhaill. A poem from Dr Irvine's manuscript printed in *Leabhar na Féinne*, but of late composition, makes repeated mention of Dùn Mac Tuathail on Drummond Hill and states:

Ann an sealladh Dùn Mhic Tuail
Bha Dùn Fhìnn gu uarach ard, etc.

'In sight of Dùn Mhic Tuail was Fionn's fort, proud and high'. Elsewhere in the poem the fort is called An Dùn Bàn.

A well known verse has it—

'Bha dà chaisteal deug aig Fionn
An Cromghleann dubh nan Clach.'

We are now in the Vale of Fortingall, but before going further we may mention some names on the south or right bank of Lyon above Comrie. Achadh Laogh or Ach Laogh, calves' field, is on maps Achloa; other forms are Achleys, Auchinleys. Further up is Cinn Ghealainn, the second part of which appeals again as Gealainn at Miggernie above Bridge of Balgie. Duneaves is on record as Tuneve, 1598; Tynnaiff, 1598-9; Tennaiffis 1602 (RMS). In Gaelic it is Tigh Neimhidh, house of the Nemet or sacred place of meeting. The fine bend or loop made by the river at this spot forms a distinctive and appropriate meeting-place. Above Duneaves is the small farm of Tynayere (stressed on -yere), in Gaelic Tigh Neimh' Ghearr, house of the short Nemet; its river frontage is short compared with that of Duneaves. The plural form of Duneaves is due to the fact that Tigh Neimhidh applied to the two places or farms. Near Tigh Neimh' Ghearr are the remains of a meal mill known as Muileann Airc, probably from *airc*, a water passage or conduit. It is just below a big deep pool in Lyon called Linne Lonaidh[1], otherwise known—for a time—as Peter's Pool, after Peter Dewar, gamekeeper, who lived at

1 From *lonaidh*, a path.

Gealainn when I used to frequent that district. Immediately above Linne Lonaidh is the old ford over Lyon, Ath Mo-Ghriam, whatever that means. The pool itself has been the scene of several drowning disasters, caused by the swamping of the coble used in crossing, or by the force of the current carrying down people who were crossing by the ford, or owing to some other cause. It was by this ford that the body of Dugald Buchanan was taken from Rannoch to Strathyre in 1768. The funeral procession was witnessed by the father of a man in Fortingall who was still living in my own time.

A little way above the ford and on the left bank of Lyon is the site of Tigh Chunnairt, house of danger, where once the MacGregor pipers lived.

Bridge of Lyon bears the inscription: Archibald Bannatyne: His Work: 1783.

Song on the building of the Bridge of Lyon ('Archibald Ballantyne: His Work: 1793'), as recorded by the late Alexander Campbell of Borland, and given me by his brother, John Campbell.

> 'S coma leam am bàta dubh,
> Chan 'eil mi 'n diugh 'na eisimeil,
> O 'n chaidh an drochaid air an t-sruth
> Gum faigh sinn aiseag saor ann.
>
> An t-urram (Mo bheannachd) aig a' Bhallandach
> Chuir suas an drochaid ealamh dhuinn;
> Chan ionann e 's na clachairean
> Nach leanadh clach ri aol dhoibh
> (Nach seasadh clach no aol dhoibh).
>
> 'S iomadh oidhche mhuladach
> A bh' agam an Tigh Chunnarta;
> Cha toir sinn oidhche tuille ann
> O 'n tha an drochaid saor dhuinn.
> O 's coma leam am bàta dubh, etc.

Tigh Chunnarta was on the left bank of the river, leading to the ford known locally as Ath Tigh Chunnairt.

The western end of Drummond Hill opposite the farmhouse of Achtar (Ach-tearra) is An Cromradhar, the bent outfield; it is part of the pasture of Fearnan village.

On the west side of the public road from Fearnan to Fortingall there are two pleasant small farms, Ach-tearra, Achtar, which seems to mean 'tar-field', and Croit Gharbh, the rough croft. Adjacent to Croit Gharbh or Croftgarve, and on the same side of Lyon, is the sunny, sheltered farm of Cùldoir Mór, a charming retired spot right at the mouth of Glen Lyon; 'back-copse', or possibly 'nook-copse', 'corner-copse'.

Fortingall is in old records Forterkil 1240, Fertirkil, Fertirgill (RMS), Forthirgill 1488 (RMS), and such like; it is now in Gaelic Fartairchill, meaning 'Forter-church'. A very similar name is Kirk-forthar in Fife, and as I have said elsewhere (CPNS p69), 'forter' is most probably a Gaelic form of Welsh *gwerthyr*, a fortress. Fartairchill means 'fortress church', with reference to the ancient fort of Dùn Geal on the bluff close by. See further CPNS, p433.

It was the custom of the early Celtic Church to plant a church on or near the site of a pagan holy place, and Fortingall seems to be an example of this custom. In favour of this view three facts may be noted.

(1) The church is in the immediate neighbourhood of the ancient Nemet of Duneaves. The Nemet is defined as 'a holy place or shrine in a wood' (CPNS p244). It was a place of worship and of judgment among the pagan Celts.

(2) In pagan times tribal meeting places were often marked by a sacred tree; some of these trees, yew trees among others, were very famous, as is known from early Irish sources. According to the Book of Armagh, St Patrick founded one of his churches hard by the Tree of Tortiu (*iuxta Bile Torten*). The yew tree which grew and grows still right at the western end of the church of Fortingall is of immense age. In Pennant's time it measured fifty-six feet in circumference (1772). If, as authorities state, this yew is fully 3,000 years old, and 'probably the oldest authentic

specimen of vegetation in Europe', it must have been well grown before the Romans set foot in Britain. Its proximity to the Nemet strongly suggests that it was a sacred tribal tree.

(3) In the field across the public road from the church and the yew tree there are three groups of standing stones, indicating a pagan place of burial, probably of chiefs or great men. One of these groups consists of three stones; the second has also three, two of which are very massive and shapely, broad and rounded at top; the third has four stones, all water-smoothed, one comparatively small. On Dail an Fhraoich, about half a mile west of the church, there is a most interesting and rather elaborate burial place, circular in shape, with three concentric rings or walls, the third containing the burial—as I suppose—being depressed in the centre. The diameter overall is 43 feet: the diameter inside the outer wall is 40 feet. The sepulchre goes by the name of Uaigh an t-Seanalair, the general's grave, and is popularly supposed to be the grave of Pontius Pilate's father or of Pontius Pilate himself[1]. How this absurd notion arose I have no idea, but it is doubtless connected with the alleged 'Roman Camp' on Dail an Fhraoich. Lying on the outer wall of the grave is an approximately cigar-shaped stone about 8 by 3 by 2 feet. It has nine cupmarks on the side facing west and one cupmark on the end facing north. It is likely that this stone was originally upright. A little way to the south west and near the river there is a standing stone.

---

1 For the Pontius Pilate tradition see Mr Alexander Stewart's *A Highland Parish*, p39; he discusses the 'Roman camp', at p40. At the eastern end of Dail an Fhraoich there is a rectangular earthwork, the surface of which is somewhat higher than that of the adjoining level moor. It measures about 120 feet by 87 feet, lying east and west. The entrance was on the east side, and elsewhere all round there is a ditch measuring about 50 feet from lip to lip. The earth from this ditch appears to have been spread on the top of the enclosure, thus raising it as mentioned. This, so far as I could judge, is the only artificial structure on Dail an Fhraoich, except the ancient grave described above. When in full repair, with its ditches clean and a palisade along their inner edges, it must have been an extremely strong little post.

The hamlet of Fortingall consists of the Clachan (Clachan Fartairchill) next the church, and Baile a' Mhuilinn, Milltown, a little way to the west. A massive, roughly pyramidal stone in one of the gardens, and visible from the public road, is called Clach Mo Luchaig, to which, according to local authority, scolds were wont to be fastened—the iron insets are still visible. In a field to the south of the road is Carn nam Marbh, where the victims of a plague are said to be buried (see *A Highland Parish*, p36). The burn skirting the west side of Baile a' Mhuilinn is Allt Odhar (no article), which the late Rev Charles M. Robertson considered— probably correctly—to be for Allt Dobhar, the original name having been simply Dobhar, brook, water. On its right bank is Tulach a' Mhuilinn, Mill Hill, where James MacGregor, the Dean of Lismore and Vicar of Fortingall, was born towards the end of the fifteenth century. It is now the site of Glen Lyon House. West of it and near the entrance to Glen Lyon is Ard-tràsgairt, the second part of which is from Welsh *traws*, across, and *garth*, a field, enclosure; the meaning is thus 'height of crossfield'.

Some names of Saints are connected with Fortingall. On the farm of Duneaves are Dail Chiarain, St Ciaran's meadow, and Dail Mo Choid (or Mo Choide), St Coedi's meadow; while a ford on Lyon below Duneaves is Ath Bhreanaidh, meaning St Brendan's ford. A church or chapel of St Ciaran formerly stood on the farm of Borland on Loch Tay, just over the parish march. The Fortingall fairs were Feill Ceit nan Gobhar, St Catherine's Goat Fair, on December 6 and 7; Feill Ceit an Fhrois, St Catherine's Seed Fair, on April 28; and Feill Mo-Choide on August 9 (old style), the lamb market.

In addition to the cupmarked stone on Dail an Fhraoich, there is a cupmarked standing stone in the enclosure beside the yew tree at the church where Sir Donald Currie is buried. I do not know whether this stone is in its original position or not. There are many cupmarks on a big flat-topped boulder on the hillside above Tynayere. Cups occur on several of the stones on Fearnan pasture opposite the farm of Achtar, and also on a flag near the upper end of the lane that leads uphill at the north end of the farmhouse of Croftgarrow. I know of only one cupped stone in Glen Lyon, the inference being either that the folk of the 'castles' did not make cupmarks, or that, if they did, they came down to Fortingall to make their magic. I am convinced that the cups on stones are due to a process of sympathetic magic; stones so marked are often found near a sacred place, e.g. at Kilchoman in Islay the cups are actually on the base of the High Cross.

The low part of the dyke in front of Fortingall Hotel immediately west of the gate, is Guala Làidir, strong shoulder. Here men used to sit of an evening (e.g. in my time John MacDougall, famous for feats of strength, especially at Féill Ceit).

The magnificent Pass of Lyon, about two miles long, begins near Ard-tràsgairt and opens out at Chesthill. On its north side, running far up the mountain side, is A' Choille Dhubh, the black wood, strictly applied to the wood above the eastern end of the pass, the limit of which is marked by the name Ceann na Coille, Wood-end. The old name for the Pass is Cumhang Dhubhghlais, the narrow of the black stream, where the epithet *dubh* may be due to the river's thickly-wooded course rather than to the colour of its water. I have suggested the same explanation of Abhainn Teimheil, river of darkness, anglicised as Tummel (CPNS, p451).

The brook that comes down at Ceann na Coille is Allt a' Ghobhlain, burn of the forklet. Some make Allt a' Ghobhlain the beginning of Glen Lyon.

Chesthill, Sestill 1502 and 1603 (RMS), is in Gaelic Seasdul or Seasdal, which I have explained as *seas-dul*, bench-dale (CPNS, p415); *dul* being here the old Celtic term seen in *Dul*, Dull, not from Norse *dalr*, a dale. Opposite Chesthill comes down Allt dà Ghob, burn of two beaks, so named because at its junction with Lyon it has formed a tiny delta which splits its waters in two. In time of spate Allt dà Ghob is something worth seeing, plunging down in a series of steaming leaps or cataracts. Betiveen the head of Gleann dà Ghob and Coire nam Buidheag, corrie of the yellow flowers, is Binnean, so spelled by the Rev C. M. Robertson, but I have not heard it pronounced.

Balintyre, west of Chesthill, is Baile an t-Saoir, the wright's homestead. On the plateau, a little west of it and behind a roadside cottage, is a circular fort.

Further along on the same plateau, where the road bends up the brae, are the remains of the mansion or castle of Duncan Campbell, Donnchadh Ruadh na Féile, 'Red Duncan of generosity', who died in 1578. It is known as the Castle of Carn Bán, and its first stone was laid in 1564.

An Carn Bàn Beag and An Carn Bàn Mór are close by the castle.

Dericambus, Derycammys 1502 (RMS), is in Gaelic Deireacamas, is explained as from *deireadh* and *camas*, a bend or bight; it is on the last bend made by Lyon before entering the gorge of the Pass.

Between Carn Bán and Invervar and on the north side of the road is the ancient cemetery of Cladh Chunna, St Cunna's graveyard. The saint's well is nearby, and behind the graveyard is Radhar a' Chluig, the outfield of the bell. On the Loch Tay side the saint's name is preserved in Coire Chunna, St Cunna's corrie, anglicised Carwhin. In the north-west part of Cladh Chunna is the burial place of the Lothians of Glen Lyon, capable and intelligent people, one of whom was Duncan Lothian, the hymn and proverb writer, who taught in Rannoch during and after the time of Dugald Buchanan.

Invervar, Inverbarris 1502, is Inbhir Bhara and Inbhir Bharra, at the junction of Allt Bhara or Allt Bharra with Lyon. The second term may be the old *bara*, wrath, anger, rather than the genitive of *barr*, a summit, top.

Inverinain on the south side of the Glen is Inbhir Innein the mouth of Allt Innein, with Eas Innein, coming from Coire Innein, while above Inverinain is a hill named An t-Innean, the anvil, from which burn, mouth, etc, are named. *Innean* or *inneoin*, anvil, is not uncommonly applied to flat-topped eminences high or low. A well-known instance is the Innean of Glencoe, absurdly made in English 'the Study'. There are also the Inzeon hills in Fife. A low flat-topped ridge east of Ardochy on Loch Etive side is An t-Innean, and gives its name to the adjacent farm. It is perhaps necessary to say that Inbhir Innein, etc, have no connection with St Ninian!

On the north side of the road between Invervar and Ruskich is Dun Oisein, supposed to mean Oisin's or Ossian's Fort.

Ruskich, Ruskich 1502, is Rùsgaich, the dative-locative of *rùsgach*, a marshy place, common in Ireland. In Glen Urquhart there is Rùsgaich with the same meaning.

Slataich, Slattich 1502, means place of wands, from *slat*, a rod.

Roro is Ruadhshruth, red stream. It is a fine large flat on the south side of Lyon, once well peopled. One of the old 'castles' is on Roromore (Ruadhshruth Mór), and its walls not so long ago sheltered the local school. The burn which flows along the west side of Roromore is Allt Caoir, from *caor*, a blaze, a live coal, so named from its sparkling water. It is the equivalent of the Eibhleag of Evelix, near Dornoch. A well-known local saying is:–

> Caor is Cadan is Conghlais,
> Trì uisgeachan na h-Alba.

'Caor and Cadan (of Inbhir Chadain in Rannoch) and Conghlais (above Tyndrum) are the three (best) waters of Scotland.'

West of Roromore is Roroyare, i.e. Ruadhshruth Ghearr or short Roro. From its western march to the march between Inverinain and Dericambus lies the district known as An Tòiseachd or the Thanage, the mensal lands, so to speak, of MacGregor of Glen Lyon. A poem in the Dean of Lismore's Book has:–

> MacGriogoir na ngreasa ngéar,
> taoiseach as tréan ar gach tír;

'MacGregor of sharp encounters, a chief who is mighty over every land.' In the same poem he is styled 'seabhag déidgheal na dtrí ngleann', 'white-toothed hawk of the three glens', i.e. Glen Orchy (or Glen Strae), Glen Dochart and Glen Lyon. Also he is 'flath Ghlinne Líomhunn na lann', 'prince of Glen Lyon of the sword-blades'.

Balnahanaid, Baile na h-Annaid, homestead of the Annat, which denotes an ancient church. The present farmhouse stands on an old burial ground. West of it is Baile Meadhonach, middle-town.

Craigianie, Crageny, 1502, is in Gaelic Craig Ianaigh, also Craig Fhiannaidh, with supposed reference to the Fianna. The former is more likely to be correct: *ianaigh* is probably the old genitive of *ianach* (i.e. *eunach*), the act of fowling or hunting birds. On the rock which gives the farmhouse its name there is a mark which looks like the mark of a man's foot, ascribed by tradition to the ùruisg or water-demon Peallaidh, and called 'caslorg Pheallaidh', 'Peallaidh's foot-track'. Peallaidh was king of all the numerous uruisgs of this region and of Breadalban. A stretch of the hill above Camas-bhrachdain, west of Craigianie, is called Ruigh Pheallaidh, Peallaidh's reach or slope. In Moness Den at Aberfeldy there is Caisteal Pheallaidh, Peallaidh's Castle; and the junction of the Moness Burn with Tay is Obar Pheallaidh, Aberfeldy, Peallaidh's confluence. The name Peallaidh is from *peall*, a skin or hide (Latin *pellis*), and means 'the shaggy skinned one'. Hence *peallach*, rough-haired; *peallag*, a rough tuft of hair; a shaggy skin; *peallagach*, shaggy-haired. All these become dialectically in Lewis *piull-*, while Piullaidh in Lewis means the Devil. The water-demon has of course been equated with St Palladius, a proceeding which the saint would hardly regard as a compliment.

A little way beyond the rock and on the south side of the road stands a low slab of stone with a cross on each side; the hollow immediately beneath the stone is Lag a' Mhòid, the hollow of the moot, and the chief is said to have sat at the foot of the cross. A few yards from this, but on the other side of the road, is a stone pierced by a round hole. This hole was made by St Adamnan's crozier when he stayed the plague in Glen Lyon from advancing beyond that spot—so one form of the tradition. Mr Stewart gives another form (*ib.* p24).

Camas-bhrachdain, the next place as one goes west, is not clear to me.

Innerwick is Inbhir Mhuice, the meeting of Allt Mhuice, swine burn, with Lyon. There are also Làirig Mhuice, swine pass, going to Dall on Loch Rannoch, and Meall Mhuice, swine hill. A fair named An Fhéill Muice was held here of old on Là na Féill-Muice. *Muc* as a stream name occurs in Eadar-a-mhucaidh, Edramucky, 'between two swine burns', on Loch Tay side. Another term found for streams is *banbh*, a pig, whence the Banbhaidh of Blair Atholl and Banbhaidh, Banavie, near Fort William. Banw, with the same meaning, is the name of a river in Wales. The idea, in some cases at least, is that of rooting or digging like a hog (CPNS, pp441, 442). Besides Làirig Mhuice another pass, Làirig Chalabha, goes from Innerwick to Carie on Loch Rannoch (Càraidh); I do not know the meaning of *Calabha*.

Kerrowmore, An Ceathramh Mór, the big quarter, is on the south side of the river; there is also Kerrowclach, Ceathramh Chlach, Keroclauchy 1502, Kerauchlauchie 1632: the record spellings indicate Ceathramh Clachaidh; 'quarter of stones' or 'stoney quarter'. Two or three of the old 'castles' are in this neighbourhood.

Bridge of Balgie is Drochaid Bhalgaidh, named after Linne Bhalgaidh, a big rounded or bag-like pool in Lyon. *Balgaidh* is an adjective formed from *balg*, a bag, a sack, with the suffix -*da,* aspirated -*dha*, thus giving *balgdha*, 'baggy', which becomes with us *balgaidh* in the same way as *diadha*, godly, becomes *diadhaidh*; *fuardha*, chill, becomes *fuaraidh*, etc. Similarly Abhainn Bhalgaidh in Applecross and in Strathbogie (Srath Bhalgaidh) means 'baggy river', i.e. river with bag-like pools.

Làirig Bhreislich, pass of confusion, connects Dùn Chroisg in Glen Lochay, fort of the crossing, with Bridge of Balgie. It is a perplexing pass.

Làirig Luaidh, pass of lead, enters into Làirig Bhreislich, so called from a vein of lead (and perhaps silver), which was formerly worked.

On the flat near Linne Bhalgaidh there lived an old lady named Mór. On the occasion of an unusually heavy spate in Lyon the river entered Mór's cottage and brought with it a salmon. A poem commemorating the event has:–

> Thain' bradan tarrgheal a Linne Bhalgaidh,
> An aghaidh earbaill a choimhead Móir;
> Ars' Mór 's i 'g éirigh, 'Ochón mo léireadh,
> Nach cum thu a' Bhéist gus am faigh mi 'n tuagh?'

The sites of some of the houses can be traced on the south side of the pool below the bridge. Ath Bun na Seann Drochaide, a ford across Lyon directly in line with the Manse, commemorates an old bridge, one of whose piers still stands in the south bank of the river. 'Kendrochard', mentioned in Macfarlane's *Geographical Collections*, may have been situated here.

From Bridge of Balgie a road goes to Loch Tay side through the pass called Làirig an Lochain, so named from a lochlet known as Lochan na Làirce. In the mouth of this pass are traces of one of the 'castles'. Near the 'castle' is Dail an Tèadhaich, the Menteith man's meadow, where one of a raiding party from Menteith was slain by an arrow shot from the 'castle'.

Creag Eilig (OSM Creag nan Eildeag!), Cragilk 1502 (RMS), on Kerrowmore means 'rock of the *eileag* or deer-trap'. This is the furthest south instance of *eileag* that I have noted; the common term in Perthshire is *eileirg*, anglicised Elrick (see CPNS, p489). The fact that Creag Eileig is included in the charter of 1502 ('the two merklands of Cragilk') shows that it was a place of some importance.

Milton Eonan, Baile Mhuileann Eodhanain or Eodhannain, Myltoun 1502; Mylntoun cum molendino Eonan nuncupato (Mylntoun with the mill called the mill of Eonan) 1632 (RMS); St Adamnan's mill-town, as distinguished from Baile Mhuileann Ruadhshruth, Milton of Roro. Adamnan, says Mr Stewart, 'is believed to have been the evangelist of Glen Lyon, and the instructor of the people in many useful arts. He is said to have erected the first mill on the Milton stream. A mill was in operation there till about 1880 ... About the above date it was denuded of its covering of Ben Lawers slates, and a few years ago its walls were carried away to repair Meggernie Drive'—an almost incredible act of vandalism. A local poet (the late Mr Duncan Campbell of Balnacraig) says of Baile Mhuileann Eodhanain:

Far nach 'eil creach no claidheamh no cùirt

with reference to the sanctity attached to St Adamnan's Mill. Mr Campbell also refers to a mysterious power possessed by the Mill of inflicting a *beum-sùla* or stroke of the evil eye when need for such a proceeding arose (beum-sùla an am feum), and gives an example of this power having been exercised.

On the north side of the river, over a mile west of Camas Bhrachdain, is Bruthach nam Bord—so Mr Stewart, p25—Bruichtbuird 1631; Brughbuird 1648 (RMS), brae of the boards; the record forms suggest Bruach or Bruthach Buird, bank or brae of (the) board. 'Here, up till 1881, a flourishing little community of crofters and craftsmen lived contentedly' (*ib*. p25).

Cladh Bhranno is an ancient graveyard on the south side of the river a little way below Bridge of Balgie, where there was once a church or chapel, the font of which is still there, while the bell is now in the custody of the Minister of Glen Lyon. In 1502 we find 'the two merklands de la Brandvoy', indicating perhaps the old patrimony of the church. I have taken the second part to be Branbhoth, genitive of Branubh (CPNS, p312). The Rev C. M. Robertson, who served for some time in the district, gave it to me as Bràinibh or Brèanaibh, with long vowel; but as I heard it pronounced in Gaelic the vowel was short.

Meggernie, Meggarne 1502; Milgarny 1620; Mylnegairnie 1632, is in Gaelic Migearnaidh, and is to be compared with Migear, a boggy place near Comrie; Welsh *mign*, a bog (see further CPNS, pp374-76). The later record forms suggest etymologising. Near the Castle of Meggernie is Leac nan Abrach, the Lochaber men's flagstone, where thirty-six Lochaber raiders were hanged on one tree by Cailin Gòrach, who died about 1587. The tradition, as given by Mr Duncan Campbell in the poem referred to, is that the Lochaber men were going home with their *creach* when Donnchadh Ruadh, son of Cailin, son of Donnchadh Ruadh na Féile, encountered them and, taking them prisoners, shut them up in Meggernie Castle. While Donnchadh Ruadh was debating what course should be adopted with the prisoners, his father took them out and hanged them on the hillside below Meggernie. Cailin Gòrach slew Dugald, the leader of the raiders, with his own hand; his cairn, Carn Dughaill, is still to be seen near Bridge of Balgie.

Gealainn, Gallyn 1502, Gallyne 1620 and 1632 (RMS), is near Meggernie. It appears to be a compound of which the first part is *geal*, white, bright. It may perhaps be compared with Ruadhainn, Ruthven, a compound of *ruadh*, red, and *maighean*, dative *maighin*, a spot, place: 'red spot or place'. As already noticed, the term occurs in Cinn-ghealainn near Duneaves, 'at-head of white-spot'.

An Ros, the point, is the point formed where Conait joins Lyon. It is now uninhabited.

Dail an Tàchrain, the ghost's meadow, is between Conait and Ceannchnoc. Its story is unknown to me.

Ceannchnoc, anglicised Kenchnoc, head-hill, divides the lower part of Glen Lyon from the upper part. The exact middle of Glen Lyon is said to be Fóid Lìomhunn, the sod of Lyon, near the lower end of Dail an Tàchrain. From it, says Mr Duncan Campbell,

> Tha cóig-deug de mhìltean gu Allt a' Ghobhlain,
> Is cóig-deug eile gu Lón a' Chuaille.

[It is fifteen miles to Allt a' Ghobhlain, and another fifteen to Lón a' Chuaille.] Lón a' Chuaille is at the summit of the Pass between Beinn a' Chaisteil and Cam-Chreag, and is regarded as the western extremity of Glen Lyon.

Mor Shios and Mor Shuas, Lower and Upper Mor: Mor is for Mothar, a clump of trees, a place overgrown with brushwood, which is probably the reference here.

Conaid, the stream from Lochs, is from *cù*, a hound, stem *con-* with the extension *-id* discussed in CPNS, pp445-6. The part of it between the two lochs is Conaid eadar dà Loch, printed in Macfarlane's *Geographical Collections* as Tonaig-Etera-loch. With Conaid may be compared the Welsh river Cynon, our Conann of Strath Conon.

Lochs gets its name from the two lochs, Loch Giorra and Loch Damh. It used to be an excellent sheep farm. The tenant, Mr John MacNaughton, a man as generous as Donnchadh Ruadh na Féile, told me that first-rate barley used to be grown there in a place called Ach Tors at a height of about 1,350 feet above sea level. A pass between Lochs and Rannoch is called Làirig Mheachlainn: possibly for Mhaoil-Sheachlainn.

Stronuich, in Gaelic Sròn Iuthaich, is on the south side of Lyon, south-west of Mor Shuas, probably from *eó*, a yew, meaning 'point of yew-wood'.

Allt Loingsich, Loingseach's burn, is the march between Stronuich and Dalchiarlaich. Loingseach means a mariner and an exile. Compare Torr Loingsich in Glenshiel, Ross-shire. There is also Coire Loingsich, spelled in Macfarlane's *Collections* Coryloinshick. The Rev C. M. Robertson reported to me that he had heard it as Coire Mhaoislich and as Coire Laoighein, the former, in his opinion, a substitution of an understood term for one—Coire Loingsich—not understood.

Dail Chiarlaich, on south side of Lyon, by contraction from Dail Chiarthulaich, meadow of swarthy knoll.

Cashlie is in Gaelic Caislidh, properly Caislibh, the dative plural of *caiseal*, a stone fort, as in the Munster Cashel. Four or five of the circular stone forts are concentrated here within a distance of about a mile. One of them is Caisteal a' Chonbhacain, the castle of the hound-tether-stick or perhaps rather of the hound-bendlet. The conbhacan is a stone which stands about 2 feet 6 inches above the surface, and is shaped rather like the figure 7. Viewed sideways it looks very like the head and neck of a grim hound. Local tradition says that the Fianna who inhabited the adjoining round fort used to tether their dogs to this stone. It has no great hold of the earth, and I was told that on one occasion it was accidentally uprooted and replaced. More authentic is the report that at no very distant date expectant mothers used to pass prone under the 'jaw' of the stone in order to ensure safety in delivery. In 1913 the late Dr Alexander Ross and Mr James Barron accompanied me to see the Glen Lyon forts, and Dr Ross made a careful drawing of An

Conbhacan, both by itself and in relation to its surroundings, of which he gave me a copy in water colours.

Another is called Caisteal Mhic Rèill, MacNeil's castle. This is the regular form of MacNèill in Strath Tay and district, e.g. Clach MhicRèill on Borland Farm; Bàta MhicRèill, a ferry on Tay below Ballinluig; Tom MhicRèill, Tomcrail, on the right bank of Garry opposite Killiecrankie Station.

A third is Caisteal an Deirg, the red man's castle, and a fourth is Caisteal an Duibh, the black man's castle, but Mr Duncan Campbell's poem has Caisteal an Duibhne. Speculation as to these names is useless. Mr Campbell says truly:

> Tha móran eachdraidh air a call
> Mu Chaislibh 's Chamas-làidh,
> Dail an Tulchainn is Dail na Fóid,
> Dail Chiarthlaich 's Dail nam Bard.

[Much history has been lost about Caislibh and Camas-làidh, etc.]

The last of the forts is, or rather was, at the head of the glen, about two miles west of Tom a' Chaorthainn, at the foot of Beinn a' Chaisteil, but I have never been at this spot.

Puball (no article) on north side; behind it is Meall Phubaill, lump (massive hill) of the tent.

Lùb Riabhach, Lubreoch, brindled loop, on south side, is the starting point of Làirig nan Lunn, pass of the bier-poles, between Glen Lyon and Glen Lochay. Here the dead were carried across on biers.

Seasgarnaich, sheltered place, is near the lower end of Loch Lyon; also Lùb Sheasgarnaich, loop of S., and the hill Beinn Sheasgarnaich.

The stream Meuran flows through Gleann Meurain and joins the Lyon at Inbhir Meurain, as the latter leaves its loch. Here *Meuran* probably means small branch.

Fionnghleann, bright glen, with its stream Allt Fionnghlinn, on the south side of Loch Lyon. *Fionn* in place-names not uncommonly means holy, and may do so here, connected with Beinn Mhanach, monks' peak, on its north-west.

Some Place-Names of the North

Our knowledge of antiquity is derived partly from literature and partly from material objects formed and fashioned by the hands of the men of old. Names of places consist of words which, whether they are intelligible to us now or not, were certainly understood by the people who first gave them and used them; they are a form of literature. Further, just as ancient writings are liable to corruption from the carelessness or ignorance of later transcribers, so the names of places suffer change and corruption in the process of tradition. In the case of names, however, there is another very important factor to be reckoned with, namely, change of language. When the language of a country changes there is almost inevitably a period of bilingualism, which tends to preserve the old names, or at least the more important of them and those that are most in common use. But as time goes on and the new language becomes established, the number of old names, now unintelligible, becomes smaller; they are displaced by terms from the new language. Thus we have successive strata of nomenclature, the oldest stratum being represented by comparatively few names, and these hard or impossible to understand now, while the later strata are richer and easier to understand. Such, in outline, is the general course of events, subject to qualification in particular investigations.

In the North two strata, Celtic and Norse, are readily distinguished. Seeing that the coming of the Celts cannot be placed much earlier than BC400, it is possible that our more ancient names may contain a pre-Celtic element; absolutely nothing, however, is known for certain regarding the pre-Celtic speech.

Celtic Names—British

The Celtic names belong to the two great divisions of Celtic, one (the earlier) represented of old by Gaulish and British, now by Welsh, Breton, and Cornish; the other represented by Irish, Manx, and Scottish Gaelic. This was the view held by the scholars of last generation, including Dr Alexander Macbain, of Inverness, and though some now would assert the complete absence of the British element, one of the most competent Celtic scholars of the present day, Professor Julius Pokorny of Berlin, states that 'for all practical purposes we can safely assume an almost purely British substratum under the Gaelic surface, with perhaps occasional pre-Celtic remains looming in the background'. Or as the late Kuno Meyer put it: 'No Gael ever set his foot on British soil save from a vessel that had put out from Ireland'.

Our oldest names come, some of them, through tradition derived from the Greek navigator Pytheas (c BC 320), the Columbus of his day. Others come from the geographer Ptolemy of Alexandria (c AD 140), who had the benefit of the knowledge of the North acquired through Agricola's campaigns and circumnavigation of North Britain in the latter part of the first century. Here it must suffice to mention only such as are still extant.

One of our very oldest names is the Norse-Gaelic hybrid Orkney, in Old Norse *Orkneyjar*, 'isles of the Orcs', a tribal name meaning 'boars'. It first appears as an adjective, *Orcan* (a Greek neuter form), applied to a cape in the far north, probably Dunnet Head. The Orcs are mentioned in very old Irish poetry.

In later literature we find the *Caitt*, 'Cats', inhabiting Shetland, which in Irish literature is *Inse Catt*. '*I Cataib*', 'among the Cats', was the old descriptive term for Caithness and south-east Sutherland, whence Sutherland is now in Gaelic *Cataibh*.

One of the northern tribes mentioned by Ptolemy is the Smertæ, who occupied the basin of the Oykel and probably of the Carron adjoining. Their name survives in *Carn Smeart*, a hill above Braelangwell Lodge in Strath Carron.

Three northern rivers mentioned by Ptolemy, Nabaros, Ila and Varar, are now represented by the rivers *Nabhar*, Naver, *Ilidh*, the name of the Helmsdale river, and *Farar* of Strath Farrar, now the Beauly river, all difficult names, but probably Celtic. Another ancient name is *Oiceal*, the river Oykel, whose high bank, on the north side, is in Norse Ekkjals-bakki, 'Oykel's bank', corresponding to Ptolemy's ὄχθη ὑψήλη, 'Ripa Alta', 'High Bank'.

The name *Oiceal* may be connected with Gaulish and British *uxellos*, 'high', whence Welsh *uchel*, our Ochil, Ochiltree.

The British term *aber*, a river-mouth, is found in three northern names to the west of the watershed: (1) Applecross, of old Apor-crossan; (2) Loch-aber, which Adamnan has as *Aporicum Stagnum*, or in modern Gaelic (*an*) *Loch Abrach*, and *Stagnum Aporum*, where *Aporum* is genitive plural; (3) Aber-calder on Loch Oich. East of the watershed there are Aber-calder in Stratherrick and also in Badenoch; Aber-arder in Strath Nairn and on Loch Laggan; Abriachan on Loch Ness, the full form of which is heard in the well-known 'Bodaich Obar-Bhritheachan', 'the carles of Abriachan'; and Aber-tarf, in Gaelic *Obar-thairbh*, at the west end of Loch Ness, making six instances, or nine in all.

Calder, in Gaelic *Caladar*, is a purely British name, as I have proved elsewhere, found in Wales as *Calettwr* (i.e. *caledlwfr*) and *Clettwr*, representing Early Celtic *caleto-dubron*, 'hard water', 'rocky water'. It occurs in Scotland from Scots-calder in Caithness to Galloway.

Early Celtic *dubron*, water, stream, becomes in Welsh *dwfr*, and is taken over into Gaelic as *dobhar*. It occurs often in stream names from Dover on the English Channel to Dofyr in Strathnaver (1260, RM). The Aldourie Burn, not far from Inverness, is in Gaelic *Dobhrag*, 'streamlet', a diminutive in form, but probably a reduced form of a compound name. When *dobhar* forms the second part of a compound, and is therefore unstressed, it is shortened to *-dar*, *-der*, or if aspirated it becomes *-ar*, *-er*. Thus *ard-dobhar*, 'high-water', becomes Arder on Loch Laggan, whence Aber-arder, 'high-water mouth'. *Mór-dhobhar*, 'big water', becomes Mórar.

Strath-peffer is in Gaelic *Srath-pheofhair*; the town of Dingwall, near the mouth of the Peffray, is *Inbhir-pheofharan*, 'mouth of Peffran', which latter is in form a diminutive of *Peofhar*. A number of streams called Peffer or Peffray are found along the east coast from Lothian northwards; the name is British, connected with Welsh *pefr*, radiant, beautiful. In Peterculter parish, Aberdeenshire, there was a brook called Peferyn or Paforyn, now Silverburn, which is practically a translation of the old name.

Urquhart of Glen Urquhart is written about AD700 as *Airchartdan*, a compound of the preposition *ar* (common to Gaelic and Welsh), and the old form of Welsh *cardden*, 'a thicket, copse'. The meaning is 'wood-side'. The Gaelic equivalent is *Urchoill*, Orchill, from *ar* and *coill* or *coille*, a wood. Another name which seems to be British is Erchite, from *ar*, 'on', and Welsh *coed*, a wood.

The river Conon, which flows through Strath Bran, but gives its name to Strath Conon, is probably the same as the Welsh river Cynon, meaning 'hound-stream'; the reference may be to otters, as in Con-eas in Glen Glass, Ross-shire 'dog-waterfall'. Otter is in Welsh *dyfr-gi*, 'water-dog', in old Gaelic *dobhar-chú*.

The Ness is in Adamnan's Latin (cAD700) *Nesa*, genitive *Nisæ*. The former appears in Loch Ness and Inver-ness, but in Gaelic these are *Loch Nis* and *Inbhir Nis*, or, in fifteenth-century poetry, *Inbhir Nise*, corresponding exactly to Adamnan's form of the genitive. The name is doubtless very old, and most probably Celtic, but the exact meaning is uncertain.

The Nairn of Strath Nairn gives its name to *Inbhir Narunn* (or *Narann*), the town of Nairn. It is to be compared with the river Naro in Dalmatia, with the town of Narona at its mouth, and with the Italian Nar, with its town Narnia. Nairn is certainly pre-Gaelic.

Cantray is in Gaelic *Cantra* or *Canutra*, and is most probably an ancient British name, meaning 'white or bright stead', 'bright settlement'.

The second part of Doch-four is the aspirated form of a term equivalent to Welsh *pawr*, pasture, grazing. A derivative of it is *Pórainn* in Strath Conon. In Ross-shire there is Inch-fuir, pasture meadow, in Kilmuir Easter, and there is Pit-four, in Gaelic *Baile Phùir*, Avoch.

Doch-four means 'the davach of pasture'; and Delfour, near Kincraig in Badenoch, is 'dale of pasture'.

The term 'Pit', which appears so often at the beginning of names, is in old Gaelic *pett*, and is equivalent to the Welsh *peth*, a part, a share. From *pett*, later *peit*, comes *Peitigh*, Petty, 'place of "petts" or shares of land'; also *na Peiteachan*, in Killearnan, 'the place of shares'. *Blar-pheitigh*, Blairfettie, near Struan, is 'moor of (the) place of shares'. The names beginning with Pit are found as far north as Rogart in Sutherland. A few occur, or appear on record, in Glenelg and Loch Carron. In Easter Ross and the Black Isle there are a dozen or more; they are not so numerous in Inverness-shire.

In Gaul there were holy places of worship and of judgment called *nemeton*. The *nemeta* were usually placed in groves, and an eighth-century list of pagan rites and superstitions has a heading, 'de sacris silvarum quæ nimidas vocant', 'concerning shrines in groves which they call *nimidæ*'. The ancient Britons also had holy places so named. When the early Church obtained a hold, its policy was to take over these places for Christian use. In Scotland we have traces of many such; the term is in Gaelic *neimheadh*, gen. *neimhidh*. It is not unlikely that some at least of the places so named were places of assembly in pre-Gaelic times.

In Inverness-shire the only instance is *Creag Neimhidh*, 'rock of the Nemet', above Temple Pier, Glen Urquhart, near which stood the ancient church of St Finan and the 'Temple' of St Ringan or Ninian.

In Ross-shire there is *Cnoc Neimhidh*, Knocknavie, in Rosskeen, with a cairn on top called *Carn na Croiche*, 'the Gallows Cairn', indicating a tradition of judgment and execution. On the south slope of the hill is the old church of *Neimheadh na Cille*, Nonakiln, with a glebe attached till recent times. Low down beside the river is *Innis Neimhidh*, Inchnavie, 'the meadow of the Nemet', and on the north side of the hill is *Dail Neimhidh*, Dalnavie. Further east along the same ridge is *Neo' Mhór* (for *Neimheadh Mhór*), Newmore, on record as Nevyn Meikle, which belonged to the church of Tain, and which corresponds exactly to the Gaulish *Nemetomāros*, 'great Nemet'.

215

On the South Souter behind Cromarty is *Neamhaidigh*, Navity, the same as Navitie in Fife. The formation is from *neimheadh* with a suffix or extension, and means 'place of the Nemet'. Navity was church land, and had chapels of St Duthac of Tain and of St Michael. The firm tradition in Cromarty was that the final judgment is to take place on the moor of Navity; Hugh Miller records a striking instance of the effectiveness of this belief.

The above may be taken as specimens of the pre-Gaelic or British element in our northern names, which includes a number of important names, especially names of rivers.

Gaelic Church Names

Among our oldest Gaelic names are those connected with the early Scoto-Irish Church, which, owing to the zeal and wisdom of Columba, obtained a footing among the hitherto pagan Northern Picts about AD565. 'Columba,' says Bede, 'was the first teacher of the Christian faith to the Picts beyond the mountains northward, and the first founder of the monastery in the island of Hii, which was for a long time much honoured by many tribes of the Scots and Picts. The said Columba is now called by some Colum Cille, the name being compounded from "Columba" and "Cella".' Western commemorations of Columba usually employ the compound form, e.g. Iona was known as *I Choluim Chille*, and churches named after him are called *Cill Chaluim Chille*. At Largs, however, the great fair held on his day, June 9, was known as St Colm's Fair. In the east, though we have Cill Chaluim Chille in Strath Brora, the form regularly used is Colum, e.g. Inch-colm in the Firth of Forth. Columba is the patron saint of Petty, which possessed a girth or sanctuary, in Gaelic *tearmann* or *tearmad*, whence Termit in Petty. The church of Kingussie occupies the site of an ancient foundation dedicated to Columba.

Lughaidh, commonly known as Mo Luag, a contemporary of Columba, whose chief church was in Lismore, is supposed to have founded Rosemarkie. His name appears in *Dabhach Mo Luaig*, Davochmaluag, 'Mo Luag's davach', near Dingwall. Croftmaluag, 'Mo Luag's Croft', is now Chapelpark, at Raitts, Badenoch. *Cill Mo Luaig* and *Croit Mo Luaig*, his church and croft, are near Inverfarigaig.

Finan, another contemporary of Columba, was revered from Loch Shiel in Moidart, where is *Eilean Fhìonain*, St Finan's Isle, all along the Great Glen and in Nairn. A church bearing his name (Kilfinan) stood at the north-east end of Loch Lochy. There was another *Cill Fhìonain* near Temple, Glen Urquhart, where there are still *Lag Chill Fhìonain*, 'the hollow of St Finan's church', and *Allt Chill Fhìonain*, Kilfinan Burn. A third church named *Cill Fhìonain* may still be seen, with its ancient burial ground, near Loch Ness at Abriachan. *Seipeil Fhìonain*, 'St Finan's chapel', is the Gaelic name of Foynesfield at Nairn. The Records of the Presbytery of Inverness have, under date 23 November 1643: 'That day report was made to the Presbitrie that there was in the Paroch of Dunlichitie ane Idolatrous Image called St Finane, keepit in a private house obscurely.' At next meeting the image was delivered to the Ministers of Inverness, who ordained that it should be burned at their Market Cross next Tuesday, after sermon, which was duly done.

Still another contemporary and intimate friend of Columba was Cainneach, whose chief seat in Ireland was Achadh Bó, 'the cows' field', in Ossory (Queen's Co). He is said to have accompanied Columba on his visit to Brude, the king of the Picts, at Inverness, and to have stayed for some time in Scotland. It is not unlikely, though there is no certainty, that Cainneach's place of residence was near the old church of Laggan, near the eastern end of Loch Laggan; this church bore his name, and the parish was called *Lagan Choinnich*, 'Cainneach's hollow'.

The parishes of Killearnan and Kiltarlity, whose ministers have done much good work conjointly on the history and literature of the Highlands, are named after saints Earnan and Talorgan. Another Killearnan is in Kildonan parish, Sutherland, and Talorgan is commemorated in *Cill Taraghlain*, near Portree, in

Skye. Adamnan mentions Ernen, son of Cresen, as a younger contemporary of Columba, and he may be the saint of Killearnan; but data for proof are lacking. Owing to a misreading of a name in the list of St Donnan's community in Eigg, Talorgan has been wrongly asserted to have been one of Donnan's monks. As the name of Portree Bay is *Loch Caluim Chille*, 'Columba's Loch', it is possible that Talorgan was of the community of Iona; but we have no further trustworthy data.

Maol Rubha, or Maol Ruibhe, of Applecross is, next to Columba, the most famous saint of the Scoto-Irish Church. He was abbot of Bangor in Ulster, and in AD 671 crossed to Scotland and founded the monastery of Aporcrossan, now Applecross, where he died in AD 722. In Loch Carron the site of the present parish church was known as *Clachan Ma-Ruibhe* (*Maol* in unstressed position becoming *Ma* owing to assimilation of the *l* with *r*). The stream that flows by the church is still known as *Buadhchag*, 'the little one of virtue'—once a holy stream of power to cure diseases. He was the saint of Contin in Ross-shire, where a famous fair was held on his day at the end of August; later *Féill Ma-Ruibhe* was shifted to Dingwall. *Preas Ma-Ruibhe* near Strathpeffer is the burial place of the family of Coul. *Loch Ma-Ruibhe*, Loch Maree, has superseded the older name of Loch Ewe. *Eilean Ma-Ruibhe*, Maol Rubha's Isle, is in Loch Shin; he was the saint of Lairg. Keith in Banffshire was of old called 'Maol Rubha's Keith' (Kethmalruf); his fair there was 'Summareve's Fair', i.e. Saint Ma-reve's Fair. Amulree in Perthshire is in Gaelic *Ath Maol Ruibhe*, 'Maol Rubha's Ford', on the river Braan. The people of Harris and of Skye still asseverate by his name: 'Ma Ruibhe tha!'; 'By Maol Ruibhe it is so!' The account of the rites performed in his honour in the seventeenth century by the people of Loch Carron and Gairloch is given in the *Records of the Presbytery of Dingwall*, edited by Dr William Mackay.

Curitan, Bishop of Rosemarkie, was contemporary with Maol Rubha. He was a cleric of high position and great importance, for in AD 697 he and Bishop Ceti or Cœddi of Iona were the two clerical sureties from Alba for the fulfilment of Adamnan's Law forbidding the employment of women in battle. The other Scottish surety was Brude, son of Derile, king of the Picts. *Cladh Churadain*, St Curitan's graveyard, is at the lower end of Loch Ness, and between the Loch and Caiplich is *Suidhe Churadain*, Curitan's Seat. At the church of Corrimony in Glen Urquhart there is another *Cladh Churadain*, with *Croit Churadain* and *Tobar Churadain*, Curitan's Croft and Well, the latter on Buntait. A third graveyard of the same name is at Struy in Strathglass, and a fourth lies at the top of a field above Assynt farmhouse, Novar. A hillock north of Ardoch, Alness, once, I believe, church property, is called *Cnoc Churadair* (for *Churadain*). The Minister of Wardlaw states that the saint of the old church of Farnua, near Beauly, was Corridon, i.e. Curadan.

Comgan was son of Caointighearna (Kentigerna), daughter of a king of Leinster; she died in AD734. Comgan was therefore contemporary with Curitan. He was connected with Loch Alsh, and was revered about Dingwall and the Aird. An interesting tale in the Wardlaw Manuscript makes Lord Lovat's shepherd asseverate by St Coan about the year 1570. In 1603 or soon thereafter, Macdonald of Glen Garry, having been taken to Edinburgh for his part in the Raid of Kilchrist, was proved by Mr John Mackenzie, parson of Tollie near Dingwall, to be a worshipper of St Coan, whose image was afterwards taken to Edinburgh and burned at the Cross. Mountrich near Dingwall is in Gaelic *Cill Chomhghain*.

Baile Dhubhthaich, the Gaelic name of Tain, is St Dubhthach's Town; the old church of St Dubhthach or Duthac stands on Tain Links. He appears to have lived long after Curitan, but the pilgrimages made to his shrine by Scottish nobles, and at least one king of Scotland (James IV), and the reverence in which his relics were held, show that his cult was extensive and powerful. He is commemorated in *Clachan Dubhthaich* in Kintail, whence Loch Duich beside it. A pass from Kintail to Glen Affric is called *Cadha Dhubhthaich*. His fair, the Féill Dubhthaich, at Tain used to be largely attended.

The saint of Dornoch was St Barre of Cork, who died early in the seventh century. The Dornoch market or fair was held on his day, September 25. No place-name in Sutherland is known to commemorate him; but the Isle of Barra is a Norse hybrid meaning 'St Barr's Isle'; Barra and adjacent isles were called by the Norse *Barr-eyjar*. His church there is *Cill Bharr*.

Some general terms connected with the Church may close this section. Applecross is in Gaelic *a' Chomraich*, the sanctuary, formerly *a' Chomraich Abrach*, where *abrach* is the adjective from *abar*, of old *opar*, a river mouth. The bounds of the sanctuary were marked by stone crosses, one of which was entire about 1872, when a mason engaged on building the new school smashed it in a fit of religious zeal. The other great sanctuary of the North was *Comraich Bhaile Dhubhthaich*, the girth of Tain. It too was marked by stone crosses.

An interesting instance of a river deriving its name from a church connection is the Orrin of Glen Orrin, which flows near by the church of Urray in Ross-shire. *Oirrinn*, Orrin, is the genitive singular of *oifreann*, an offering (Lat. *offerendum*). The river mouth was once known as Inverafferayn (from *aifreann*, another form); thus we have the unusual circumstance of river, glen, and confluence obtaining names through Church influence. The offering was doubtless a grant of land to the early church of Urray.

In regard to Clachnaharry, near Inverness, the Minister of Wardlaw wrote: 'The battle of Clach-ni-Harry, i.e. the Repentance or Pennance Stone, happened June 27, 1378.' Dr William Mackay, who edited the manuscript for the Scottish History Society, preferred the popular explanation, *Clach na h-Aire*, the Stone of the Watching. Old men, however, uninfluenced by ideas about the meaning, have given the name in Gaelic as the minister spells it, and refused the pronunciation *Clach na h-Aire*. It appears therefore that the minister was right, and that the last part of the name is *aithrigh* or *aithrighe*, repentance, a term which was formerly current, now displaced by *aithreachas*. The stone was in all probability so named because it was used as a penitential station, like *Clach a' Pheanais*, 'the Stone of Penance', hard by the old church of Cill Chatriona in Colonsay.

Dobhach nan Cliar, Dochnaclear, in Fodderty, probably means 'the Clerics' Davoch', i.e. land that belonged to the Church, like its neighbour, Davochmaluag.

A' Chananaich, Fortrose, means 'the place of Canons', Chanonry. This is the only name by which Fortrose is known in Gaelic, just as Tain is known only as *Baile Dhubhthaich*. We have thus lost valuable data for the derivation of the names Tain and Fortrose.

Two places in the North are known as *a' Mhanachainn*, 'the Monastery', Beauly and Fearn. The former is differentiated as *Manachainn MhicShimidh*, 'Lord Lovat's Monastery'; the latter as *Manachainn Rois*, 'the Monastery of Ross'. Markets held at both places were called *Féill na Manachainn*. Beauly itself is French *Beaulieu*, 'beautiful place', from Latin *bellus locus*. The Monastery or Priory was founded by John Byset, lord of Lovat, in 1230, and the monks were of the order of Valliscaulians, who delighted in gardening. Hence an old bard of the Mackenzies calls it 'Manchainn nan Lios', 'the monastery of gardens'. Chanonry he styles 'Cananaich nan Clag', 'Chanonry of the bells'.

An old and important term connected with the Scoto-Irish Church is *annaid*, earlier *andóit*, explained by the Irish learned men as a patron saint's church, or a church which contained the relics of the founder. The derivation has not been settled, but it may come from late Latin *antas*, genitive *antāt-is*, a shortened form of *antiquitas*, with the not uncommon change from abstract to concrete, i.e. from 'antiquity' to 'an antique place'.

Our Annats are often situated in rather remote places, and can be very seldom associated with any particular saint. But in, I think, all instances they show traces of an ancient chapel or cemetery, or of both. Often, too, the Annat adjoins a fine spring or a clear flowing stream. The nominative is *an annaid*, 'the Annat', fem., gen. *na h-annaide*.

North-east of Duthil church is Achnahannet, with remains of what seems to have been a round stone cell; also a magnificent spring. Another Achnahannet is near Spean Bridge, 'where there was a chappell builded of ancient, not two mylls from Kilmanevag'. Another Achnahannet is in Glen Urquhart. An *Annaid* is at the head of Glen Roy, also on Allt Dotha, west of Corpach, in Kilmallie. Near Beauly there is Groam na h-Annaide. Here 'Groam' is an ancient term for a swamp or bog, and the Annat was apparently constructed in the bog; similarly in Ireland it is recorded in the Latin Life of Carthach or Mo-chutu that a certain saint had made his cell *in gronna deserti*, translated in the Irish Life by *ar móin fhásaigh*, 'on a desert bog'.

On the Ross-shire mainland there is Achnahannet in Kincardine, near *Cill Mo-Chalmaig*, the ancient church of St Colman, with its cemetery, near Kilmachalmag Burn. In Strath Conon there are two Annats, one near Balnault in the lower part of the strath, the other much further up, opposite Invermany. The parish of Nigg has, among other memorials of the early Church, an Annat and *Loch na h-Annaide* on Nigg Hill. On the west there is an Annat at Kildonan on Loch Broom, and another at Torridon.

Achadh na h-Annaide in Durness is mentioned by Rob Donn. There is also Annat and Annat Bay in Loch Cabhaidh, off Loch Laxford. I know of no Annat in Caithness.

Ruilick in the Aird and near Beauly is from *reilig*, a graveyard or cemetery, which is borrowed from Latin *reliquiæ*, whence English 'relic'.

'Ireland' Names

Early Gaelic influence is indicated by the name Findhorn, for *Find Eirinn*, 'white or bright Ireland', primarily denoting the bright sandy district about the mouth of the river. The river valley is *Srath Eireann*, Ireland's Strath, with the five Coigs or Fifths at its head. The Gaelic saying regarding these is almost too well known to need repetition: 'Tha cóig cóigimh an Eirinn, agus tha cóig cóigimh an Srath Eireann, ach is fhearr aon chóigeamh na h-Eireann na cóig cóigimh Srath Eireann'—'There are five fifths in

Ireland and five fifths in Strathdearn (Ireland's Strath); but better is one fifth of Ireland than the five fifths of Strathdearn'. A large fort near Dulsie Bridge on Findhorn is named *Dùn Eireann*, 'Ireland's Fort'. Strathdearn is identical with Strathearn in Perthshire.

Opposed in meaning to Findhorn is Deveron, which, in view of the old spellings, is plainly 'Black Ireland'; nor can it be without significance that at the mouth of Deveron is Banff: Banbha is an old name for Ireland.

Allt Eireann, Auldearn, means 'Ireland's Burn', and the old name of Auldearn parish appeals to have been Eren or Eryn.

Another ancient name for Ireland was *Elg*, dative *Eilgg*. This appears twice in the north—(1) in *Gleann Eilge*, Glenelg; (2) in *Eilginn*, Elgin, the capital of Moray. The latter used to be styled by way of distinction *Eilginn Moireibh*, 'Elgin of Moray'. An old rhyme has:–

> Elgin Moray on the coast,
> From whence good comes but rare, etc

This rhyme was, of course, a product of the northern side of the Moray Firth.

Old Customs

Some names preserve the memory of old customs. A name which must have a history, now lost, is *Cnoc nan Giall*, Knocknagael, 'the hill of hostages', near Inverness. This name must have arisen from some memorable occasion or occasions.

Cnoc an Tionail, now the site of the Cameron Barracks, is 'the gathering hill', or 'the rallying hill', probably a rendezvous in times of stress.

Innis a' Bhàirigh, Inchberry, is 'the hurling meadow', where young men played shinty. Similarly near Callander there is *Achadh an Làmhaich*, 'the field of casting', where the young men practised casting spears of old, a regular part of their training.

223

The old term for an assembly or market is *aonach*. Hence comes *Tigh an Aonaich*, Teaninich, near Alness, 'house of the market or assembly'. Blarninich, near the church of Fodderty, is 'moor of the market'. Aonachan, not far from Spean Bridge, is 'market place', and an old writer reports that adjacent to it 'selling and buying wyne, ale, aquavitæ, and sundry drinks and merchandice' went on. Spean Bridge is in Gaelic *Drochaid Aonachain*. One of our best known *puirt-a-beul* is entitled 'Gobhainn Druim an Aonaich', 'the Smith of market-ridge'.

The hunting of the deer of old was practised not by stalking but by driving and gradually surrounding the deer over a wide area, and finally forcing them to pass through a narrow defile, sometimes artificial. The gentlemen were assigned stations on either side (*tom sealga*), whence they shot the game with arrows, or later with guns. This narrow pass or deertrap was called *eileirg*, or in northern Gaelic *iolairg*, whence our numerous Elricks. The Elrick nearest to Inverness is near Flichity, in Strath Nairn. There is also an Elrick in Glen Affric, the furthest north known to me. Another name for much the same thing was *eileag*, and this is the regular term north of Inverness. 'Eileag na Baintighearna', 'the Lady's *eileag*', was on Caiplich moor, east of Abriachan, and appears to have been so named after a Lady of Lovat, described by the Minister of Wardlaw as 'a stout bold woman' and 'a great hunter'. That the *eileag* was not always a narrow defile appears from some remarks in the *Old Statistical Account* by the Minister of Assynt with regard to a place in his parish called *Feith na h-Ardeileig*, 'the bog of the high *eileag*', explained by him as 'a track of soft boggy moor in which, in times of old, the natives gathered deer, and when entangled they killed them'. It may have been from a similar unsportsmanlike but effective practice that we have *Bog na h-Eileig* and *Loch na h-Eileig* on Lettoch in Killearnan parish.

A name that has roused the curiosity of at least one classical scholar—a late Inspector of Schools—is Achpopuli on the moor of Abriachan. In Gaelic it is *Achadh Poible*, field of the *pobull*. The *pobull* was a hunting or herding hut, formerly feminine, genitive *poible*. Belisarius, says Procopius, used a tent of heavy cloth, commonly called a παπυλεῶν (pavilion), when on his campaigns. A stream in Kincardine parish is called *Abhainn Poible*, river of (the) hut or booth.

Another name which has come to have much the same meaning is *longphort*, originally a ship-station, then an encampment, then a dwelling or even a palace, then a hunting booth; in Aberdeenshire a 'lunkart' was the name used for the circle of stones containing an open-air fire for washing. A well known example is Loch Luichart, 'loch of (the) encampment or booth'. In Kintail there are Camas Longard on Loch Long, and Lungard and Loch Lungard. Here the meaning is probably 'ship station'. The term is widely distributed and assumes various forms, e.g. Luncarty (dative pl.) near Perth; Craig-lockhart in Edinburgh; Longford in Midlothian. Hence also Gaelic *lùchairt*, a palace.

Both, a hut, gives Boath in Nairnshire and Boath in Alness parish; the latter is *na Bothachan*, 'the hut-places', in Gaelic. This term is rather common along the Great Glen: '*Both Neachdain*', Bunachton, 'Nechtan's booth'; Boleskine; *Both Lobhach* (anglicized, I think, as Bulloch) in Brae Lochaber, meaning 'rotten hut', with reference perhaps to the ground around it; Bohuntin and *Both Chàsgaidh* in Glen Roy. Another 'epidemic' of *both* occurs in north and north-west Perthshire.

Names of Persons

Place-names often involve names of persons. Instances have been given already of the numerous names containing names of saints; a few containing names of laymen may be added.

Gleann Fhionghuin, Glen Finnan, is 'Fingon's glen'; *Fingon* is a very old personal name, whence *MacFhionghuin*, Mackinnon.

Fearann Domhnaill, Ferindonald, comprising the parishes of Alness and Kiltearn, is 'Donald's land', the *dùthchas* or homeland of the Munros. Who the Donald in question was cannot now be determined. Similarly a long strip on the north side of the Kyle of Sutherland was *Fearann Cosgraigh*, 'Coscrach's land'.

Dail Fhearghuis, Dal-arossie in Strathdearn, means 'Fergus's holme or flat'. The old genitive of Fergus was *Fergusa, Fearghusa*, the final *a* of which is represented by *-ie* in the anglicized form; this shows that the latter is old.

A number of names containing names of persons appear under the other headings.

The Davach

The old measure of land in the north was the *dabhach*, now pronounced *do'ach*, meaning primarily a vat, a large tub. The mash-tub used by smugglers of whisky was *an do'ach*: I have heard it so called by one of the fraternity. As a land measure the davach was not a fixed number of acres: it denoted the amount of land, infield and outfield and pasture, which would maintain a certain amount of stock. The davach was the largest unit of land, and the term was probably so applied because it was the largest measure of capacity among the Gaelic people of Scotland and Ireland. It is worth noting that according to tradition Garbol in Strathdearn was so named because its infield required a big boll (*garbh bolla*) of seed. There is another Garbol in Breakish, Skye. The davach, as is known from the Book of Deer, was the unit of assessment for all the various burdens effeiring [=pertaining] to land tenure. It was also the unit for military service even in the eighteenth century; when men were needed for *feachd* or *sluaghadh* (expedition or hosting), the numbers were so many for each davach.

Near Inverness there are Doch-four, 'the davach of the pasture'; Doch-craig, 'the davach of the rock'; and Dochgarroch, probably 'davach of the rough land'. Dochanassie on Loch Lochy is 'the davach of the station or stance' (*fasadh*). Strath Conon, from Leac a' Bhradain at the Eas Dubh of Scatwell to Creag a' Chaoruinn above Scardroy, towards Ledgowan, comprised three half davachs (*leathdach*): *Leathdach Bun an t-Sratha*, the half davach of Bunantra (foot of the strath); *Leathdach Méinn*, the half davach of Main, in the middle of the strath; and *Leathdach Ceann Loch Beanncharain*, the half davach of the lower end of Loch Beanncharan.

Leathdach is anglicised as Lettoch, whence Lettoch in Killearnan and elsewhere. With the first part (*leath*) translated we have Halfdavach, which becomes Haddo in Aberdeenshire.

The eighth part of the davach was *ochdamh* or *ochtamh*, whence Ochto on the Kyle of Sutherland opposite Rosehall, and a number of other names, such as Ochdavullin, for Ochdamh a' Mhuilinn, the octave of the mill. Ochdamh a' Bhlair, Achterblair, near Carr-Bridge, is the octave of the moor.

The fourth part of the davach is *ceathramh*, anglicized as Kerrow and Kerrie, e.g. Kerrow-more, the big quarter; Kerrow-aird, the high quarter; Kerrow-gair, the short quarter. Kirriemuir in Angus may be for *Ceathramh Muire*, the Virgin Mary's quarter—churchland; but *Cill Mhoire*, 'Mary's Church', is also possible. The Kerry river in Gairloch is Norse, 'copse water'.

Forts and Brochs

The chief defensive structures north of the Grampians fall into two classes, brochs and forts. North of the Kyle of Sutherland there are hosts of brochs, but very few forts. Between the Kyle and Inverness, at the mouth of the Great Glen, there are, or were, some half-dozen brochs, but a large number of forts, three of which were of first importance, namely, Craig-phadraig at Inverness, the fort on the Ord of Kessock, and the great fort on Knockfarrel above Strathpeffer. Similar to these in position and structure, there is the Dun of Creich on the north side of the Dornoch Firth. All four are vitrified. Of brochs south of the Kyle, one is at *Achadh na h-Uamhach*, 'field of the cave', so called doubtless from an underground structure connected with the broch; the place is now Birchfield in English. A little way further down the Kyle there is a small broch on Kilmachalmag Burn. The next was at Edderton, named Dun Alaisgaig, 'fort of Ali's strip', the latter part being Norse. There are remains of broch-like structures on Scotsburn farm and in Boath, Alness. One at least is at Struy, Strath Glass, and another, called Castle Spynie, near Lentran. Between Inverness and the Grampians there are no brochs, and not very many forts. As to distribution elsewhere, I know of no fort or broch between Knockfarrel and Strome Ferry, i.e. in Strath Conon, Strath Garve, Strath Bran, and so on by Achnasheen. Nor does there seem to be any fort between Garve and Braemore on the way to Ullapool. On the other hand, the lower part of the Beauly basin is well supplied with forts. The next line of forts is along the Great Glen, from Inverness to Fort William. It would be interesting to speculate on the reasons that underlie these facts of distribution.

The period of the brochs has been so far settled that they are proved to have been in use during the Roman occupation of Britain. Of course they were not all built at the same time, and their construction may have begun even before the beginning of the Christian era. The approximate period of the northern forts is so far quite undetermined, and will remain so until some of them have been thoroughly excavated. When this takes place we may be in a position to compare the early civilisation of the north with that of the south of Scotland as revealed by the excavations on Traprain Law in East Lothian.

The brochs are called by the Gaelic people sometimes *dùn*, a fort, and sometimes *caisteal*, a castle; but an older Gaelic name for them and for the broch-like structures in Perthshire and Argyll was *caiseal*. This is proved by the place-names Casley in Sutherland and Cashlie in Glen Lyon, both of which have brochs or similar structures. These names are for *caislibh*, the dative-locative plural of *caiseal*, a stone fort. The most famous broch in Sutherland is Dùn Dornaigil in Strathmore, ludicrously made into Dun Dornadilla. *Dornaigil* is Norse, meaning 'thorn gully'. An account of 1726 in Macfarlane's *Geographical Collections* says: 'It's called by tradition Dundornigil', as it is now in Gaelic.

Forts are sometimes named after men, sometimes from some other circumstance. Knockfarrel is in Gaelic *Cnoc Fearghalaigh*, 'Fearghal's (or Fearghalach's) Hill', an old name. The fort thereon is traditionally connected with the burning of the women of the Fiann by Garadh mac Morna, and appears to be referred to in several Fenian ballads under the titles of *Bruth Farbairn* (i.e. Brugh Farbraoin), 'the Mansion of Fairburn': *Tigh Farala* and *Tigh Fharmail*, 'House of Farala' or 'Farmal'. When the disaster was in progress, the Fiann were in Skye hunting. They made haste to leap the strait on their spears, but one small member of the band, named Mac Reatha, fell short and was drowned, whence *Caol Reatha*, Kylerea, 'Reatha's Strait'. One rather dislikes to suggest that Caol Reatha may mean 'Strait of the Race or Current', from *rith*, old genitive *reatha*, still used in Irish.

Craig-phadraig is 'Patrick's Rock', but the name may not be old.

A very large fort on a hill at the east end of Strathrory in Ross-shire is named *Dun Gobhal*. A local authority considered it to mean 'Goll's Fort', Goll being a famous warrior of the Fiann. This was of interest as showing survival of the Fenian tradition in Easter Ross; but the meaning must be 'Fort of (the) Forks', from its situation on the brink of a double gully at its eastern side.

Dun Dearduil, perched high on a rock at the Pass of Inverfarigaig, is traditionally connected with the heroine Deirdre, who eloped from Ulster with Naoise, the son of Usneach, about the beginning of the first century, and came with him and his two brothers to Scotland. There is no doubt that Deirdre's name became Dearduil in Scotland, for it appears so in poetry, probably through an intermediate form, Dearduir or Deardair. The great tale was widely known, and several versions or redactions of it were made from age to age. One of these connects the heroine with various places in Argyll. A poem which is not ancient, though fairly old, mentions Naoise as returning from the host or hosting at Inverness. In this case, as in the other famous and parallel case of Diarmid and the boar, a widely known tale tended to be localized in more than one place: Diarmid's story is placed in Sutherland, in Kintail, in Skye, in Lochaber, in Perthshire, and doubtless elsewhere in Scotland. *Grianan Dearduil*, traditionally understood as 'Deirdre's sunny spot', is near the head of Glen Etive. An old account of Glen Lyon states: 'Item upon the northsyde of Glenlyon, Grinen-dair-dyr, a hie steep hill'. This is of course for *Grianan Deardair*, now *an Grianan*, a most beautiful shapely hill far up Glen Lyon, the tradition of which is now apparently lost. The *Old Statistical Account* of Kilmalie describes a fort spelled Dundhairghall 'upon the very summit of a green hill, about 400 yards perpendicular in height', commanding part of Mamore and the whole of Glen Nevis, and within sight of the castle of Inverlochy. This seems to be another Dun Dearduil, but I have not heard the name in Gaelic. It has to be mentioned that there is a word *deardan*, with variant *deardal*, meaning 'storm'; this might explain Dun Deardail well: 'Fort of Storm'; but it leaves us with the Glen Lyon name.

Dun Eireann, the large fort on Findhorn, has been mentioned. In Daviot there is Dun Deimhidh, explained by Dr Macbain as British or Pictish, the equivalent of the British tribal name Demetae, from the base *dem*, sure, strong; Gaelic *deimhin*. There is another Daviot in Aberdeenshire.

Strathdearn has no forts; in this high-lying valley the people appear to have dwelt quiet and secure, like the Zidonians.

In Laggan there is the important hill fort of *Dùn dà Làmh*, 'the fort of two hands', so named for some reason unknown to me. It resembles the name *Dùn dà Ràmh*, 'the fort of two oars', near Inverary, the old MacNaughton stronghold.

Names round Inverness

A few of the names around Inverness may now be mentioned.

Abban Street in Inverness is from *àban*, explained to me by the late Mr Hugh Maclennan, Hilton, as a backwater, or a small creek running off from a larger body of water. *Clach an Abain*, 'the stone of the creek', is a large boulder in Petty Bay. A small creek off Loch Dochfour is called *an t-Aban*. I have not met the term except in Inverness and neighbourhood.

Affric of Glen Affric is a compound of *ath*, intensive, and *breac*, mottled, meaning 'very speckled or mottled'. It was once a not uncommon woman's name: two Abbesses of Kildare were named Affraic, dying in AD743 and 834 respectively. A poem in *The Book of the Dean of Lismore* is by Affraic nighean Chorcadail (daughter of Corcadal, whence MacCorquodale). The Affric of the Glen was regarded by Dr Macbain as a stream goddess; but it may well have been the name of a mortal woman who was in some way connected with the glen.

Ard na Saor, Ardersier, is probably 'cape of the wrights', the final *n* of *nan* (gen. pl. of the article) being lost before *s*, as is usual.

Ashie of Loch Ashie is in Gaelic *Athaisidh*, for *ath-inse*, from ath in the sense of 'worn out', as in *atach* for *ath-aodach*, 'worn out clothes', and *inse*, gen. sg. of *inis*, a meadow. Loch Athaisidh thus means 'the loch of the worn out meadow', i.e. the meadow poor in pasture. The ridge running close by is *Druim Athaisidh*, anglicised as Drummossie.

Avoch means 'stream-place', from *abh*, a river, with the suffix *-ach*. *Abh* was often sounded *obh* (even in Old Irish we have *oub* for *ab*, a river), and Avoch is in Gaelic *Obhach*. Another example is *Loch Obhaich*, Loch Oich, 'the loch of stream-place'; the river that enters the loch was of old called *Abh*, and the higher ground on one side of it is still called *Uachdar Abha*, 'the upland of Awe'. The river Awe in Argyll is in Gaelic *Abha*, and its foot is *Bun Abha*, Bunawe or Bonawe: but the loch is *Loch Obha*, Loch Owe. A side loch off Loch Awe is *Loch Abhaich*, Loch Avich, 'loch of stream-place'. There is another Loch Awe in Sutherland.

Bona, at the lower end of Loch Ness, is in Gaelic *am Bàn-ath*, 'the white ford', from some white stones in the old ford there before the construction of the Caledonian Canal. But Bonar in Sutherland is *am Bann-àth*, 'the lowest ford', originally *am Bonn-àth*. The old ford may still be noted a little way below the bridge.

Castlehill near Inshes is *Caisteal Still*, 'castle of (the) strip', with reference to some strip of land.

Cùil na Càbaig, Culcabock, is 'nook of the cheese'.

Cùil lodair, Culloden, is for *Cùil lodain*, 'nook of the puddle'; the final *n*, preserved in the English form, has changed to *r* in modern Gaelic.

Cùil-daodhail, Culduthel, is an obscure and difficult name. The first part is *cùil*, a nook; the second part is the same as *Daodhal*, Duthil, the parish name. As far as sound goes, the names might be spelled *Daoghal*, but *gh* would hardly become *th* in the anglicized forms; in these *gh* often appears as *v*; e.g. *na Ruighean*, Rhives, 'the slopes'.

Cùil Challaigh, Kilcoy, is 'hazelly nook', from O.Ir. *collde*, 'hazelly', the adjective of *coll*, hazel. In Gaelic the old *o* has become *a*; 'Kilcoy' has come down through Cul-colly, Cul-cowie, the *ll* becoming almost or quite lost in Scots. Similarly Dun-coll in Dumfriesshire is now Duncow; the Colly burn in Angus is now Cowie; Tolly in Aberdeenshire is Towie. *Bealach Collaidh*, 'hazelly pass', to the west of Wyvis, preserves *o* of O.Ir.

Dores is in Gaelic *Duros* or *Duras*, for *Dubh-ros*, 'black wood'; ros means primarily something 'fore-standing', either vertically (whence a wood) or horizontally (whence a cape or promontory).

Errogie in Stratherrick is *Air-aghaidh*, 'east face', from its aspect.

Essich, near Inverness, is 'place of waterfalls'.

Flichity is 'place of wetness'. Flichity Hotel is called in Gaelic *Tigh an Ailein*, 'the house of the green'.

Dun-telchaig is *Dun-tseilcheig*, 'fort of (the) snail'. This prefixing of *t* before the genitive sg. of nouns beginning with *s* is an old custom, seen, for instance, in *Ceann tSaile*, Kintail, 'head of salt water'. The hill above Loch Duntelchaig, as viewed from Abriachan, looks exactly like a huge snail.

Foyers is in Gaelic *Foithir*, 'a terraced slope'. There are several 'Foyers' in Stratherrick, whence the English plural. The Falls of Foyers are in Gaelic *Eas na Smùide*, 'waterfall of the vapour or spray'.

An Leacainn, the Leachkin, the fine slope north by west of Inverness, is 'the hill-side'; it is the dative sg. of *leac*, a cheek: the nominative is sometimes used in the same sense, e.g. *Leac Ruaidh*, Leckroy, the hill side at the head of Glen Roy.

Loch na Seanais, the favourite curling loch near Inverness, is 'loch of the old meadow', and its anglicized form should be rather Loch na Shanish than Loch na Sanais. The name is shortened from *L. na Sean-inse*.

Mun-lochy means 'at foot of (the) loch', from older Gaelic *i mBun-locha*. Here the nasal of the preposition *in* combines with the following *b*, and the result is *m*; the final *a* of *locha* becomes *y* or *ie*, as often. An exact parallel is Monessie in Brae Lochaber, for *i mBun-easa*, 'at foot of waterfall'; similarly Mon-ess at Aberfeldy is for *i mBun-eas*, 'at foot of waterfalls'.

Norse Names

The Norse overlordship and partial occupation of the northern mainland appears to date from about AD875, when Thorstein the Red, together with Sigurd of Orkney, conquered and ruled over Caithness and Sutherland, Ross and Moray, according to *Islands Landnamabok* (the Book of the land-take of Iceland). After the death of Thorfinn in 1064 the Norse dominions gradually contracted to Caithness. The Norse supremacy over the northern parts ended finally in 1200, in the reign of William the Lyon.

Norse influence is strong in Caithness, rather less in Sutherland, and still less in Ross and Cromarty. Its limit on the eastern side is the Beauly Valley, where we have Eskadale, 'Ash-dale'. No names of Norse origin occur further along the east coast.

The examples of Norse names that follow are taken chiefly from the mainland of Ross and Cromarty and Sutherland.

á, a river, genitive *ár*, is seen in *Brùra*, Brora, for *Brúar-á*, 'bridge-water'. The genitive occurs in Arscaig, for *ár-skiki*, 'river's-strip', in Sutherland. Amat of Strath Carron, Kincardine parish, is *á-mót*, 'river-meet'. There are also Amat in Strath Oykel and in Strath Brora, all at confluences.

bol-staðr, a homestead, assumes more than one shape when taken over into Gaelic; in our examples it is regularly bol, except in Scrabster, which is *Skara-bolstaðr*, 'seamew-stead', in the *Orkneyinga Saga*. In Sutherland there are *Unabol*, Unapool, 'Una's or Uni's homestead'; Kirkibol, 'kirk-stead'; *Crosabol*, Crosspool, 'rood-stead'; Erribol, 'gravel-beach stead' (*eyrr*, gen. *eyrrar*, a gravel beach); Tor-boll, 'Thori's stead'; Skelbo, 'shell stead', like Gaelic Sligo, Sligachan, Pitsligo; *Sgìobul*, Skibo, either 'Skithi's stead' or 'firewood stead' (*skíð*, firewood).

In Ross and Cromarty there are *Ullabol*, Ullapool, 'Ulli's stead'; Cadboll, probably 'wildcat's stead'; Arboll, perhaps 'seal-stead', and Culbo, Gaelic *Cùrabol*, for *kúla-ból*, 'knob-stead', from *kúla*, a ball, knob, rounded hillock.

dalr, a dale, is common. In Sutherland, Armadale in Farr is either 'arm dale' or 'bay dale'. Helmsdale is in the sagas Hjalmund's dale. Swordale is 'sward dale'; it recurs in Kiltearn parish, Ross-shire, and in Skye, all in Gaelic *Suardal*. Torrisdale is 'Thori's dale'. Spinningdale, in Gaelic *Spaingdal*, is doubtful.

The chief Ross-shire dales are: Alladale, 'Ali's dale'; *Dìobadal*, Dibidale, 'deep dale', a well-deserved name; Strath-rusdale, 'strath' being prefixed by the Gaelic people to *Hrúts-dalr*, 'Hrútr's dale' (the personal name Hrútr means 'ram', whence Gaelic *rùta*); Earradale in Gairloch, 'gravel-beach dale'; Attadale in Loch Carron and Applecross, probably *at-dalr*, 'fight-dale', with reference to horse-fights; Tarradale, 'bull-dale'.

fjörðr, a firth, appears in Lax-ford, 'salmon firth', and in Gruinnard, Loch Broom, 'shallow firth'; the same name occurs as Greenyards (English plural) in Kincardine.

nés, a cape, headland, forms the second part of Duirinish, 'deer cape', in Lochalsh; the name recurs in Skye and near Bunawe in Argyll; also in Sutherland as Durness (*dyra-nés*). Hence *Dìùra*, Jura, for *dyra-ey*, 'deer island'.

vík, a creek, bay, gives *Sìldeig*, Shieldaig, 'herring bay' (*síld-vík*). *Dìobaig*, Dibaig, 'deep bay' (*djúp-vík*), in Applecross and Gairloch; *Mealabhaig*, Melvaig, 'bent-grass bay' (*melar-vík*), in Gairloch.

völlr, a field, appears often as *-well*. In Sutherland, Rossal is for *hross-völlr*, 'horse field'; its grass is still regarded as hurtful to cattle but not to horses. Brawl is in Gaelic *Breithal*, for *breið-völlr*, 'broad field'. Musal, formerly Moswell, is 'mossy field'. Langwell is *lang-völlr*, 'long field', a common name.

In Ross-shire the chief example is Ding-wall, 'Thing-field', the seat of the Norse Thing or court of justice. Langwell in Strath Carron, Kincardine, and in the Black Isle, is 'long field', Scatwell is *skatt-völlr*, 'tax-field', or 'tribute field'. Katewell in Kiltearn, in Gaelic *Ciadail*, is doubtful.

Some miscellaneous names may be added. Assynt in Sutherland, and near Novar Station in Ross-shire, is probably Norse, but difficult; the usual derivation from *áss-endi*, 'rock end' (Ceann na Creige), is unsatisfactory in respect that the initial *a* of Assynt is short in Gaelic. Golspie, in 1330 Goldespy, and now in Gaelic *Goillsbidh*, has as its second part *byr* or *baer*, a stead or village; but the first part is uncertain. Cyderhall, near Dornoch, is in 1230 Sywardhoth, i.e. 'Sigurd's howe' (*haugr*). It is the burial place of Earl Sigurd, who died from the effects of a scratch from the bucktooth of Mael Brighde, Mormaer of Moray, whose head he carried at his saddle-bow. The sagas state that Sigurd was buried at Ekkialsbakki (Oykel Bank), the date being about AD 890. Strome is Norse *straumr*, a current, a tide-race; Strome Ferry is in Gaelic *Port an t-Sròim*. The great bar at the mouth of the Dornoch Firth, whose roar may be heard miles away on a frosty night, is called 'the Gizzen Briggs', for Norse *gisnar bryggja*, 'leaky bridge'. Tradition has it that this is all that is left of a 'bridge' which once reached from Ross to Sutherland. In Gaelic I have always heard it called *Drochaid an Obh* (pronounced long, like *ow* in cowl). A malicious water sprite or hag is called a 'vow' in Easter Ross English.

Varia

(Reply to a Review)

Dr E. G. Gwynn's courteous notice of *The History of the Celtic Place-Names of Scotland* contains some points on which I should like to remark.

First as to the Picts. Professing to summarise my views on these people, he writes:– 'They came first as pirates.' I have expressed no opinion as to how they came first. There is evidence that some of them, at least, practised piracy in the sixth century (probably still earlier) and also later.

'They penetrated southwards until they became the dominant people among the British population, whom Dr Watson supposes to have covered the whole island.' From this the natural inference is that in my view the Picts became lords of all Britain, an idea against which I have protested (p67).

'He holds, apparently, that the Picts themselves were of Celtic origin.' I hold that the ruling race among the Picts was of Celtic origin; further, that 'under them were the pre-Celtic people, forming doubtless the bulk of the population, and themselves of more than one racial origin' (p66).

Dr Gwynn suggests that granting the existence of non-Gaelic names in the far north, 'there is nothing to show that any of these names are traceable to the Picts rather than to any other part of the British speakers who occupied the country at an early date'. If by this he means that the early tribes mentioned by Ptolemy were British but not Pictish, and that the Picts invaded and occupied that territory at some period later than Ptolemy's time (early second century), he should show some reason for so holding. My position is that the term Picts (which occurs first at the end of the third century) was collective, and included all the tribes of the far north, without connoting any substantial change in the population from what it was in Ptolemy's time. But I can only guess at Dr Gwynn's meaning.

'Dr Watson always gives the benefit of the doubt to the British side, and claims for it many a name that might equally well be regarded as genuinely Gaelic. Thus at p367, Carmoyle is explained as Caer Moel, although it would have been simpler to equate it with Cahirmoyle, that is, Cathair Mhaol ... in Co. Limerick.' Such a tendency on my part deserved full illustration: the single alleged example chosen is unfortunate. Carmyle (not Carmoyle), in Lanarkshire, part of the British kingdom of Strath Clyde, is Kermil in 1240, and reference to pp222, 223, 366ff, where *cathair* and *Ker-*, etc, are discussed, will absolve me from Dr Gwynn's charge. I venture to say that the instance is typical of my alleged partiality. As a matter of fact I have been scrupulously fair, and have assigned to Gaelic names (e.g. Geldie, Dores) which had been regarded as British or Pictish.

In regard to early Gaelic settlements in Scotland, I have drawn attention to certain indications of settlement from Munster, in the eastern Midlands. The primary authority for this is the Psalter of Cashel, as quoted in four of the great Irish manuscripts (p219); but in addition there are collateral lines of evidence. One of these is the sporadic ogham inscriptions found in the East. Munster is well known to have been the great centre of the ogham cult in Ireland; Professor Eoin MacNeill states that of the Irish inscriptions, numbering about 300, five-sixths belong to the counties of Kerry, Cork and Waterford, and adds that 'the distribution of the inscriptions' (in Wales, Devon, etc) 'clearly corresponds to the region of Gaelic ... influence in the period that followed the withdrawal of the Roman legions from Britain'. In Ulster there are only sporadic instances, and I have pointed out that this explains the all but total absence of oghams in the West of Scotland, which is known to have been settled from Ulster. On the other hand, the presence of oghams in the east supports (as I consider) the statements of the Psalter of Cashel. On this Dr Gwynn makes the following criticism:— 'Neither does the sporadic occurrence of ogham inscriptions give much support to Dr Watson's contention, for these inscriptions are found, with one exception, in the east and north, not in the south-west, where colonisation would naturally begin.' The relevance of this is not apparent to me.

'The essential weakness of the book ... is simply this, that the Celtic place-names of Scotland have no history.' By this he means, so far as can be judged, that the early record forms of our place-names, found in increasing quantity from the twelfth century onwards, are all of them anglicized forms and therefore of little or no philological value. To discuss this proposition fully would take a paper to itself. It is true that Scotland does not possess a literary tradition at all comparable to that of Ireland, and I have made this clear enough. On the other hand, Dr Gwynn's sweeping statement requires much qualification. The scribes who wrote the names on early record may or may not have understood Gaelic, but in any case when the names on early record were written Gaelic was freely spoken over—it is not too much to say—the greater part of Scotland, while in certain districts Welsh, if not still actually spoken, had been spoken quite recently. In other words, the early record forms had not yet time to become anglicized, and they are far from deserving Dr Gwynn's contempt. One striking instance of this is Gleann Freoin (Glen Fruin), with which he would have us compare the Irish Freamhainn, now Frewin. But in 1225 we find on record the lands of Neved and Glanfrone, i.e. of the nemed (later neimheadh) of Rosneath, and Glenfruin[1]. Here Neved is as clear to the understanding as if it had been written in Middle Irish spelling, while Glanfrone proves (1) that the name was pronounced then as now; (2) that it had no *mh*, for if the *mh* is preserved in Neved, why not also in Glanfrone? Many similar examples occur in the book; to take three at random: Glencorse, in 1336 Glencrosk (Gaelic); Calder, circ. 1170, Kaledofre (British); Orrin, in 1257 Inver-aferan, in 1660 Glen-avaryn (*aifreann* from Lat. *offerendum*). In face of the facts it is idle to say that our names of places have no history.

Similarly with the suggestion that our Allan, a river name, is to be equated with Allen, the name of a height in Leinster, of old Almu, later Almhain: such early spellings as Aloent, Alwente, are

---

1 Also Nemhedh 1225, Glenfreone c. 1250 (Orig. Paroch.)

decisive against it, especially in view of Alowent of 1238, now Alwent, a river in Co. Durham, and the Welsh river Alwen. When Dr Gwynn further suggests the hypothetical Early Celtic Alovinda, 'white-stoned one', as a probable early form of Elphin in Roscommon, he violates the elementary rule of stress. Elphin is of old Ail Finn, 'white rock', where *finn*, being the specific, descriptive, or qualifying term, bears the stress; in a true 'strict' compound like Alovinda the stress falls on the first part, exactly as in Gaelic *busdubh*, 'black as to the muzzle', a common terrier name of the same formation as Gaulish *Busso-māros*, 'big-mouthed'.

Further examples of the same error are Dalry, Ceannruighe (Kinrive), and the suggestion that our Moireabh (Moray) should be compared with Irish Tráig Eba, etc, later Tráigh Eabha. In the first two the stress on the second part, duly noted in the index to the book, proves this part to be the specific or qualifying element, i.e. either a noun in the genitive or an adjective. Dr Gwynn's *-raige*, suggested as the second part, would demand stress on the first syllable, as in Dart-raige, now Dartry, in Oriel (Hogan). If Moireabh contained as its second element the woman's name Eba or Eabha, it would presumably mean 'Eba's Sea', stressed on the Eba, like Dun Domhnaill, Donald's Fort. Moireabh is morth-reabh, composed of the same elements as the Welsh Trefor, i.e. tref-for, from *tref*, fem., and *mor*, with initial soft mutation after the fem. noun. The former is the older formation, meaning 'sea-settlement'; the latter is 'homestead or hamlet by-sea'. His third example of a possible *-raige* ending is Carberry, stressed indeed on the first part; but the early spelling Crefbarrin (1143) proves the first part to be *craobh*, tree, while the second part, with initial *b*, is most probably *barran*, a top-fence or hedge (p143), certainly not *-raige*.

'Dunira, again (explained by Dr Watson as Dun-iaráth, "Fort of Westford"), might recall Duniry, in Galway, which is in Irish Dun Daighre.' On this all that need be said is that Dunira is in Gaelic at the present day Dun-iaráth, as I stated. A well-known phonetic law forbids aspiration of initial *d* after *n*, e.g. 'mo nighean dubh'.

'It would be perhaps as plausible to equate the name of Loch Hourn, which the Dean of Lismore wrote as Sowyrnni, with Sabhrann, which is the older form of the river Lee, and is also the Irish form of the Severn, as to explain it by a form Subh-bhairne, "gap of berries", for which there is no collateral evidence.' But the name is Subhairne, which really cannot be 'equated' with Sabhrann, the Lee, or Severn (in Welsh Hafren). As for 'collateral evidence' there are the facts which I have mentioned: (1) that at the head of the loch is Coire Shubh, whose waters flow into the loch-head; (2) that Loch Hourn lies in a tremendous *bearn* or gap. A legitimate objection to my explanation would be the phonetic one that subh-bhearna should result in Subairne; that, however, would only hold if the name were ancient, which is not necessary to suppose; there is not the slightest trace of *bh* in *subh* as pronounced in Gaelic.

'Inber Scene has nothing to do with scian, "a knife". MacNeill has shown that it is not a genuine name at all, but a literary fiction, borrowed from Orosius.' And where, one may ask, did Orosius 'borrow' it from? Did he invent it, or, being an honest man, did he report a bona fide name then existing? Orosius (fl. 415) says that the parts of Ireland one comes to first (partes priores) look towards Brigantia (Corunna, in NW Spain), especially from that promontory where is the mouth of the river Scena (Scenae fluminis ostium), and where the Velabri and Luceni are situated (et Velabri Lucenique consistunt)—a definite and circumstantial statement. Ptolemy places the Vellabori in the south-west corner of Ireland, and Professor MacNeill has shown that the name occurs in LL 23, a.17 in the place-name Luachair Fellubair. The Luceni are not otherwise known, but that Orosius invented them is unlikely. Thus two of the three names mentioned by Orosius appear in Irish literature: why accept Luachair Fellubair and reject Inber Scene? There can be no doubt that the one is as genuine as the other; and in all probability Inber Scene, as Kuno Meyer stated long ago, is 'the knife-like slash of the Kenmare river'.

'The word mormhoich, which Dr Watson regards as equivalent to muir-mag, "sea-plain", is really a deformation of the Irish murbhach; the second element is the verbal noun of bongim, as in combach, tobach, etc.' The word *murmag* occurs in Irish literature, and naturally becomes in Scottish Gaelic *mormhoich* (dat.-locative), as *ár-mag*, slaughter plain, battle-field, becomes *áraich* (dat.), both feminine (cf 'Tighearna na Moighe', 'the lord of Moy', i.e. Mackintosh). *Murmag* is Welsh *morfa*, and the various places in Wales called Morfa correspond in position to the places called Mormhoich with us. It is by no means certain that Irish *murbhach* is not a 'deformation' of *murmhach*, just as M. Ir. has *árbhach* for *ármach*, earlier *ármag*, Old Welsh *aerua* (for *aerfa*), 'locus proelii'.

'He is a little too ready to trust to O'Reilly, who is a very unsafe guide.' So far as I recall, I have made no use of O'Reilly except on p358, which gives a much-needed correction of a term from him which misled Skene, and again on p516, where he is quoted for a gender. My *eabar* was not from him, but from my own Scottish Gaelic; all the same the passage should be amended to read 'Ir. abar, Sc. G. eabar'. Cormac's derivation of *anart* and *adart* from *irt*, 'death', is of course nonsense; but when he says 'is ainm irt do bás', and quotes from a source now lost, that is quite another thing; and in view of the whole circumstances detailed on pp97-99 of the book, I still believe that he was telling the truth.

I have to thank Dr Gwynn for his note on Verubium: 'Point of a sword' is *ug* not *ub*. The name must be divided, as a friend has pointed out, Veru-bium, not Ver-ubium. But of the review as a whole it must be said with all deference 'is ceannach air an ubh an gloc'.

Annaid

Our *annaid* is O. Ir. *andóit*, later *annóit*, a patron saint's church, a church that contained the relics of the founder, a mother church. The meaning is well known from O. Ir. onwards; the derivation is uncertain. Stokes refers it to Low Latin *antitas* for *antiquitas*, 'ancient church'. Any connection with Anaitis is phonetically and otherwise impossible. Anaitis was an Asiatic divinity, whose name is written variously (Anaea, Aneitis, Tanais, Nanaea). Her worship prevailed in Armenia and elsewhere in Asia. Greek writers sometimes identify her with Artemis, sometimes with Aphrodite (Smith's Classical Dictionary). See further CPNS, pp250-254, etc. Wherever there is an Annat there are traces of an ancient chapel or cemetery, or both: very often, too, the Annat adjoins a fine well or clear stream, like that sung by Duncan Bàn Macintyre:–

> 'Fiòn uillt na h-Annaid,
> Blas meala r'a h-òl air.'

'The wine of the burn of the Annat, its taste was of honey to drink it.' He goes on to say that the water was an unfailing remedy: its virtue came from the Annat by which it flows.

Index of Places and Tribes

Index of Personal Names